THE PRACTICAL ENCYCLOPEDIA OF
BEADING & RIBBONWORK

THE PRACTICAL ENCYCLOPEDIA OF

BEADING & RIBBONWORK

CRAFT TECHNIQUES • MATERIALS • PROJECTS

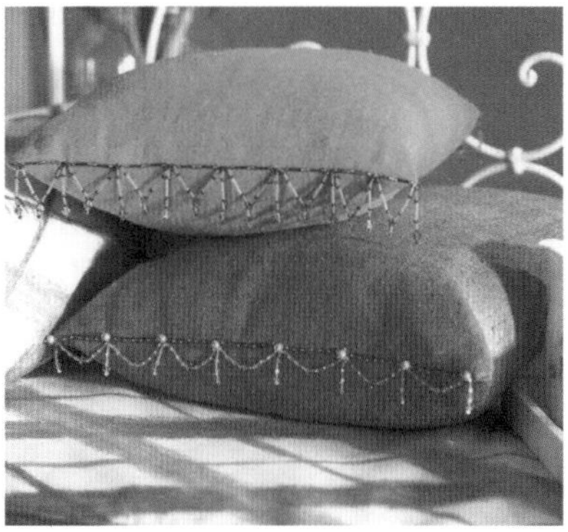

LISA BROWN AND ISABEL STANLEY,
WITH CHRISTINE KINGDOM

LORENZ BOOKS

This edition is published by Lorenz Books

Lorenz Books is an imprint of Anness Publishing Ltd
www.lorenzbooks.com; www.annesspublishing.com
info@anness.com; Twitter: @AnnessLorenzBks

If you like the images in this book and would like to investigate using them for publishing, promotions or advertising, please visit our website www.practicalpictures.com for more information.

A CIP catalogue record for this book is available from the British Library

Publisher Joanna Lorenz
Editorial Director Helen Sudell
Executive Editor Joanne Rippin
Designer Ian Sandom
Introduction by Lucinda Ganderton
Beadwork projects by Lisa Brown and Isabel Stanley
Ribbonwork projects by Lisa Brown and Christine Kingdom
Tassel projects by Annabel Crutchley
Production Controller Ben Worley

The Publisher would like to thank the Bridgeman Art Library for permission to use the following images:
10 both; 11; 12 both; 13 both; 160 both; 161.

PUBLISHER'S NOTE
Although the advice and information in this book are believed to be accurate and true at the time of going to press, neither the authors nor the publisher can accept any legal responsibility or liability for any errors or omissions that may have been made.

Contents

Introduction

Beadwork and ribbonwork, in all their many and varied forms, have never been more fashionable, or more sought after, than they are today. On the catwalk, in sophisticated interior stores, in bijou boutiques and even in some toy shops, an ever-increasing amount of beaded or be-ribboned jewellery and accessories is to be found, and specialist suppliers now stock a vast and enticing array of materials for making your own original creations.

As we embark on a new century, contemporary craft workers are looking back to the traditional techniques of previous generations, but reinterpreting and reworking them into something new and original. Bead weaving, for example, has been practised by Native Americans for centuries, but was also all the rage with Victorian ladies, who made intricate strips of beadwork on their wooden looms. Similarly,

bead- or ribbon-embellished lampshades were a favourite design detail in Art Nouveau room schemes. Beautiful accessories and decorative objects inspired by many of these styles can be found here, along with contemporary new looks and ideas, including

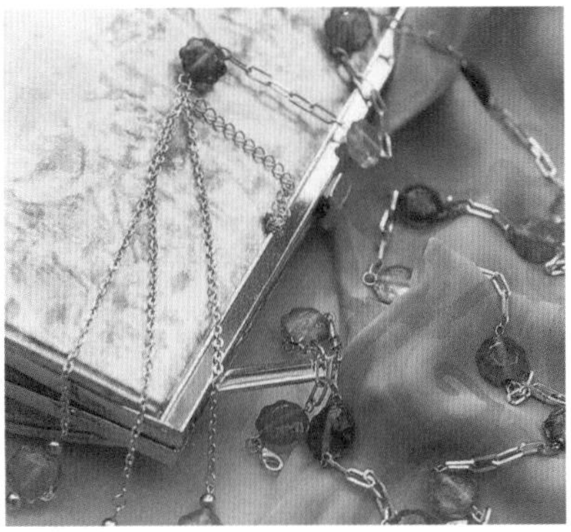

projects for making jewellery from some of the most up-to-date materials on the market, which have brought new life to jewellery in particular.

This book is full of many imaginative and exciting beading and ribbonwork ideas from leading designers, with chapters covering jewellery, fashion accessories and desirable items for the home. Each section also has an informative introduction, which covers all the basic techniques, materials, tools and equipment required. The step-by-step instructions are straightforward and each project is clearly illustrated. The ●●● symbol indicates how complex a project is. One ● means the project is straightforward and a beginner could tackle it with ease. Projects with ●●● indicate that a more advanced level of skill is required.

Whether you are a complete beginner or an experienced stitcher, you are bound to find something to make for yourself, or as a special present. The ornamental qualities of beads and ribbons are irresistible. They will add glamour, colour, sparkle and texture to your work, and the creative possibilities are endless.

Beadwork History and Techniques

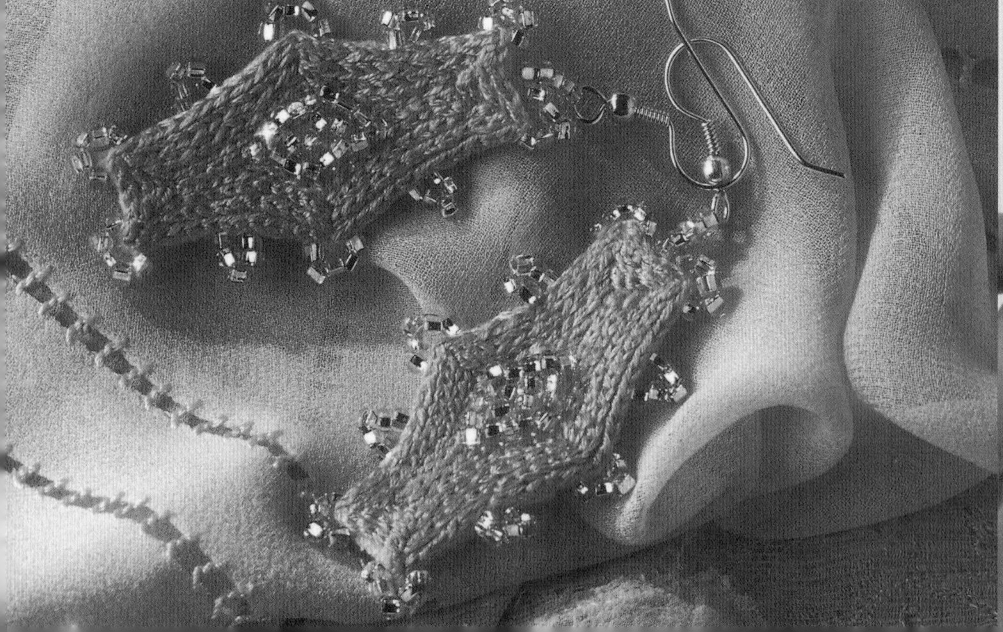

The appeal of beads has many aspects and their history holds far more than their use as purely decorative objects. They have been used as currency, worn as status symbols and regarded as talismans imbued with mystical powers. Collectors appreciate the skill involved in the creation and manufacture of the myriad types available, while designers enjoy their weight and shimmering qualities as well as the richness and depth they add to any creation.

Historically, the role of beads in society has not been as mere ornaments; across the world they have had great cultural significance as artefacts that reflect economic, religious and social conditions.

History of Beadwork

In the earliest societies, beads were used as currency, and in Africa, even in modern times for the Zulu people and the Ndbele-speaking people, beads are still a symbol of wealth and status. Men and women still wear necklaces, head bands, belts, bangles and anklets made from narrow lengths of bead-weaving and beaded, wrapped rope, worn with skins and fur. Women of different status are distinguished by heavily beaded girdles, aprons, cloaks and hats. Young women send colour- and pattern-coded messages in beadwork to their lovers when they are far from home.

In Europe, during the 15th century, beads became an important trading currency. Explorers to the Americas used them as gifts to the indigenous peoples to initiate friendship and trust. As trade grew between the Native Americans and European merchants, beads and steel needles were exchanged mainly for skins. The imported glass beads soon replaced locally made bone and shell beads, which had been applied to hides with moosehair and porcupine quills. The Native North American Indians in particular adopted the fluid floral

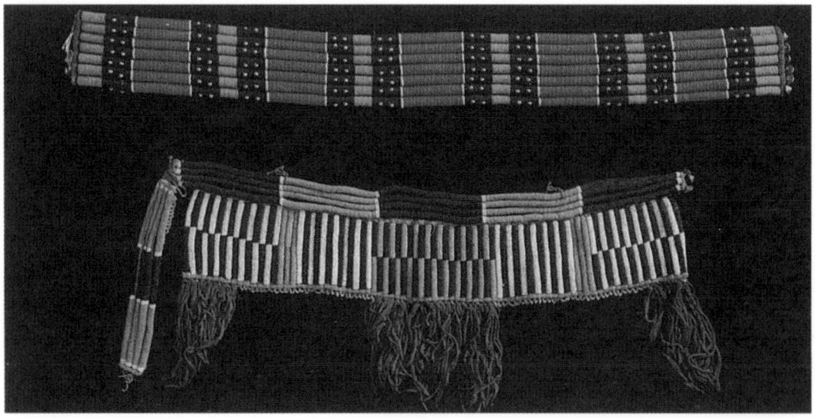

Above: These highly decorated Native American beaded moccasins use the tiny beads that European traders first brought to the American continent. These glass beads were known as "trade" or "pony" beads, and were used as a form of currency. The North American Indians took to them with enthusiasm and integrated them into their existing artistic traditions.

Left: An example of the traditional beadwork of the Zulu people. Work like this acts as a statement of wealth and status for whoever wears it.

Right: The richly worked dress of this Elizabethan woman is encrusted with beads, and proclaims her position in England's highest social echelons.

styles of the foreigners and assimilated them with traditional patterns to make beautiful and distinctive moccasins, pipe bags and skirts.

Commercially manufactured beads were first introduced to Africa in the 15th century by Asians and Europeans. Caravan routes carried the easily portable currency deep into the continent. Merchants traded their glass beads for ivory, skins and even slaves. The more valuable and rare beads quickly became prized possessions, indicators of the wealth and status of the wearer. Such was the social significance of certain beads that only the upper strata of society was allowed to wear them. The etiquette of beads highlighted other differences apart from social hierarchy. Particular combinations and patterns, as well as the exact position of a given piece, identified the married and the unmarried, the young and the old. Furthermore, these differences reflected the personal achievements and the birthplace or village of an individual. Certain elaborately beaded costumes took on special significance and could be worn only by participants during ceremonial performances, weddings and initiation rites.

In medieval England, the wearing of beads and embroidery had a ceremonial function. The first manufactured beads were made from expensive raw materials, such as precious and semi-precious stones. They were available only to the nobility and the Church. Professional embroiderers embellished rich fabrics during the first great period of excellence in English embroidery, the "Opus Anglicum". Drilled pearls and coral were applied with metallic threads to make elaborate and heavy ecclesiastical vestments. These garments must have been a wondrous sight as they sparkled and gleamed in the candle-lit churches. The beads used were so valuable that, when the importance of the Church declined, the prized beads were removed and recycled. In the early years of the 16th century, some of these stones were then embroidered on to the extravagant costumes of the Tudor nobility. This ushered in a second period of superior craftsmanship. Travelling needlewomen created fabulously rich costumes, which were stiff with embroidery and heavy with pearls, spangles, sequins and corals. These gloriously impractical outfits indicated the importance of the

wearer and rendered them virtually helpless, needing a coterie of servants to dress them.

In the middle of the 17th century, young ladies were encouraged to practise and display their needle and beadworking skills by producing textile jewel boxes as part of their "education". They used a technique now known as stumpwork in which three-dimensional or padded embroidery is worked with silk thread and wool yarn and embellished with small glass beads, spangles and mica. These wonderful caskets feature houses, their elaborately dressed inhabitants and landscape gardens, a particular 17th-century preoccupation. These gardens were crammed with exotic flowers, plants and trees, sometimes three-dimensional, and worked with beads threaded on wire and bent into shape. The bizarre proportions of the features indicate that they were not observed, but copied from illustrations.

During the 19th century, embroidery and beadwork became popular hobbies among upper- and middle-class ladies. These gentle pursuits were employment enough for privileged women who did not have to work, and the results demonstrated not only the status of the women but also the qualities of femininity, patience and diligence that were then considered desirable. Victorian ladies also made delicate three-dimensional pieces, such as butterflies, flowers and

Above: A typical example of the complex beadwork produced in Europe in the 17th century by women of leisure. This one shows Adam and Eve surrounded by animals from the Garden of Eden, while, top right, Abraham prepares to sacrifice Isaac and, bottom right, Cain murders his brother, Abel.

Left: Throughout the nineteenth century, women of the leisured classes in Europe demonstrated their skill, patience and application by producing works of embroidery. Beadwork became more and more extravagant as ladies displayed their skills and creativity.

insects, by threading beads on to wire. They arranged the finished structures as a display under a glass dome or used them to make corsages, tiaras and combs for themselves and as gifts for friends and family.

A passion emerged for using scraps of rich fabrics recycled from favourite dresses to make abstract or "crazy" patchworks. These extravagant quilts were scattered liberally with embroidery stitches, ribbons, buttons, glass beads and sequins.

Beadwork was not just the preserve of women, however – sailors at sea laboured over tokens of affection for their loved ones at home. They made patchwork pincushions using scraps of wool fabric from uniforms and stuffed with sawdust, and spelt out sentimental messages of love and remembrance in beads and sequins threaded on to pins and pressed firmly into the cushion.

The most important craft, however, was Berlinwork, or canvas covered with tent or cross stitch worked in wool yarn. This craze swept across Europe and America, its popularity based upon the ease with which it could be worked.

To take advantage of such a huge market, manufacturers produced thousands of patterns and different-coloured threads and wools. Some patterns featured beadwork. Tiny brass or more often glass beads were stitched in place of yarn to give a shimmery surface to the piece. Different tones were used to give a mottled effect, known as "grisaille work". Homes were filled with bags, tea cosies, covers, bedspreads, slippers, cushions and fire-screens, all the results of the labours of women.

Throughout the latter half of the 19th century there was a fashion for heavily beaded bodices on evening dresses using jet and black glass beads, and small bags embellished with fringes and tassels.

During the 1920s, women's lives changed rapidly, as they celebrated the end of the Great War, voted for the first time and began to enter the workplace. Fashions reflected this new-found freedom. Narrow, low-waisted dresses dripped with rows of fringes of sequins, bugle, drop and glass beads. The shorter styles of dress allowed much greater freedom of movement and the swinging fringes were designed to dazzle while dancing the new jazz-age dances. The popularity of beadwork declined with the onset of the Second World War, as rationing meant that clothes became simpler and more austere. In recent years, however, beaded fashions and crafts have had a tremendous revival.

Today, beads are produced in great numbers and variety. The incredible choice on the market allows contemporary designers and craft artists to explore fully the integral beauty and creative possibilities of beads.

Above: This diaphanous silk georgette evening dress, from the 1920s, uses delicate beadwork to create a shimmering, stunning effect, in the drop-waisted, show-stopping fashion of the time. Although it is quite ornate, a garment such as this was far easier to wear than the boned, corseted gowns of previous decades. The beaded necklace is a classic accessory of the Roaring Twenties.

Below: A lovely beading detail of a floral pattern from a woman's dress c.1925–27

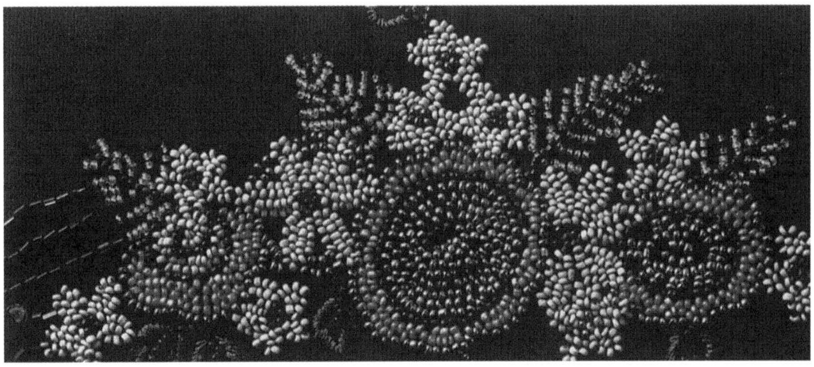

Beadwork is a centuries-old craft with a rich history. Today, designers and craftspeople are drawn to the medium for its decorative qualities, and these examples of contemporary work illustrate its versatility.

Gallery of Beading

Beadwork can be made from all types of materials, from the reassuringly traditional to the unexpectedly modern, and is just as likely to be found embellishing haute couture garments in a smart boutique as on the shelves of a craft shop. Fashionable jewellery and accessories have always made full use of glass and semi-precious beads, which are more popular than ever: there are now many shops devoted to accessories, many of which feature beadwork – scarves, bags, necklaces and earrings. Home accessories such as striking wire-wrapped candlesticks, candle jars and dramatic flower vases can now be seen in smart interior stores, along with fringed lampshades,

Below: BROOCH AND EARRINGS
The heart-shaped brooch and matching earrings are made from rich velvet fabric worked with gold machine embroidery and finished with bugle beads.
ISABEL STANLEY

Right: CANDLESTICK
This elegant candlestick has a metal base and is embellished with beads strung on wire and wrapped along the shaft.
LIBERTY

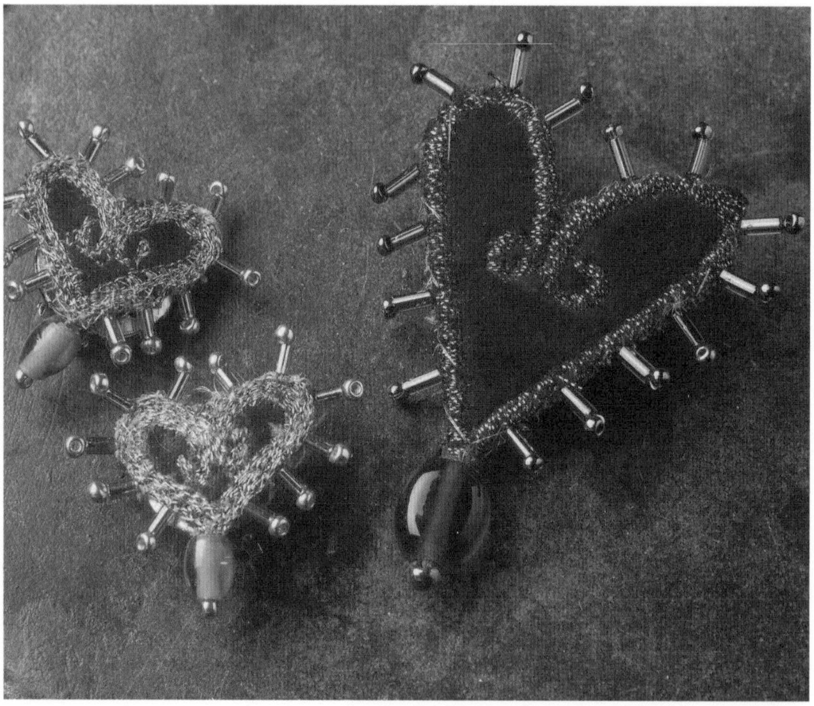

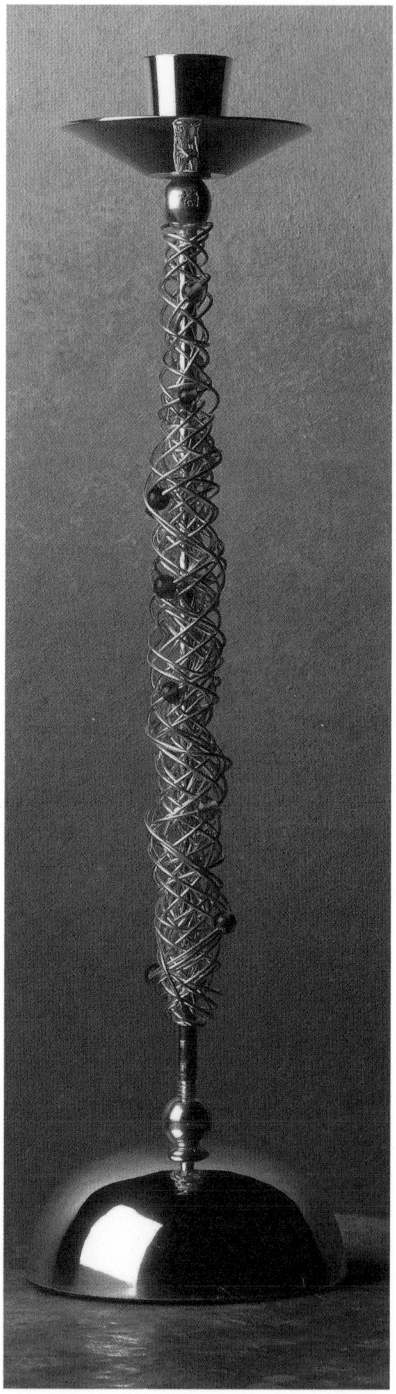

embroidered cushion covers and beaded picture frames. Most of these items are factory made, but there are many individual makers who are creating and exhibiting exquisite one-off items. Look out for their work at local art galleries and specialist craft fairs, and be inspired by the diversity of their ideas and inspirations, as beadwork takes yet another leap in its history.

Right: ROCAILLES AND PEARLY DISCS
If circumstances do not allow you to dress from head to foot in sequins and pearls, then console yourself by adding strategic detail with strips of hand-stitched gold and pearlized beads. A taste of delicious luxury, this needle-woven panel would work well on a favourite dress or an evening bag. KAREN SPURGIN

Below: BEADED FLOWERS
These decorative beaded flowers are made from crystal chips, garnets and a variety of small and bugle beads, by working out from the centre of the flower and gradually building up the wired petals. The flowers can be pinned or sewn on to garments or headgear as fashionable trims. JANICE MARR

Below: BEADED CANDLE JAR
Small red beads glow like jewels and allow the warm candlelight to show through the wire structure of this beaded candle jar. In any project that exposes beads to heat, care should be taken to use materials that are neither hazardous nor likely to melt in the heat of a flame. LIBERTY

Opposite: BEADED FRUIT
Scraps of duchesse satin and antique velvet have been beaded with cup sequins, small beads and crystal chips. For 'feel appeal' they have been filled with lentils, like little bean bags. The stems are made of twisted jewellery wire and beads, some shaped like leaves. KAREN SPURGIN

Right: BEADED BUSTIER
This stunning piece was worked on a wire base with beads woven in and out of the basic shape. DIANA LAURIE

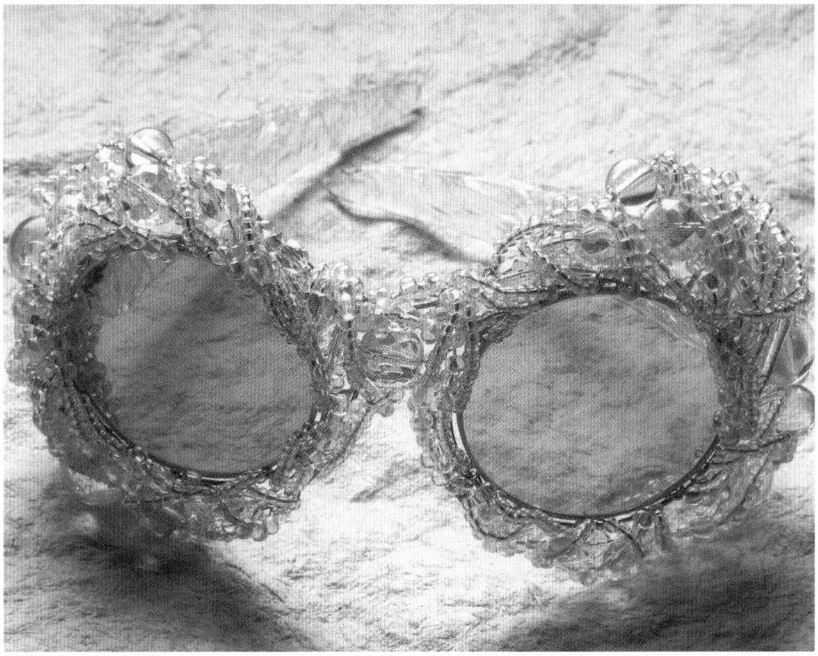

Above: SILVER SUNGLASS FRAMES
Beads are woven in and out of a wire frame for these glamorous glasses. Old necklaces found on market stalls are a good source of beads with distinctive character. DIANA LAURIE

Right: DECORATIVE DISCS
Details such as these decorative discs turn a basic fabric into something for a special occasion. KAREN SPURGIN

An enormous range of beads can be found at specialist suppliers, in a variety of styles and shapes, in materials ranging from enamel and glass to wood or semi-precious stones.

Beads

Bugle beads

These narrow glass tubes, available in many sizes, are particularly effective when used in contrast with small glass beads.

Cloisonné

These intricate enamel beads are made in China. The metal bead is covered with wire outlines, which are filled in with coloured enamels.

Crystals

Usually cut glass, these beads have a faceted surface and are available in different shapes such as hearts and diamonds. Use beeswax to protect the beading thread from their sharp edges.

Drop beads

Shaped like teardrops, with a hole at the top, these are normally used to finish a strand.

Lampwork beads

Made in India, these are decorated with molten glass trailed in intricate patterns. Some lampwork beads have a central core of silver foil, which is visible through the coloured glass.

Metal beads

These beads often have sophisticated shapes and are made of either brass or copper and may be plated with silver or gold. They are most often used in jewellery to separate larger beads or at the end of a string.

Millefiori (thousand flowers)

Long rods of coloured glass are fused together then sliced into mosaic-like cross-sections. These beads are now also available in plastic.

Natural materials

Beads made from nuts, seeds, shells, mother-of-pearl and bone are regarded as potent talismans in some countries. Soft wooden beads are more suited to jewellery than embroidery.

Pearl beads

Artificial pearl beads with a pearlized finish come in colours, white and ivory.

Pottery beads

Ceramic beads were originally made by inserting a wooden stick through the clay shapes. During firing, the stick burnt away to leave a hole.

Rocailles

These small, slightly flattened glass beads are very popular. Many varieties, such as opaque, transparent, metallic and iridescent, are available. The hole may be lined with iridescent or opaque colour, gold or silver.

Semi-precious stones

Stones such as amber, turquoise, coral and jade are expensive, but artificial imitations are also available.

Sequins

Flat plastic shapes with one or two holes, are available in different colours and finishes. Originally sequins were made from sheets of gold and silver.

Small glass beads

Small glass beads, also known as seeds, are used in many beading projects. The are spherical, but, like flatter rocailles, they come in many varieties. They are sometimes sold pre-strung, ready to transfer to a needle.

Venetian glass beads

These highly decorative beads are from one of the world's most famous beadmaking centres.

Wound beads

Molten glass is wound around a rotating metal rod to create swirling striped patterns.

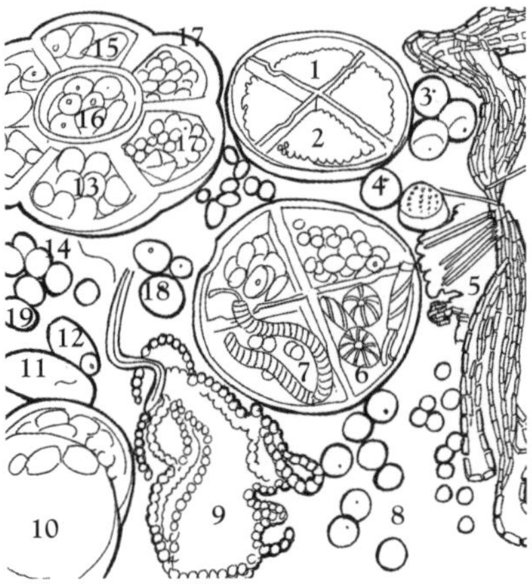

1 Rocailles; 2 Small glass beads; 3 Venetian beads; 4 Millefiori; 5 Bugle beads; 6 Bone beads; 7 Sequins; 8 Drop beads; 9 Pre-strung beads; 10 Found objects; 11 Lampwork beads; 12 Wound bead; 13 Artificial pearls; 14 Crystals; 15 Semi-precious stones; 16 Pottery beads (traditional Chinese design); 17 Metal beads; 18 Amber: 19 Cloisonné

Beadwork is an ideal small-scale hobby as it requires very few specialist tools. Basic equipment such as scissors and needles will probably already be close to hand in the sewing basket or around the home.

Equipment

Bead loom
This small loom is specially designed for beadwork. The warp threads are fitted between metal springs and wound around wooden rollers.

Beading needles
These fine, long needles are available in various sizes and can be used to thread several beads at a time. To thread beads with large holes, you can also use sewing needles.

Beeswax
This is used to run along the beading thread to increase its strength and prevent it from snagging. It is particularly useful when using faceted beads.

Craft (utility) knife
A strong knife is needed to cut out card. Use with a cutting mat for safety.

Drawing pins (thumb tacks)
These are used to pin strands of beads on to a pin board.

Dressmaker's pins
These are used to pin fabric before tacking (basting) or slip stitching.

Embroidery hoop
Two tightly fitting rings hold fabric taut. Plastic hoops are recommended for use under a sewing-machine.

Embroidery scissors
These small, sharp scissors are used to cut and trim thread and fabric.

Fabric marker
The marks made with this specialized pen fade on contact with air or water.

Graph paper
This is used to measure and check the length of fringes and tassels.

Metal scissors
Use sturdy metal scissors to crack damaged beads and remove them from a string.

Needles
Some sewing needles, called "sharps", may be small enough to pass through beads. Leather needles, with triangular points, are used to stitch beads to tough material such as leather.

Paintbrush
This is used to apply fabric paint in some projects.

Palettes
When working on a project that invoves a number of small beads, it is useful to decant the beads into white china palettes, available from most artists' suppliers.

Pin board
Fringing or macramé work should be pinned out on a board to achieve accurate results. It is important that the board is large enough to accommodate the whole design. Small pieces of work can be pinned out on an ironing board.

Ruler
This is an essential tool for accurate measuring. A metal-edged ruler is the most suitable, though not essential, for these projects.

Tape measure
Use instead of a ruler for measuring larger pieces of fabric and any kind of curved surface.

Tweezers
These are very useful for picking up individual beads, especially small ones and sequins.

Wire cutters and round-nosed (snub-nosed) pliers
These are essential for bending and cutting wire.

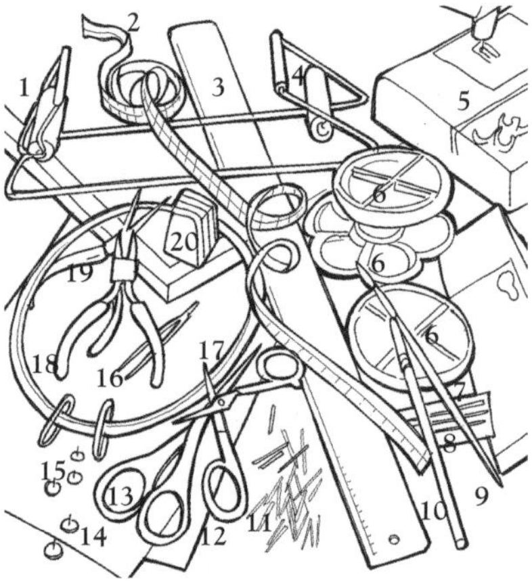

1 Pin board; 2 Tape measure; 3 Ruler; 4 Bead loom; 5 Sewing-machine; 6 Palettes; 7 Needles; 8 Beading needles; 9 Paintbrush; 10 Fabric marker; 11 Pins; 12 Embroidery scissors; 13 Metal scissors; 14 Graph paper; 15 Drawing pins; 16 Tweezers; 17 Embroidery hoop; 18 Wire cutters; 19 Round-nosed (snub-nosed) jewellery pliers; 20 Beeswax

Apart from the beads themselves, only a few other materials are needed for beadwork, depending on the project. All the materials are readily available from good craft shops and department stores.

Materials

Beading thread
Use a strong, smooth polyester or one of the many threads designed especially for beadwork.

Beading wire
This is available in gold, copper and silver, and in many diameter sizes: 0.4mm and 0.6mm are the most useful.

Bookbinding fabric
This closely woven cotton fabric has a paper backing that can be glued. It is available from bookbinding suppliers.

Brass screw binders
These are used to hold sheets of paper together to make a book.

Buttons
Mix buttons with beads for extra decorative effect.

Cord
Beads can be wrapped around a core of three-ply cord, available from furnishing suppliers and haberdashers.

Cotton spheres
These are made of compressed cotton fibres and come in various shapes and sizes. They are usually available from specialist trimmings and beading suppliers.

Cover buttons
Sold in kit form in haberdashery departments, cover buttons consist of two pieces: a top, over which the fabric is pulled, and an underside with shank attached.

Embroidery threads (floss)
These include perlé cotton (a high-sheen 2-ply thread), stranded embroidery thread (separate the 5-ply strands for fine work) and machine embroidery threads. They are available in a full range of colours, including metallics.

Fabric paints
Water-based, non-toxic paints that are fixed by ironing are recommended.

Felt-tipped pen
This is useful for marking outlines and is also used for drawing decorative patterns for beadwork.

Fishing twine
For heavy beads, such as glass, fishing twine is recommended. It is stronger than polyester thread but more difficult to work with.

Floss thread
This fibrous thread has a silk-like sheen. Use it to cover wire stems.

Fusible bonding web
Ironed on to the back of appliqué fabric, this bonds it to the background fabric before stitching.

Interfacing
Normally used as a fabric stiffener, this also makes a good background fabric for beadwork.

Jewellery findings
Hatpins, earring wires, clasps, brooch backs, jump rings and other findings are available from beadwork suppliers.

Lil pins
Shorter than dressmaker's pins, these are ideal for pin-beading.

Ribbon
Silk, satin and velvet ribbons can all be used to embellish beadwork.

Tape
Fringes are stitched to fabric tape before being inserted into seams or rolled into tassels.

Tapestry canvas and wool (yarn)
This stiff, grid-like canvas is available in various weave sizes. Stitch over it with colourful, matt tapestry wools.

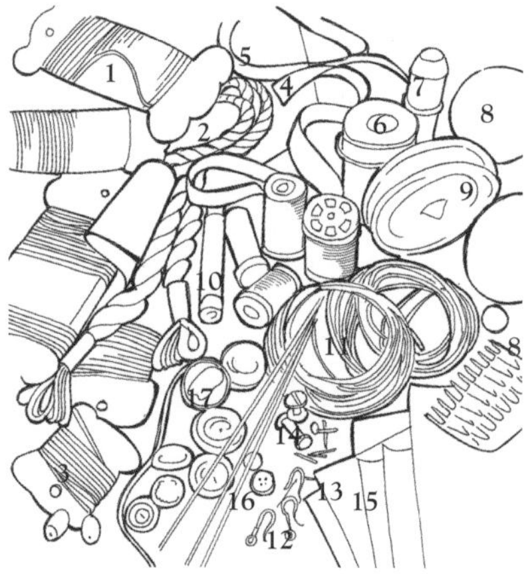

1 Tapestry wool; 2 Cord; 3 Beading thread; 4 Tape; 5 Ribbon; 6 Fabric paint; 7 Fabric paint; 8 Cotton spheres; 9 Fishing twine; 10 Floss thread; 11 Beading wire; 12 Jewellery findings; 13 Lil pins; 14 Brass screw bindings; 15 Bookbinding fabric; 16 Buttons; 17 Cover buttons.

Creating your own beads is easy, and there are several methods you can use. In spite of the massive variety of shop-bought beads available, there is still a special satisfaction in creating your own.

Making your own Beads

Clay Beads

Versatile polymer clay, which comes in a wide range of colours, is especially useful for making larger beads and beads with wide holes. The marbled effect of these beads gives a bright ethnic look.

1 Plain coloured beads can be made up by simply rolling a small amount of clay into a ball. For marbled beads, knead together two different colours.

2 To make the hole, pierce the centre of the clay ball with a large tapestry needle or a short length of thick wire. Twist gently as you pull it out.

3 To make up patterned beads from multi-coloured clay, first roll the bead shapes in layers of plain clay, one colour on top of another.

4 Using a sharp craft (utility) knife and cutting downwards, slice the multi-coloured roll of clay into very thin discs (no thicker than 2mm/ 1⁄12in).

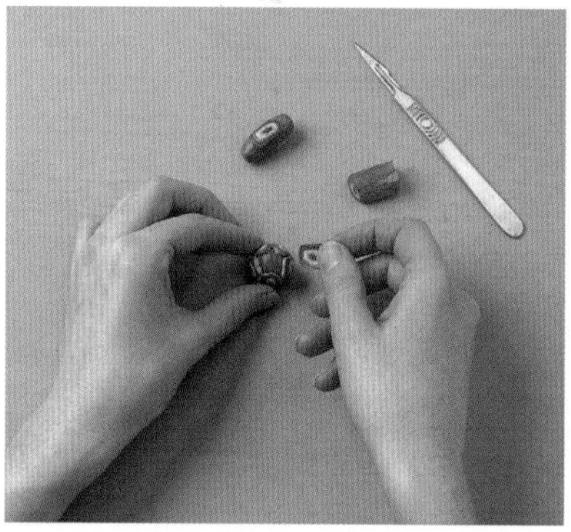

5 Press the slices on to the surface of the plain beads, completely or partially covering the surface as you wish.

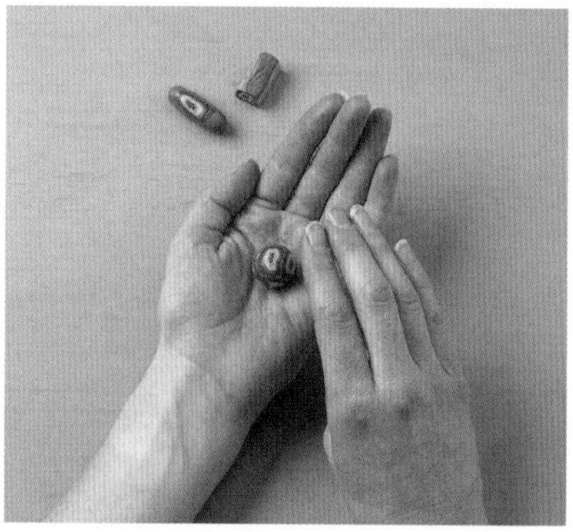

6 Roll the beads again to smooth out the surface and pierce holes through the centres. Place the finished beads in an oven to harden according to the manufacturer's instructions.

Mosaic Effects

This variation on clay beads is inspired by traditional Indian jewellery – bangles and pendants that are made by embedding beads in soft clay or plastic. Basic balls and cut-out flat shapes made from brightly coloured polymer clay can be embellished by studding the surface with patterns of tiny glass and metal beads or diamantes before they are baked. Bugles should be placed longways to make short lines and rocailles sideways, so that their holes form part of the design. Try the following mosaic-style beads and charms.

Mosaic beads

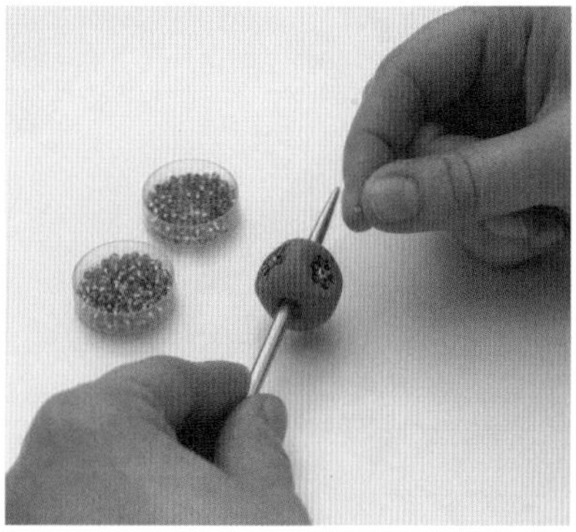

Roll a ball of clay between your palms as before to make the basic bead and pierce it through the centre with a knitting needle. Gently press rocaille and bugle beads into the clay, so that just over half of each bead is embedded below the surface.

Mosaic pendants

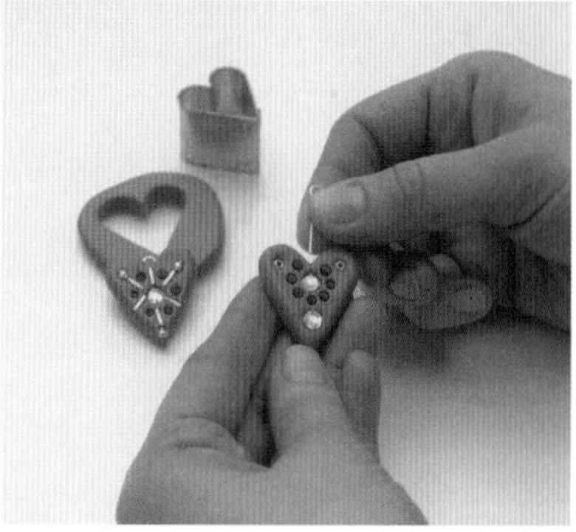

Knead the clay until it is malleable, and roll it out on a sheet of paper until around 4mm/⅕in deep. Cut a shape using a tiny cookie cutter and decorate with beads. Make a loop at one end of a 2cm/⅔in length of wire and push into the top of the shape for a hanger.

Rolled Paper Beads

These beads, made by rolling up a triangle of paper, have long been made by children, but by using interesting paper, you can achieve quite a sophisticated result. Origami paper printed with intricate patterns is ideal and the beads can then be threaded with glass beads or on their own. The wider the base of the triangle, the longer the bead will be.

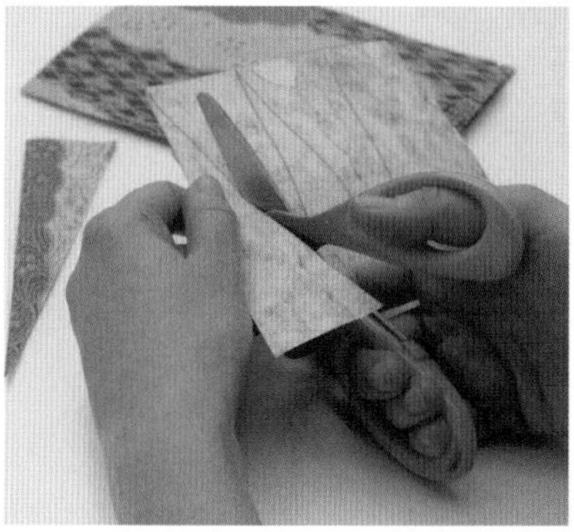

1 Use a ruler and pencil to mark the triangles on the back of the paper: the base of these beads is 4cm/1½in and the sides each measure 15cm/6in. Cut them out with scissors.

2 Apply a layer of paper glue to the back of the bead, omitting the first 12mm/½in. With the glued side facing downwards and the wide end parallel to the edge, wrap the triangle tightly around a knitting needle.

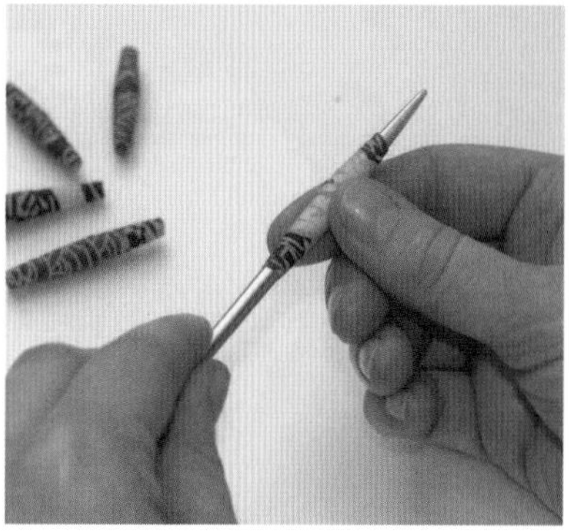

3 Slide the bead off the needle and leave to dry completely. You can then coat the finished beads with a layer of matt varnish to protect the surface.

When learning any new skill, it is worth taking time to master the basics before progressing to more complex techniques. Start with a straightforward project like stringing beads or making a short fringe.

Basic Techniques

Bead Picot

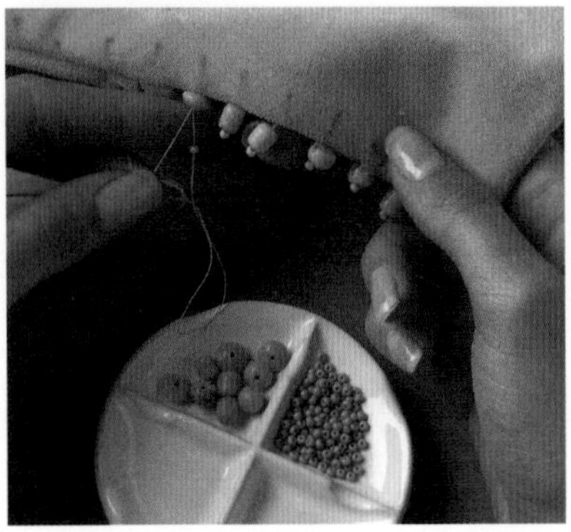

Use a tape measure and fabric marker to mark even points. Thread a needle, insert it into the fabric at one end of the picot and secure with a knot. Pass the needle through a large bead, followed by a small bead – the small bead will prevent the large one slipping off. Push both beads as far as possible up the needle then pass the needle back through the large bead. Make a stitch in the fabric to the next marked point.

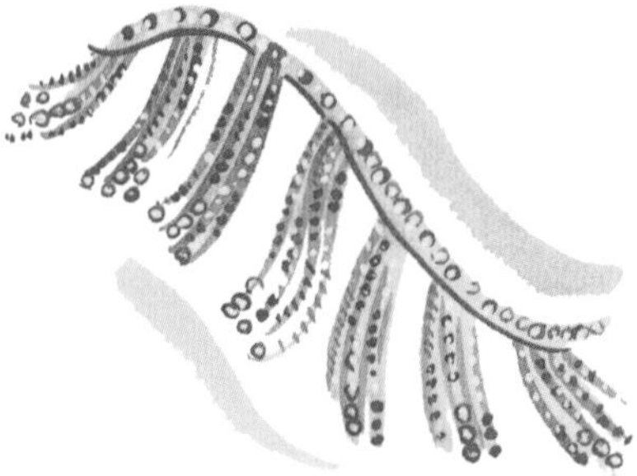

Long Fringe

1 Cut a piece of thread four times the length of the strand desired. Thread both ends through a needle. Insert into the fabric and knot. Pass the needle through the thread loop and pull taut.

2 Mark the length of the fringe on graph paper and place next to the thread. Thread on the required number of beads, pushing them up as far as possible.

3 Pass the needle through the second to last bead. Check that no thread is visible. Make a fastening-off stitch between the third and fourth beads from the end then continue up the string of beads, making fastening-off stitches every four beads.

4 Pull the strand gently to remove kinks in the thread, then trim the thread close to the beads.

Short Fringe

This is worked with a continuous length of thread. Mark the length desired on graph paper. Insert the needle in the fabric and secure the thread with a knot. Thread on the required number of beads, pushing them up as far as possible. Pass the needle through the second to last bead, then back up the full length of the string. Insert the needle back into the fabric and bring it out at the next point on the fringe.

Pointed Fringe

Thread a needle, insert in the fabric and secure with a knot. Thread on a bugle bead, a small glass bead and another bugle. Push the beads up as far as possible to form points, then insert the needle at the next point along.

Drop Fringe

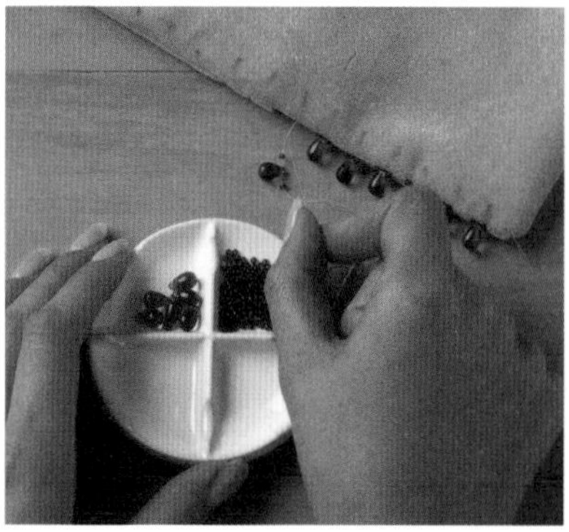

Thread a needle, insert in the fabric and secure with a knot. Thread on a small glass bead, a drop bead and another small glass bead. Push the beads up as far as possible, then insert the needle at the next point along.

Lattice Fringe

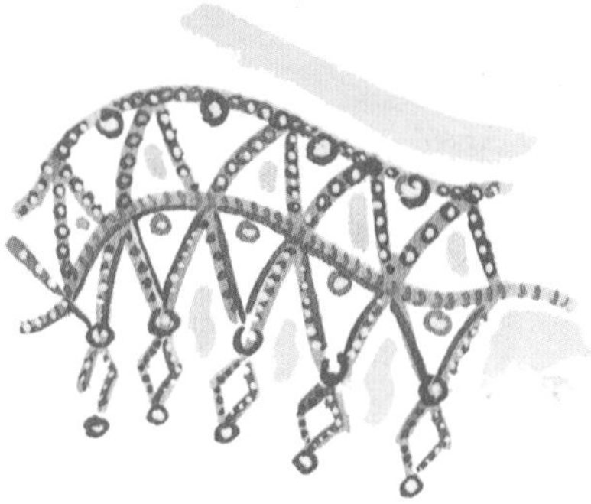

1 This pretty open diamond fringe uses long bugle beads, and can be made to any depth. It is worked on to a length of narrow petersham ribbon so that it can then be sewn on to a lampshade, bag or other accessory. Make a series of pencil marks along one edge of the ribbon, 1cm/½in apart.

2 Thread a beading needle with a long, strong thread and fasten it on at the first mark. Thread one small, one large and one small rocaille, then a bugle, a large rocaille, a second bugle, a large rocaille, a third bugle, a large rocaille and three small rocailles. Take the needle back through the last large rocaille and add a bugle, a large rocaille and another bugle.

3 Go back through the first single large rocaille of the first strand and add another bugle, a small rocaille, a large rocaille and another small rocaille. Take the needle through the edge of the ribbon at the next pencil mark, then come back through the first two beads. Add a small rocaille, a bugle, a large rocaille and another bugle, then go through the second single large rocaille of the last strand. Continue in this way to the end.

Looped Fringe

Mark points at even intervals with a fabric marker. Thread a needle, insert into the fabric at the first point and secure with a knot. Thread on enough beads to give the desired size of loop, pushing them up as far as possible. Insert the needle back at the same point to form a loop, then insert the needle at the next point along.

Looped Fringe with Stems

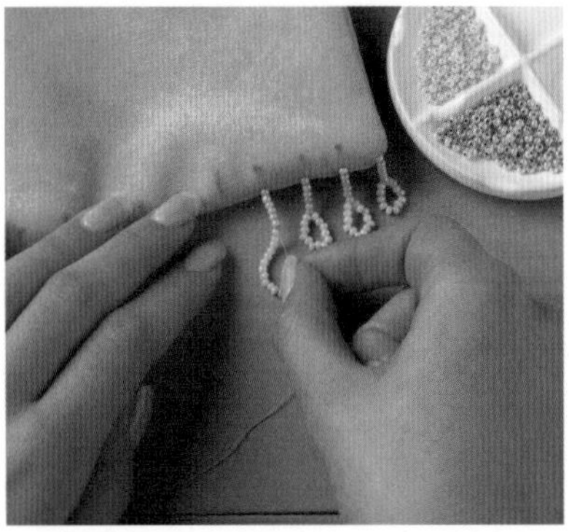

Before making a loop, thread on the required number of beads for the stem, then add the beads for the loop. Pass the needle back through the stem, then insert at the next point along.

Needle-woven Beading

Here a continuous thread runs through rounds of beads, with a second round fitting between pairs of the first, joined to the first by interweaving. The following instructions are for a three-dimensional object. For a two-dimensional design, work rows instead of rounds.

1 For round 1, thread on the required number of beads, tie around the neck of the bottle and knot the ends.

2 For round 2, pass the needle through the first bead of round 1, then thread the first bead of round 2 between the first and second beads. Pass the needle through the third bead of round 1. Continue until the design is complete.

Couching

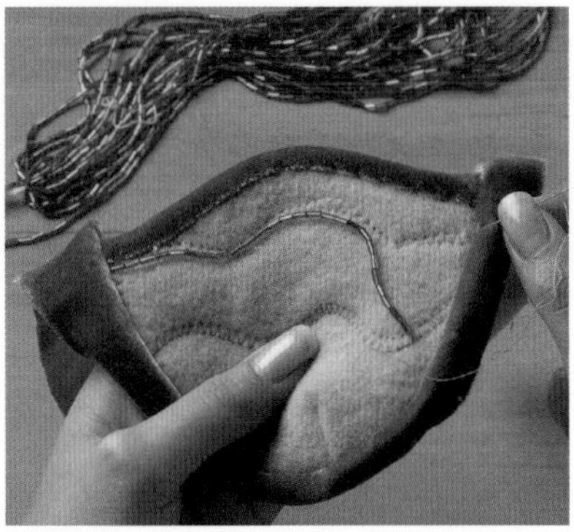

Pre-strung beads are laid down on fabric to create or embellish the lines of the design, then stitched over (couched down) with thread to secure. Add a second thread of beads on top for extra texture.

Scallops

Mark points at even intervals. Thread a needle, insert it into the fabric at the first point and secure with a knot. Thread on enough beads to give the desired length of scallop, pushing them up as far as possible, then insert the needle back in at the next point.

Bead Weaving

Bead weaving is a fascinating and easy-to-learn technique, with roots in Native American craftwork. It is used to make long strips of beadwork with geometric patterns, following charted designs in which each coloured square represents a bead. The weaving is worked on a simple loom: a wire frame that holds the vertical warp threads and keeps them under tension. The horizontal threads, or weft, that carry the beads are worked across the warp. Use long beading needles for weaving, these are fine enough to pass through the smallest beads but tend to snap easily, so keep spares to hand.

1 The warp threads run along the length of the design. They should all be the same length: the length of the finished piece of weaving, plus 25cm/10in.You will require one more warp thread than the number of beads across the design, i.e. for a 15-bead design you need 16 threads. Measure and cut the threads and tie them together at one end with an over hand knot. Knot the other end.

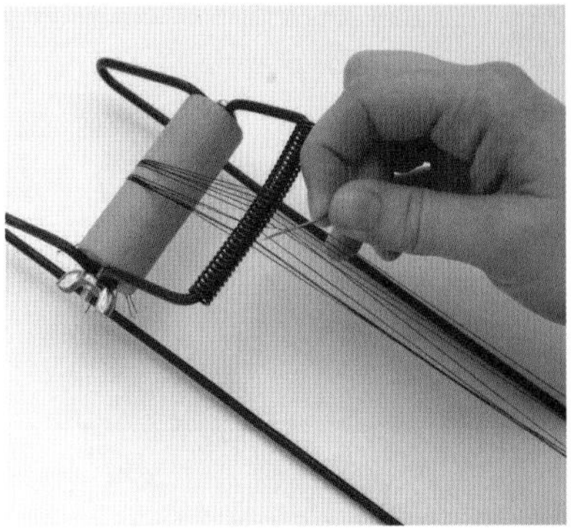

2 Divide the threads in half to form two bundles. There is a pin in the centre of each spool: slip one knot over the first of these. Slip the second knot over the other pin. Loosen the wing nut and turn the spool towards you until the threads are taut. Spread the first threads out over the wire separator so that each one lies in the groove between two coils.

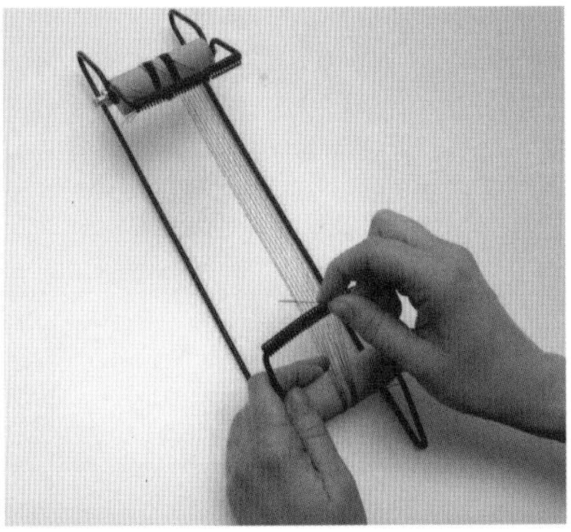

3 You may find it helpful to pick up and separate each thread with a needle. Separate the threads at the other end, ensuring that they all lie parallel. Tighten the wing nuts to maintain the tension.

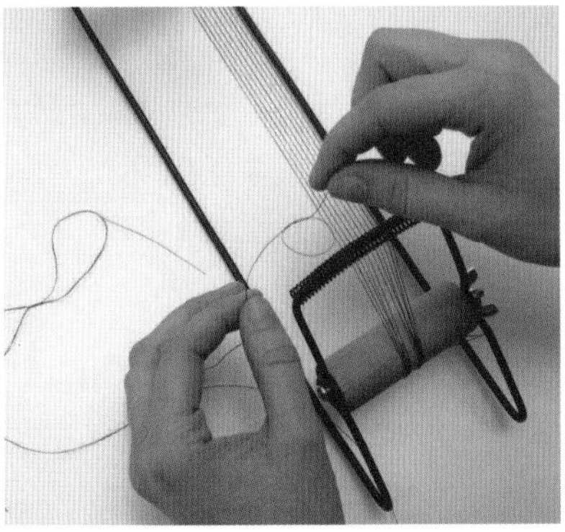

4 Position the loom so that the shorter end of the warp is facing towards you. Cut a 60cm/24in length of nymo and thread it through a beading needle. Knot the long end to the bottom of the first thread on the left, leaving a loose tail of 5cm/2in.

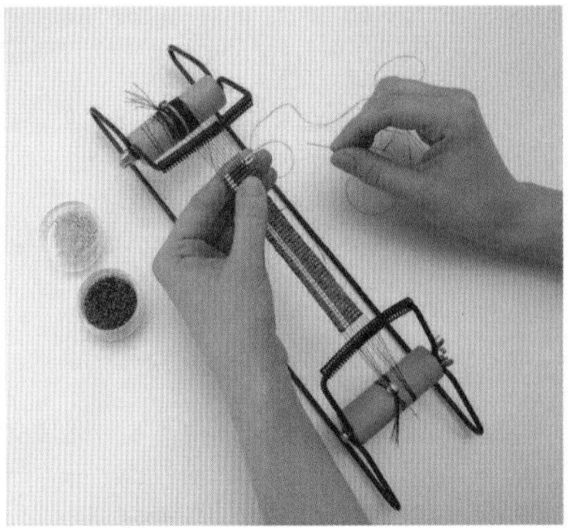

5 The patterns for most bead weaving projects are given as coloured squares on a grid. Each of these squares represents a single bead in a different colour. For the first row of the pattern, use the point of the needle to pick up a bead to match each square, working from left to right.

Wire Beading

Wire brings a third dimension to beadwork, enabling you to make more sculptural forms. It is made from many different metals, from pure silver and brass to flexible alloys, which are often plated in bright colours. The diameter of all wire is given as the gauge (g): the smaller the 'g' number the thicker it is, from 10g up to fine 40g. Use 20g for making jewellery and 24g for wrapped techniques and flowers.

Bead Chains

Individually wired beads can be linked together to make attractive necklaces or set between lengths of chain – a good way to show off just a few expensive beads. Use 20g wire and round-nosed (snub-nosed) pliers to make the loops and flat-nosed pliers to join them together. Make a loop at the end of a short length of wire, as shown on page 32. Thread on the beads, then clip the wire to 6mm/¼in. Bend this end into a second loop, ensuring that it curls in the opposite direction to the first.

1 Wire up the next beads, leaving the second loop partly open. Join the loop on to the first bead, then close it with flat-nosed pliers. Repeat until you have the required length, then add a fastener to each end.

2 Joining the beads with lengths of chain gives a pretty, flexible look to the finished piece. Cut the chain into equal-sized lengths, each with an odd number of links, then use the wired beads to join the chains together.

Wrapping

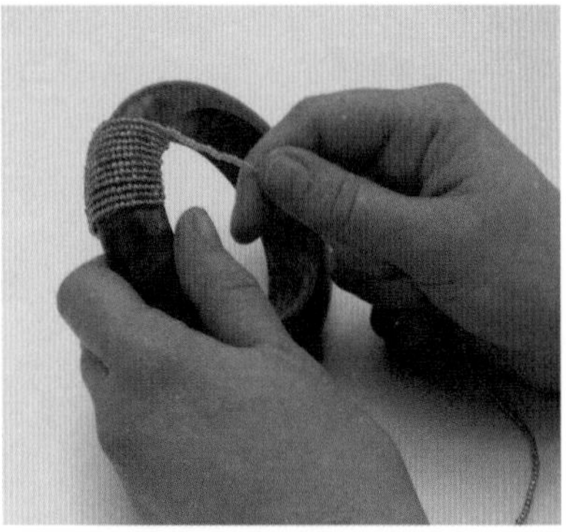

Use this technique to embellish plain bangles and headbands. Thread small beads on to fine wire and secure the end by twisting around the foundation. Slide the beads down and wrap the wire so that the rows of beads lie close together. Finish off by twisting the loose end with flat-nosed pliers.

Memory Wire

This industrial-strength coiled wire retains its shape even when stretched. It comes in three diameters for chokers, bracelets and rings. Cut it with heavy-duty wire cutters and use round-nosed pliers to make a loop at one end. Thread on the beads, then secure the end with another loop.

Tiger Tail

This strong wire is coated with a layer of plastic in a range of bright colours. It works well with crimp beads, which can be used to secure feature beads at intervals along its length to make floating necklaces and bracelets. Use flat-nosed pliers to squeeze the crimp beads into place.

Bead Flowers

These exquisite flowers have been made for centuries and were particularly popular on the Venetian glass-making island of Murano. Long-lasting and naturalistic, they were used to create garlands, posies and tiaras. Use small rocailles or short bugles threaded on fine wire. The same basic method, which is surprisingly easy to master, can be used to make leaves and petals of any size.

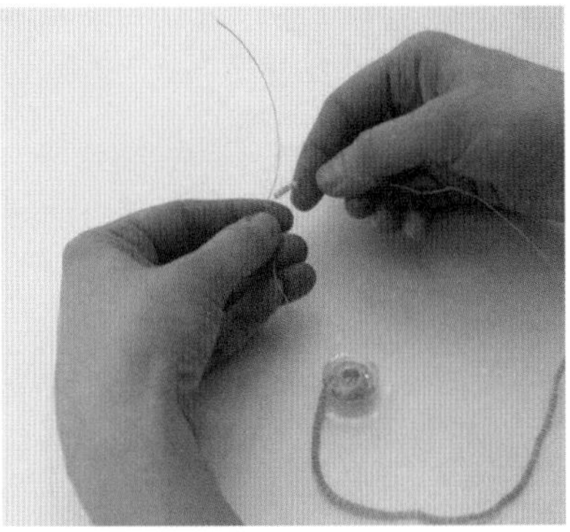

1 Thread the beads on to a reel of fine, flexible wire. Bend the last 15cm/6in into a loop and, leaving about 7cm/ 2¾in free at the end, twist the remaining wire loosely to make the stem. Slide the first five beads down the wire so they lie above the twist.

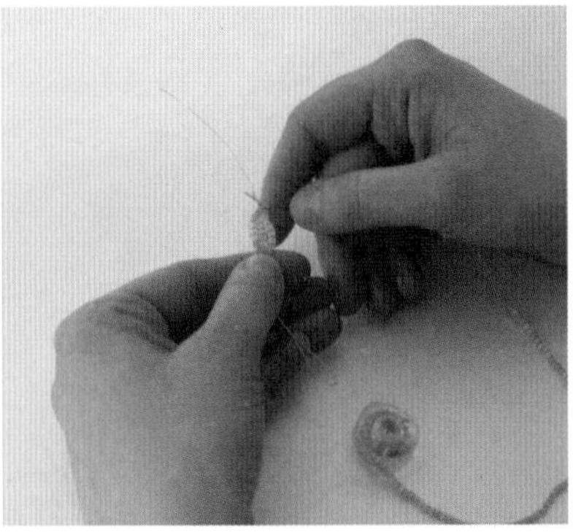

2 Wrap the working wire behind and in front of the loose end. Count off seven beads and hold them to the left of the centre beads. Take the wire once around the top of the stem below the beads, count off another seven, and bring it up to the right.

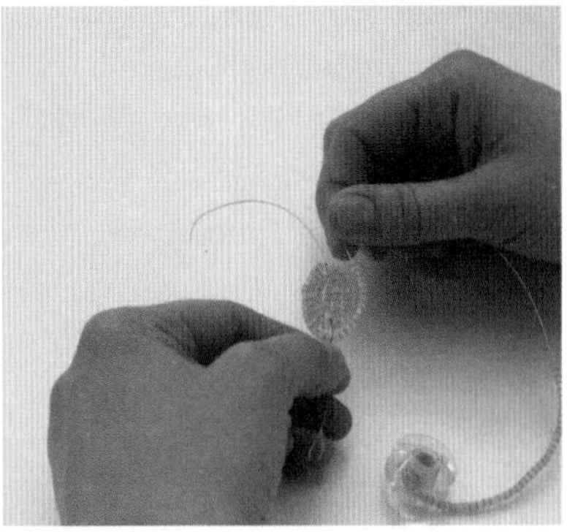

3 Wrap the wire once around the loose wire, just above the top bead. Make another round in the same way with nine beads on the left and eleven on the right. Continue adding more rounds until the petal is the required size, adding another two beads on each side as you work.

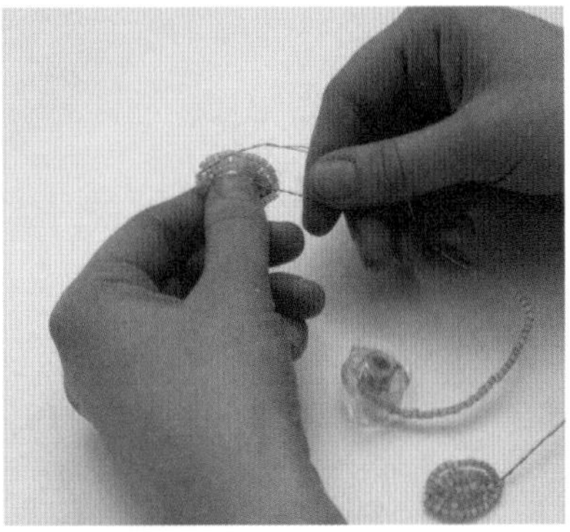

4 Finish off by bending both wires back down behind the beads. Twist all four strands together to complete the stem, and clip with wire cutters. Make another four petals in the same way and curve them gently between finger and thumb to give a natural shape.

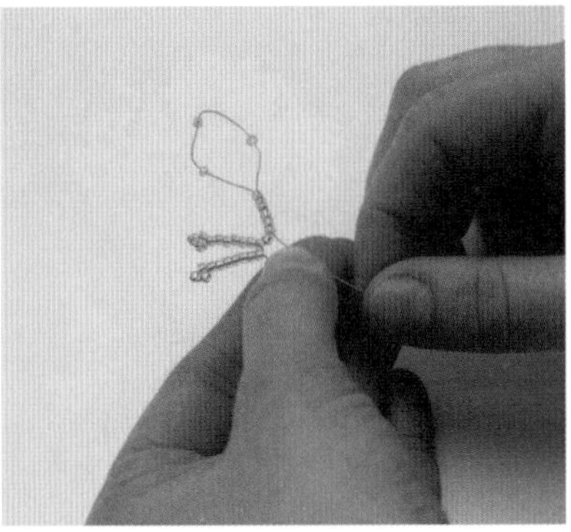

5 To make the bead stamen centre, thread ten gold beads 30cm/12in along the wire. Pass the loose end back through the first seven beads, then repeat this seven times. Twist the loose ends together and clip them.

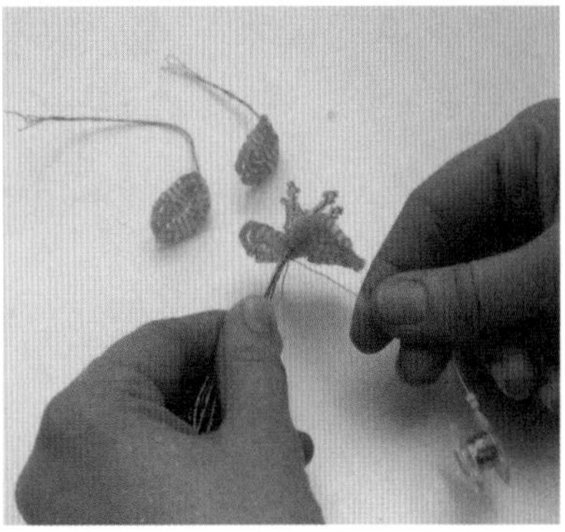

6 Hold the first petal up against the stamens and keep it in place by wrapping wire tightly around the top of the stem. Add the other petals, arranging them evenly around the centre core. Conceal the wires by binding the stalk with florist's tape (stem wrap).

Using Findings

Findings are the metal pins, clasps and loops that will transform your beads into items of jewellery. They come in a range of finishes to suit all styles from classically elegant to ruggedly ethnic.

Jump Rings

1 These wire circles are used to join fasteners to necklaces and earrings to stud posts, to link chains and droppers and to make earrings. Open sideways with a gentle twisting action, using pliers if necessary: forcing them from the centre will distort the shape.

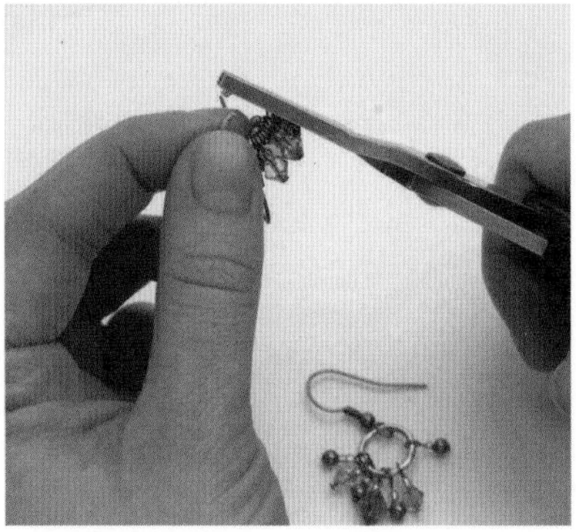

2 For an earring, thread on dropper beads and an ear hook. Close the ring by twisting it in the opposite direction so the two ends touch again. Thicker rings may require pliers to open and close them but softer, small jump rings can be carefully opened by hand.

Triangles

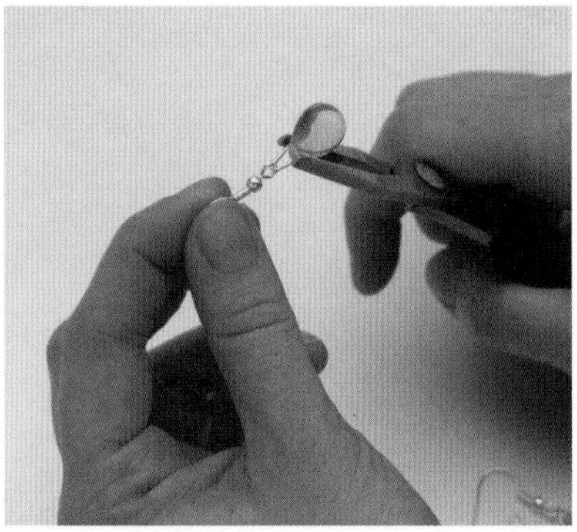

Teardrop beads have a hole at the narrow point, rather than through the centre, and are fixed to other findings with triangular links. Use pliers to open the space, slip over the top of the bead and gently squeeze the triangle shut with flat-nosed pliers.

Head Pins

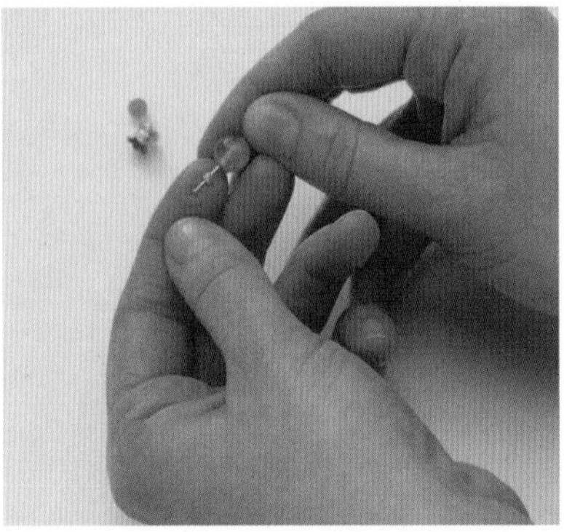

1 Head pins are for making bead drops or simple earrings. If the holes in the beads are too wide, thread on a small, matching bead first. Add more beads until there is 6mm/¼in of wire left.

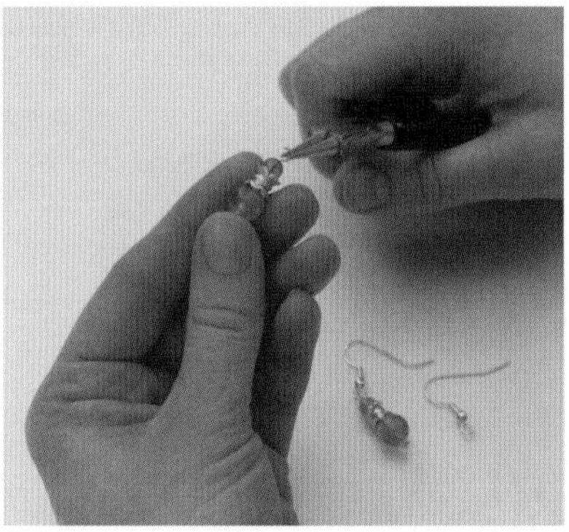

2 Bend into a loop with round-nosed (snub-nosed) pliers. Just before the loop is complete, bend the wire back to centre the loop above the pin. Thread on a dropper and ear hook and complete the loop.

Eye Pins

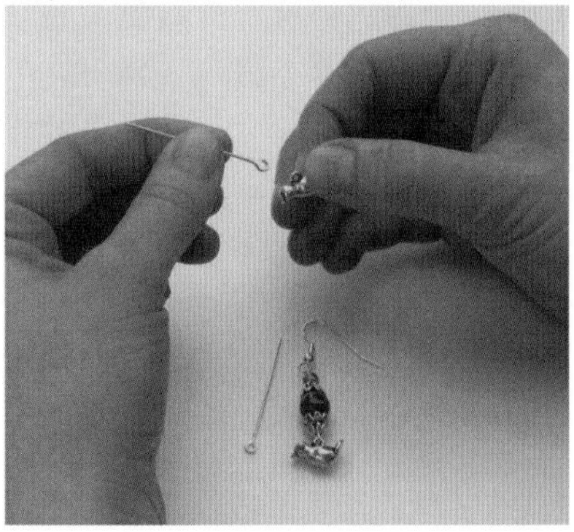

These pins have a small loop at the end for small charms and droppers. Open and close the loop with pliers. Make the top loop at a right angle so the charm will face forward.

Shell Calotte

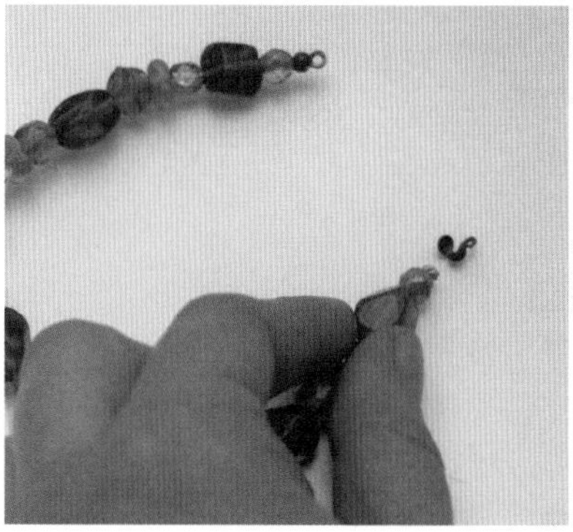

Make a knot (two or three if the thread is fine) close to the end of the thread. Seal with glue. When dry, trim to 2mm/1⁄12in. Hold the calotte over the knot and squeeze it shut with pliers. At the other end, knot the thread close to the last bead, clip the end and fix a calotte over the knot.

Crab Claw

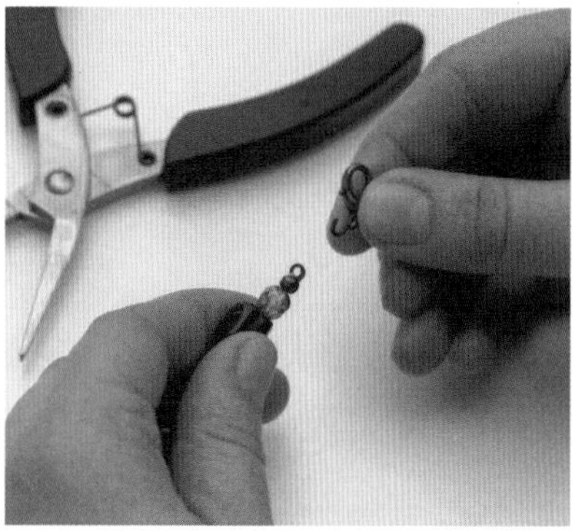

These functional, spring-loaded fasteners are joined on to a calotte with a jump ring. They come in several sizes: the smaller the beads, the smaller the crab claw should be. Fix a second jump ring to the other calotte to complete the fastening.

Hook and Eye Fastener

This fastener, which has a hollow tube at each end, is designed for use with leather thong or thick cord. Trim the cord to the required length and put a spot of superglue on the end. Insert the end into one part of the fastener and gently squeeze with pliers. Repeat at the other end.

Spacers and Bars

For multi-stranded bracelets or necklaces, the rows of beads are kept apart with these special findings, which accommodate anything from two to seven threads.

1 Tie the end of each strand securely to one of the loops on the spacer and pass the thread through the holes in a bar as you add the beads.

2 Space the bars at regular intervals – a bracelet will require two – and fasten the thread to a second spacer. For a necklace, you will need to increase the number of beads in each row so that it lies flat on the chest when worn.

Making Necklaces and Bracelets

Depending on its length, a string of threaded beads can be made into a bracelet, choker or necklace. Very long necklaces of 100cm/40in can be slipped over the head, but anything shorter will need a fastening of some kind. Each end of the thread is finished with a metal knot cover called a calotte: a small, hinged metal ball with an opening at one end and a loop at the other. The fastening is joined to the small loops.

Beaded Jewellery and Accessories

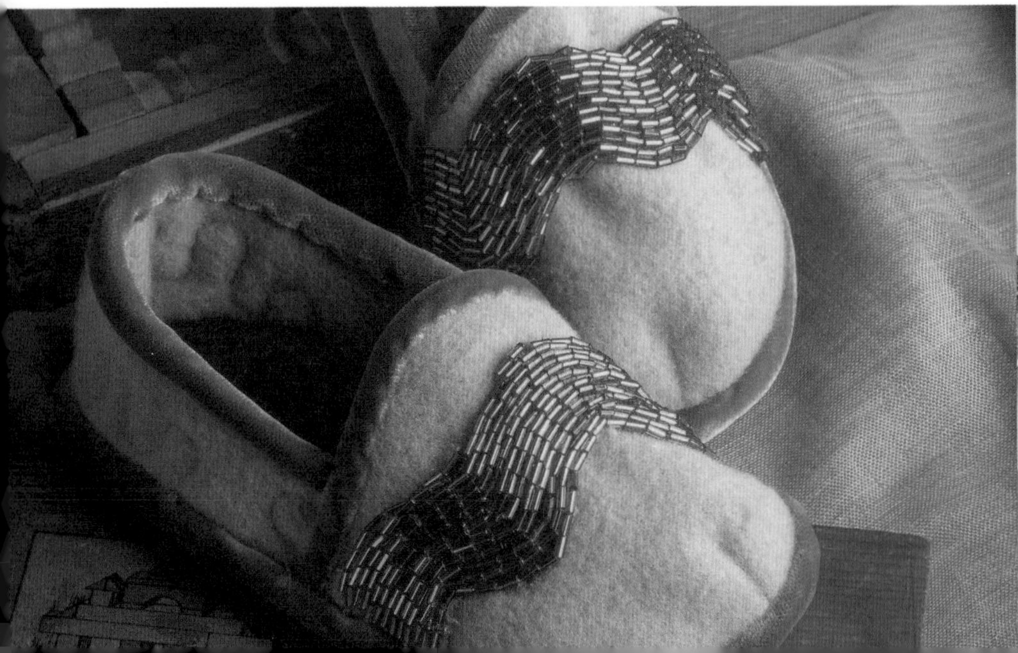
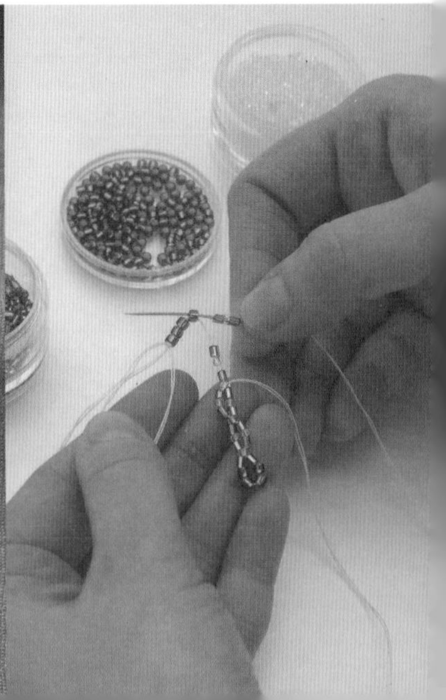

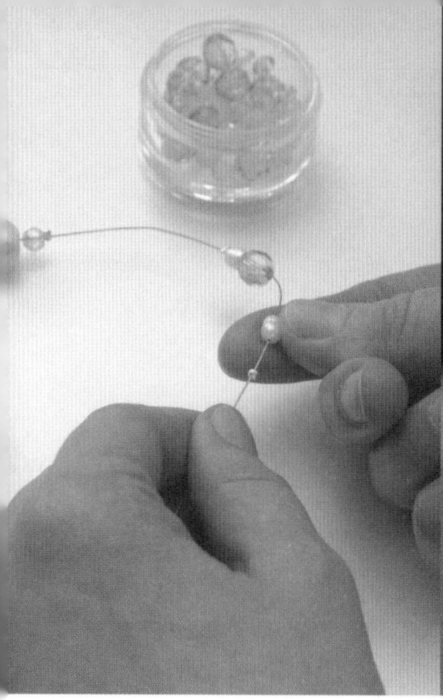

From necklaces and tiaras to belts and buttons, beadwork in all its many forms can now be found decorating the most glamorous outfits. International designers have always been inspired by the colour, patterns and textures that beads can create, and have used them to enhance their collections, as jewellery and on trimmings or accessories. The projects and ideas on the following pages make best use of the variety of beads now widely available.

Show off a few precious glass beads, like these exquisitely decorated Venetian lampwork beads, by joining them with multiple strands of smaller, more inexpensive rocailles in matching shades.

Venetian Necklace

you will need
Scissors
5m/15ft strong black nylon thread
Beading needle
6mm/¼in lilac iridescent and red rocailles
3mm/⅛in bronze and green glass rocailles
7 large Venetian glass beads
2 crimping beads with loops
Round-nosed (snub-nosed) pliers
2 6mm/¼in gold jump rings
S-shaped gold fastener

1 Thread the needle with 1m/1yd of thread and tie a bead to the end. Thread on the following beads: one lilac, 25 bronze, one green, two bronze, two green, one red, three green, one red, one lilac, one Venetian, one lilac, one red, three green, one red, two green, two bronze, one green. Repeat this sequence six times. End with 25 bronze and a lilac.

2 Cut another 1m/40in length of thread, thread through the needle and tie around the anchor bead as before. Pass the needle through the first lilac bead then thread on 25 bronze, one green, two bronze, two green, one red and three green. Pass the needle through the red, lilac, Venetian, lilac and red beads. Repeat this sequence six times, ending with 25 bronze beads and passing the needle through the lilac bead.

3 Make another three strands in the same way. Knot the threads at each end, then attach a brass crimping bead over each knot with pliers.

4 Attach a jump ring to each crimping bead and thread the fastener through them.

This simple drawstring bag, just the right size for a pair of shoes or special accessories, is personalized with a pair of initials worked in bead couching. Make a larger version to hold laundry or linen.

Monogrammed Bag

you will need

- 60 x 25cm/24 x 10in cotton, silk or linen, for the bag
- 60 x 25cm/24 x 10in cotton lawn or lightweight silk, for the lining
- Tape measure
- Dressmaking scissors
- Pencil and tracing paper
- Beading needle
- Matching sewing thread
- Glass embroidery beads in a variety of colours
- Small glass bugle beads
- Dressmaker's pins
- Sewing-machine
- 100cm/40in silk or leather cord
- Safety pin
- 2 large beads with large centre holes

1 Cut two rectangles each from the main fabric and lining fabric, measuring 30 x 25cm/12 x 10in. Draw your chosen initials on to tracing paper. Rub over the wrong side with pencil, and place it right side up over the right side of one of the main pieces of fabric. Trace over the lines to transfer the design.

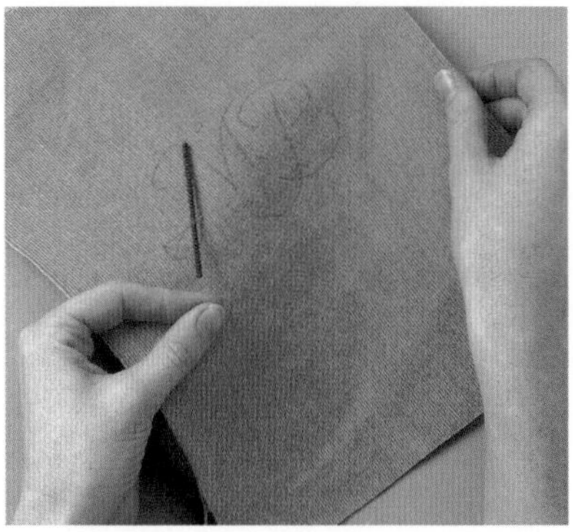

2 Thread the beading needle with sewing thread and bring it out at the top of the first letter. Thread on enough beads to cover the first line and take it down at the end.

3 Couch the beads in place by making small horizontal stitches between them, following the shape of the line exactly. Fasten off securely at the end.

4 Continue until you have completed the whole monogram. Decorate the rest of the bag with randomly placed individual embroidery beads and small bugles in a variety of colours.

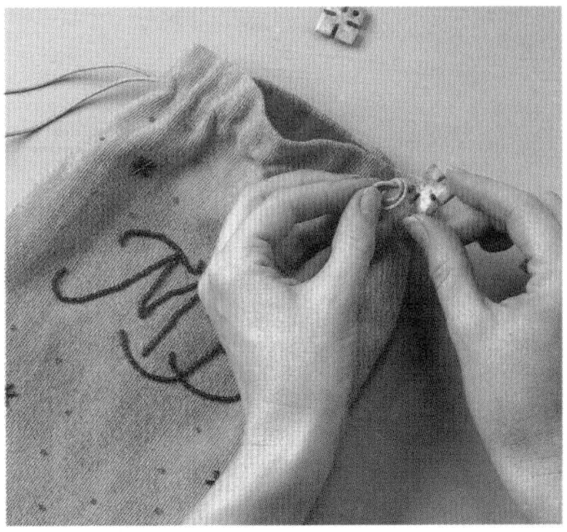

5 To make up the bag, pin the two main pieces right sides together, and machine stitch along three sides, leaving the top open. Repeat with the lining fabric. Turn the main fabric right-side out, and press.

6 Slip the lining inside the bag. Fold all the raw edges inside, pin, and slip stitch the folded edge of the lining to the folded edge of the bag. Sew two lines of stitching through both thicknesses of fabric, 3cm/1¼in and 1cm/½in from the top edge, to form the drawstring channel.

7 Snip through the stitches of the side seams between the two rows, to make gaps to insert the cords. Cut the cord in half. Use a safety pin to thread one half through from one side, and the other from the opposite side. Thread a decorative bead on to the two cords at each side, and knot to secure.

Gleaming freshwater pearls and faceted crystals in feminine shades of pink and cream come together in this graceful necklace. They are threaded on fine tiger tail wire, which is almost invisible when worn.

Pearl and Crystal Necklace

you will need

180cm/2yd tiger tail wire
Wire cutters
Selection of freshwater pearls and crystal beads in various shades and sizes
Silver crimp beads
Flat-nosed pliers
2 silver shell calottes
10 small silver jump rings
Silver head pin
Crab-claw fastener

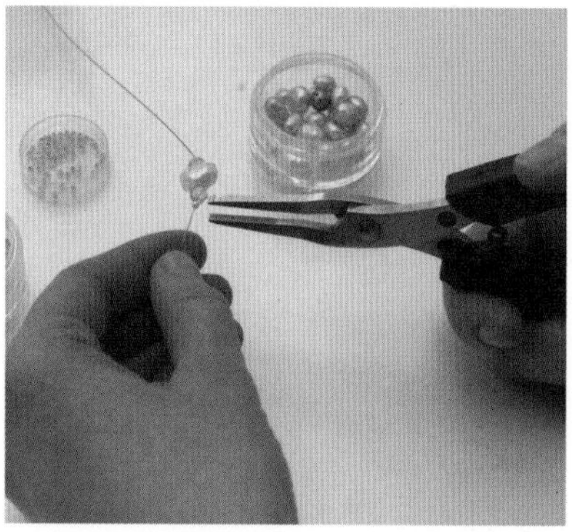

1 Cut the tiger tail into three 60cm/24in lengths with the wire cutters. Thread a pearl at the centre of one length and add a crystal and a crimp bead at each side. Squeeze the crimp beads with the tip of the flat-nosed pliers to hold them in place.

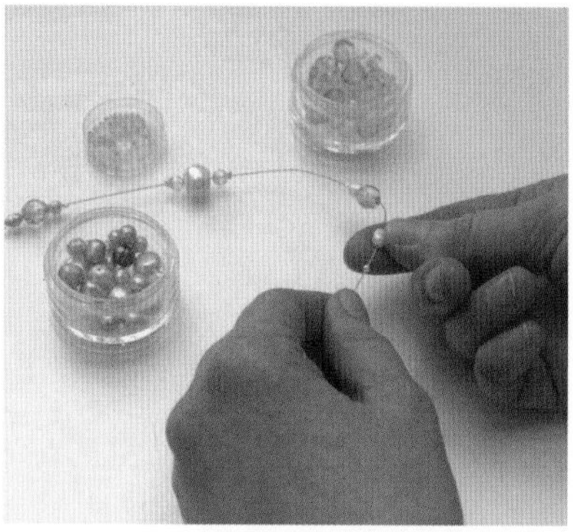

2 Fix a crimp bead 3cm/1¼in along and thread on a pearl, a crystal and another pearl. Secure with a second crimp bead. Continue adding groups of evenly spaced beads along each end of the wire.

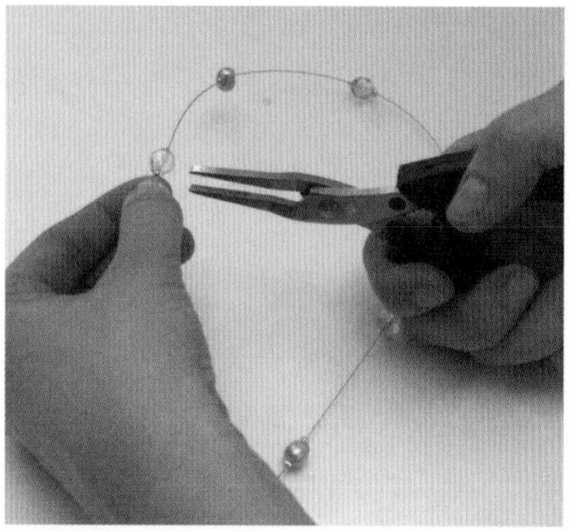

3 Thread the second wire with alternate single pearls and crystals, at the same intervals, each one held in place with two crimp beads.

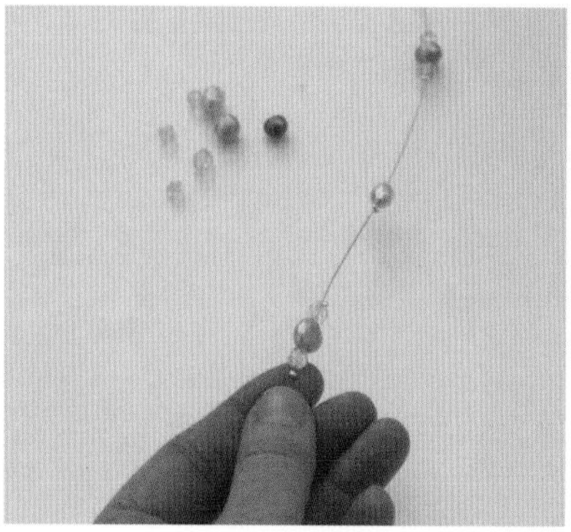

4 Add beads to the third length of wire at the same intervals, alternating the single beads with groups of three beads.

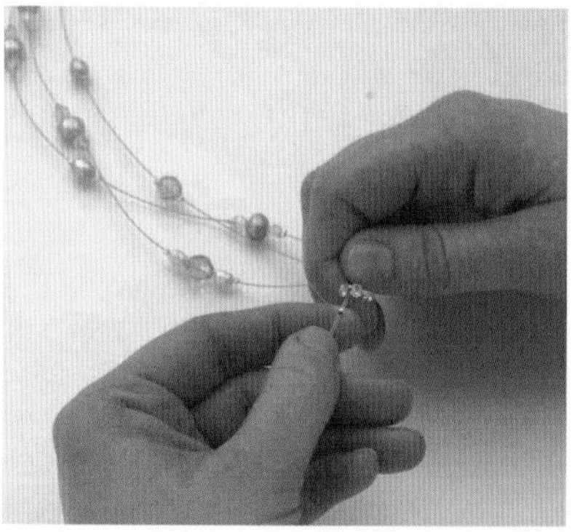

5 Lay the three strands flat and adjust them so that the beads lie within the spaces on the other wires. Thread each group of three loose ends through both a calotte and a crimp bead.

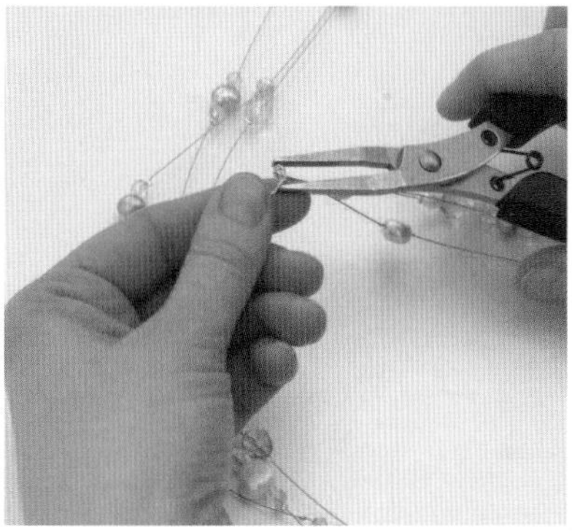

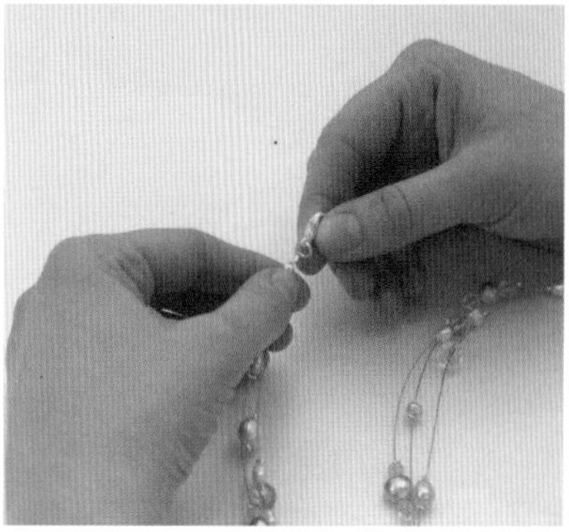

6 Use the wire cutters to trim the ends of the tiger tail very close to the crimp bead. Slide up the calotte and close it with pliers so that the ends are completely concealed.

7 Join the jump rings to make a chain. Thread two beads on to the head pin and bend the end into a loop. Add this to the chain, then fix the other end to one of the calottes.

8 Open the last jump ring by twisting it sideways with pliers and slip on the crab claw fastener. Pass the ring through the second calotte and close with pliers.

The bead droppers that hang from this pretty charm bracelet are made from an eclectic selection of pearl, iridescent glass and faceted crystal beads, in shades of amethyst and silver.

Beaded Charm Bracelet

you will need

Silver chain link bracelet
Selection of pearl, crystal and glass beads
Silver rondelles
2.5cm/1in silver head pins
A few rocailles in matching colours
Round-nosed (snub-nosed) pliers
Silver jump rings
Silver charms
Flat-nosed pliers

1 Make a dropper for every other chain link of the bracelet by threading a large bead, a rondelle and a small bead on to a head pin. Use a rocaille first, as a stopper, if the first bead has a narrow hole.

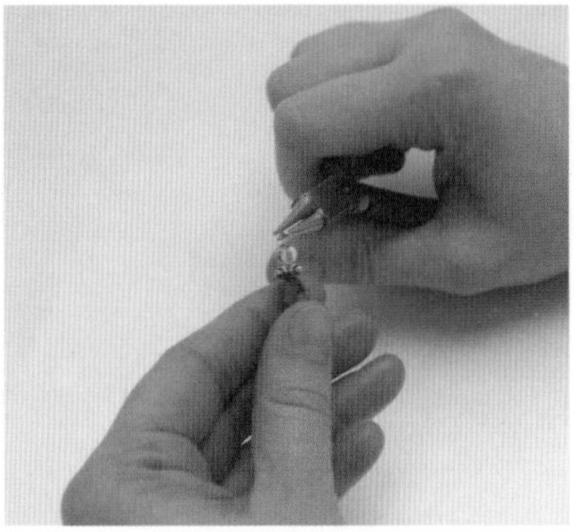

2 Bend the end of the wire into a loop using the round-nosed pliers. Gently ease the wire between the jaws to make a smooth curve, then just before you complete the ring, bend the wire at a right angle to make a question mark shape. Close the loop.

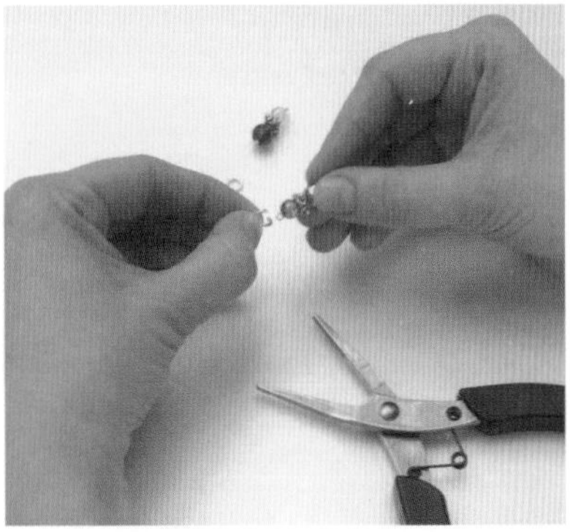

3 Add a jump ring to the top of the first dropper. Open up the ring by gently twisting the two halves apart with a sideways movement, using the flat-nosed pliers. Slip one end through the wire loop.

4 Slot the open jump ring on to the second chain link and squeeze it closed with flat-nosed pliers. Add the other droppers on to every other link along the bracelet.

5 Use a jump ring to attach a silver charm to the first empty link. To complete the bracelet, fix the remaining charms to the other links.

These bohemian earrings are made from a combination of bronze-effect wire and topaz-coloured glass beads, which give them a rich, vintage look. Try silver findings and foil-lined beads for a very different effect.

Cascade Earrings

you will need
30cm/6in chain
Wire cutters
2 small, 4 medium and
4 large oval crystal drops
12 jump rings
Medium-gauge wire
32 small bicone crystals
6 spacer beads
2 pear-shaped crystal beads
Pair of ear hooks
2 oval crystal beads
Round-nosed (snub-nosed) pliers

1 Make both earrings in the same way. Cut two lengths of chain, each of three links. Join these on to the medium crystal drops with jump rings. Cut two five-link pieces and join to the large drops in the same way.

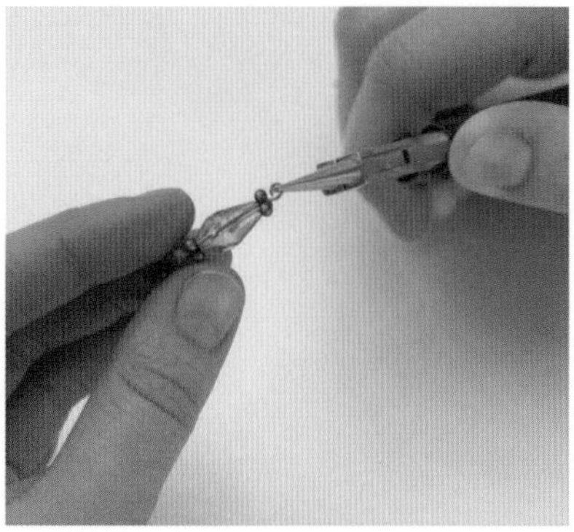

2 For the centre dropper, make a loop at the end of a 5cm/2in piece of wire and fix on a small crystal drop. Thread on a bicone, a spacer and the pear-shaped bead, followed by another spacer. Clip the end and bend into a loop with the round-nosed pliers.

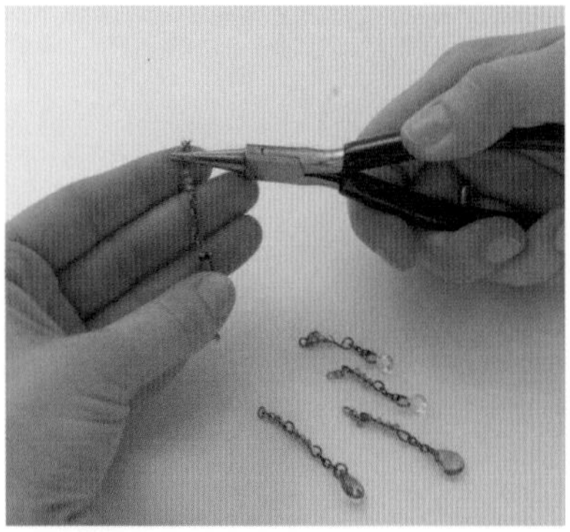

3 Make five beaded wires, each with three bicones and a loop at each end. Use a five-link chain to join one wire to the dropper. Add a seven-link length to the other end. Join the other wires to the crystal chains. Join three-link chains to the medium drops and five-link chains to the large.

4 Thread all five chains through a jump ring in the following order: medium drop, large drop, centre dropper, large drop and medium drop.

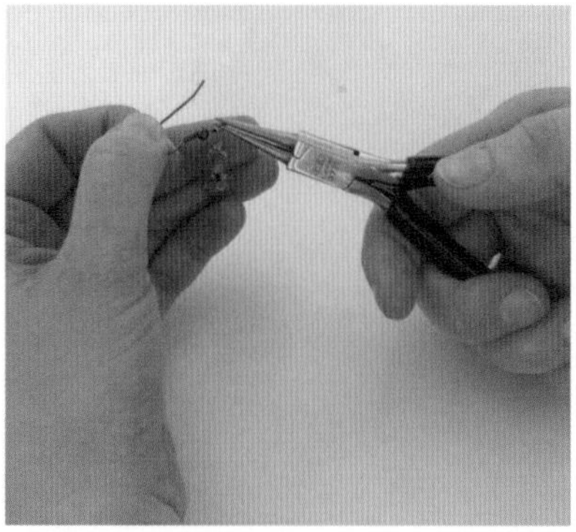

5 Make the earring head by making a loop at the bottom of a short length of wire. Add a spacer bead, an oval crystal and a bicone. Trim the other end and bend into a loop. Thread on an earring backing before closing the loop. Thread the jump ring on the other end and close.

The inspiration and starting point for this necklace was the unusual filigree pendant at the centre. The beads are strung on a core of thread, covered with naturally spiralling blanket stitch.

Chinese-style Necklace

you will need
2m/80in 2-ply silk thread
Scissors
Tape measure
Drawing pins (thumb tacks)
Pin board
4m/160in fine silk thread
2 large-eyed sewing needles
6 bone beads
2 round amber beads
2 round lampwork beads with foil inserts
4 precious stone beads
3 lampwork discs with foil insert
2 large amber beads
1 large Chinese pendant
1 clasp

1 To make the first side, cut 1m/40in of 2-ply silk thread, fold it in half and pin the midpoint to the board. Cut two 2m/80in lengths of fine silk thread. Thread each on to a needle and knot the ends so the thread is doubled. Slip both knots over the pin. Lay one length alongside the 2-ply silk and use the other needle to blanket stitch over the threads for 12cm/5in.

2 Separate out the strands of the 2-ply silk and, using the two needles, work blanket stitch for 2cm/1in down each strand. Thread a bone bead on to one strand and a round amber bead on to the other. Tie double knots just below the beads to secure them in place. Use one strand of fine silk to work buttonhole stitch over all the strands for another 15mm/⅝in.

3 Add on a round lampwork bead and knot all the threads below the bead. Work buttonhole stitch over all the strands for 15mm/⅝in, then work as two strands for 15mm/⅝in. Thread a stone bead on each strand and knot.

4 Work two strands for 15mm/⅝in, then one strand for 1cm/½in. Add a disc, knot and work one strand for 1cm/½in. Add a bone, amber and a bone bead and knot. Make the second side, thread all ends through and knot.

5 Thread all the ends through the third disc. Knot them securely and pass the threads back up through the pendant and trim. Unpin the piece, and sew half of the clasp to each end.

Inspired by ethnic beadwork, this bag is made of traditional ikat fabric from Indonesia, lined with a plain fabric that acts as a binding and casing for the ties. An ideal first project for a newcomer to beadwork.

Little Fringed Bag

you will need
30 x 15cm/12 x 6in ikat fabric
Dressmaking scissors
Tape measure
Set square or ruler
Fabric marker
Pencil
Sheet of paper
Dressmaker's pins
35cm/14in square plain-coloured fabric, in contrasting colour
Iron
Sewing-machine
Matching thread
Sewing needle and thread to match lining
Beading needle
Black beading thread
Small black glass beads
Small multicoloured glass beads
2 50cm/20in black shoelaces
12 large beads with large holes

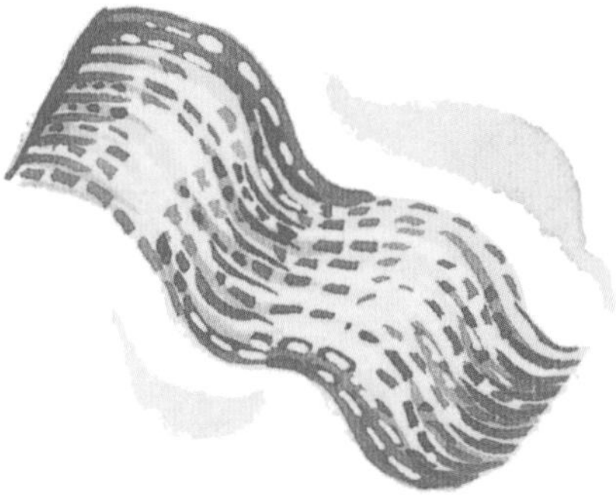

1 Cut the ikat fabric into two 15cm/6in squares. On the right side of each piece, mark a line diagonally from corner to corner in both directions, then mark parallel lines 2cm/¾in apart. Draw a bag shape similar to the bag in the finished picture on paper.

2 Pin the template to both pieces of ikat fabric and cut out. Cut two pieces of plain fabric 16 x 20cm/6¼ x 8in for the lining. With the marked lines right side up, tack (baste) one bag piece to each lining piece. Using running stitch, stitch along the lines. Trim the excess lining fabric.

3 To make the casing, cut two pieces of lining fabric 7 x 12cm/2¾ x 4½in. Press in half lengthways then press under a narrow turning all round. Pin one long edge to the top of a bag piece and machine stitch. Repeat with the second casing.

4 Place the two bag pieces right sides together. Pin, then machine stitch 1cm/½in from the raw, curved edges. Leave the top open.

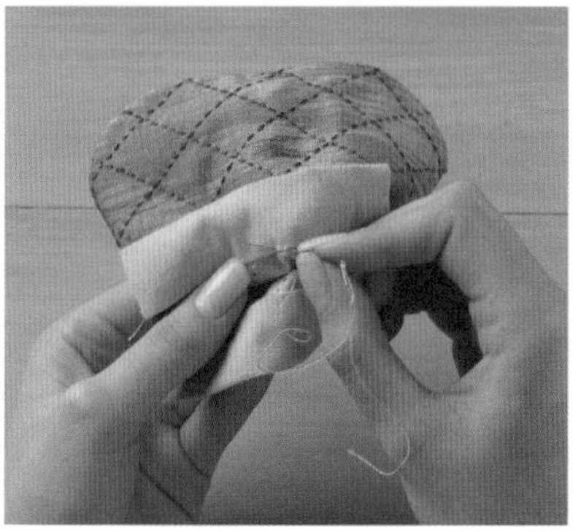

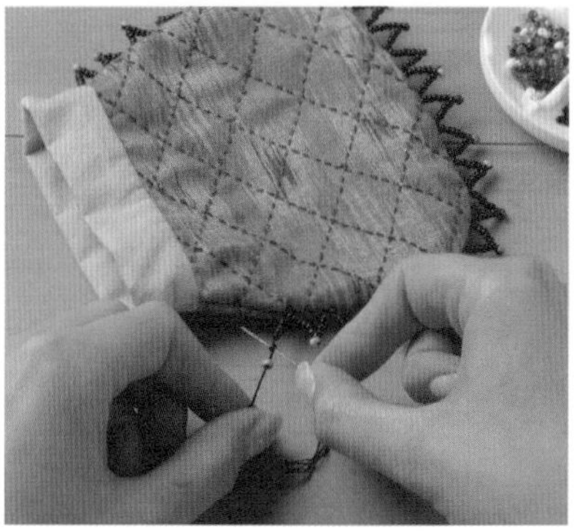

5 Turn the bag right side out. Fold the casings over the raw edges and slip stitch in place. Thread a beading needle with beading thread and fasten just below the casing.

6 Thread on seven black beads and a coloured bead, then go back through the last black bead. Thread on six black beads and make a small stitch 1cm/½in along the seam. Repeat all around the bag.

7 Thread one shoelace through each casing for the drawstring. Thread three large beads on to the end of each shoelace and knot. Tie the two shoelaces together at either end.

This deceptively simple technique, in which beads are wound around a cord, is very popular among the Zulu people of South Africa, who are some of the most skilled and prolific beaders in the world.

Cord-beaded Bracelet

you will need
Thick cord
Scissors
Sewing thread
Fabric paint, to match beads
Paintbrush
Beading needle
Matching beading thread
Small glass beads
Button, diameter to match cord

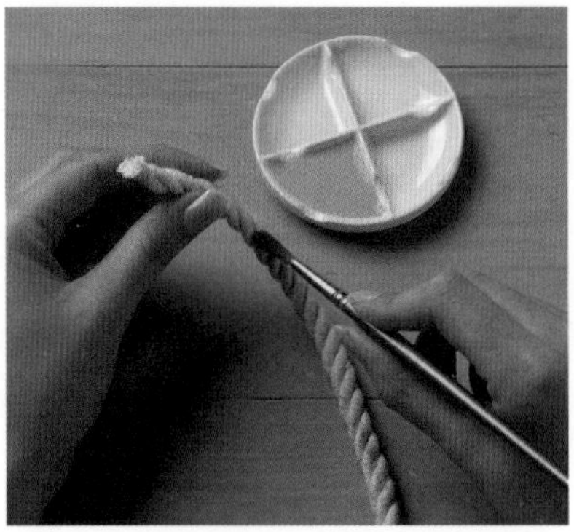

1 Cut a length of cord to fit around your wrist. Bind both ends tightly with sewing thread to prevent them unravelling. Paint the cord with fabric paint so that it is the same colour as the beads. Leave to dry.

2 Thread the needle and fasten to one end of the cord. Thread on 20 beads, holding the thread taut and pushing the beads together. Wind the beads around the cord, make a couple of stitches then pass the needle back through the last few beads. Repeat along the length of the cord.

3 To finish off the ends of the cord, thread on a few beads and make a stitch across each blunt end. Make several more stitches to cover the ends completely.

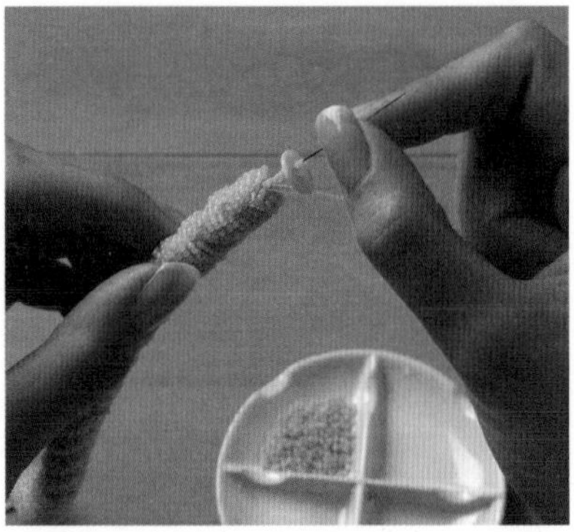

4 Make a beaded loop at one end of the cord (see Basic Techniques). At the other end, thread on three beads then pass the needle through the button. Thread on two more beads, pass the needle back through the button and make several stitches to finish off.

These delicate gold wire earrings are in the form of tiny sets of scales, the star sign of Libra, and are filled with green and blue beads. Thread the same number of beads in each so they will balance perfectly.

Libran Earrings

you will need

- Reel fine brass wire
- Fine crochet hook
- Round-nosed (snug-nosed) pliers
- Round-ended pencil
- Selection of small blue and green glass beads
- 4 jump rings
- 2 split rings
- Pair earring posts with loops
- 0.8mm/1/30in brass wire
- Pair butterfly backs
- Wire cutters

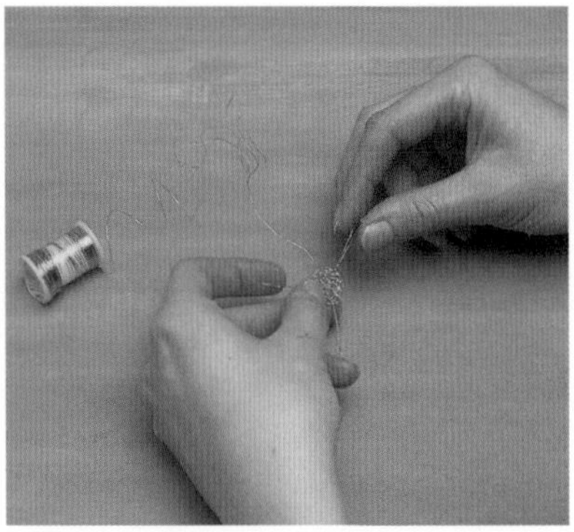

1 With the fine wire, crochet four round shapes 1cm/½in across. On the last round make three 2cm/¾in equally spaced loops with the pliers. Leave a long end of wire. Twist the loops.

2 Mould each round into a dome shape with the pencil. Thread equal numbers of beads on to each loose end of wire and secure them in each basket. Do not trim the wire yet.

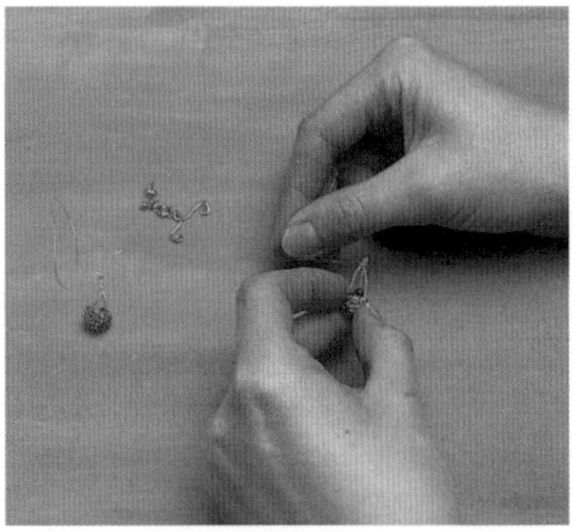

3 With pliers, attach a jump ring and split ring to each. Cut two 4.5cm/1¾in lengths of thicket wire. Twist a loop in the centre of each, then bend each end into two loops to hang the baskets from. Attach the centre loop to the split ring using another jump ring. Thread the long end of wire on a basket through the top of the twisted loops and attach to the bar. Repeat with the other baskets. Trim.

Ornate hatpins were once an indispensable accessory, used to secure the wide-brimmed headgear worn by fashionable Edwardian ladies. These contemporary versions can be pinned, brooch-style, to the lapel.

Beaded Hatpins

you will need

Decorative and diamanté beads
Hatpin bases with safety ends
Glue gun or impact adhesive
Lengths of 6mm/¼in-wide ribbon in several colours
Matching sewing thread

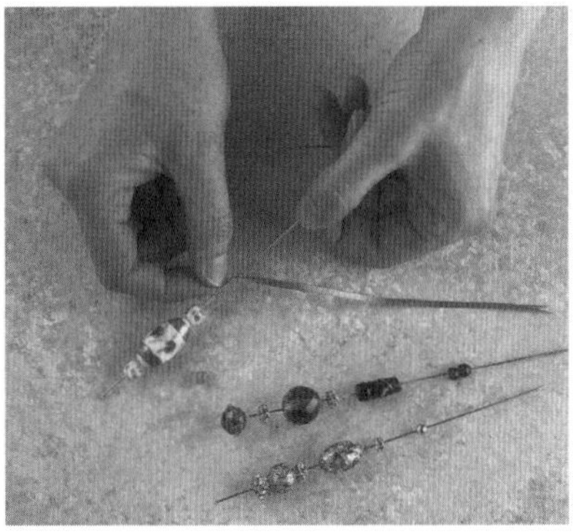

1 Choose a selection of beads in matching or complementary colours and in various shapes and sizes. Pick out a small bead to put on to the pin first to prevent the others slipping off. Smear the shaft of the pin with a very thin coat of glue, then add on the other beads.

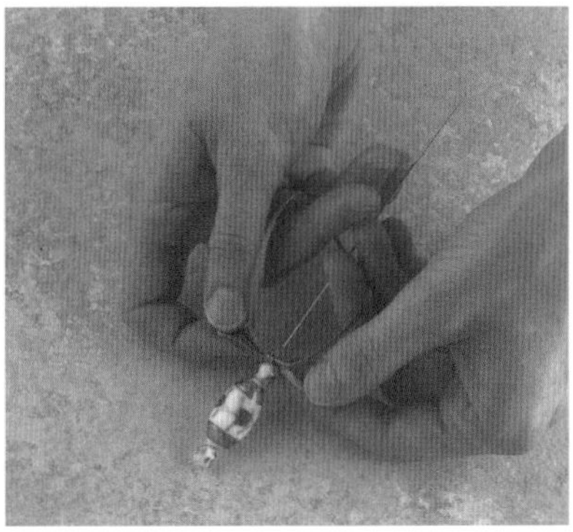

2 Streamers can be added by threading a length of narrow ribbon between the beads. Tie into a bow and secure with a few stitches.

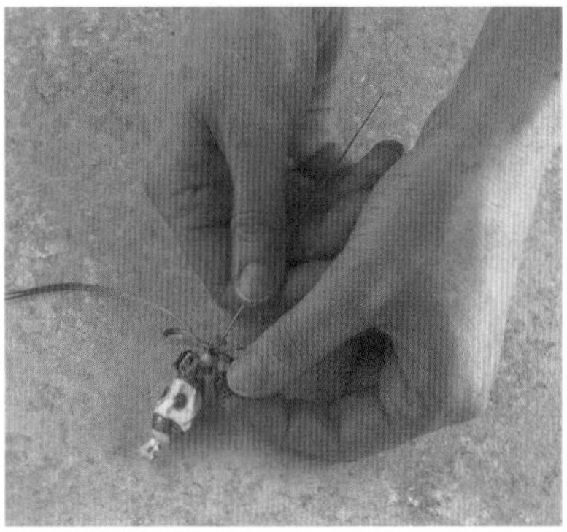

3 Make tiny roses from the ribbons, following the instructions in Basic Techniques. Sew the ends firmly and trim, before glueing the roses between the beads for a flowered effect.

These buttons are simple and satisfying to make. They would all add a unique finishing touch to a special garment, but could also be used on any soft furnishing project, from a cushion to a lampshade.

Beaded Buttons

●●

you will need

Black felt-tipped pen
Compressed cotton sphere, 12mm/½in diameter
Beading needle
Black beading thread
Small black glass beads
Fabric marker
3cm/1¼in diameter cover button
Scraps of silk
Dressmaking scissors
Sewing needle
Sewing threads to match silk and taffeta
Large transparent glass beads with silver-lined holes
4mm/3⁄16in green crystal beads
15mm/⅝in diameter cover buttons
Scraps of taffeta
6mm/¼in green glass bead
Small copper glass beads
Small transparent glass beads

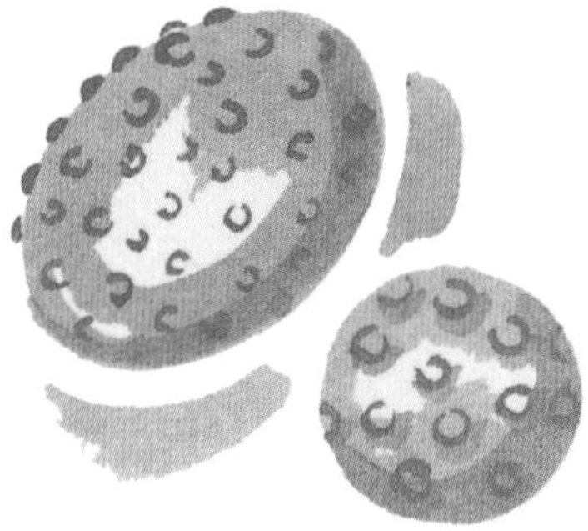

1 Colour the sphere black. Fasten the thread on at the top, stitch down a black bead, then go through the sphere. Thread on another bead and stitch it down. Take the needle around the sphere, through the top and bottom beads, then around again at right angles to divide into quarters.

2 Thread on 18 beads and pass the needle through the bottom bead on the sphere. Thread on 18 more beads, pass the needle through the top bead then around the sphere at right angles.

3 Thread on 16 beads and work from top to bottom as before, this time dividing the sphere into eight sections. Repeat with 14 beads, dividing the sphere into 16 sections, until the whole sphere is covered.

4 To make a hanging loop, fasten on at the bottom and thread on eight beads. Insert the needle back into the sphere at the same point.

5 For the flower button: draw around the large button on to a scrap of silk. Draw another circle 1cm/½in larger and cut out. Mark five equal points around the inner circle.

6 Thread a needle and fasten on in the centre of the circle. Thread on 20 large transparent glass beads, then insert the needle back at the same point to make a loop.

7 Bring the needle out at one mark. Couch down the loop with a stitch between the ninth and tenth beads. Make four more petal shapes in the same way. Stitch a green crystal bead to the centre.

8 Run a gathering stitch 3mm/⅛in from the raw edge. Place the cover button in the centre and pull up the thread. Secure with a few small stitches and attach the underside of the button.

9 For the jewelled button: cover a small button with taffeta, as instructed. Fasten on in the centre and thread on a green crystal, a few transparent beads, then go back through the crystal. Make another stitch, then repeat to cover the button.

10 For the tassel button: cut out a 3cm/1¼in circle of taffeta. Fasten on in the centre. Thread on a green glass and eight copper beads, go back through the green bead and fasten off. Gather the raw edges and cover the button as in steps 8 and 9.

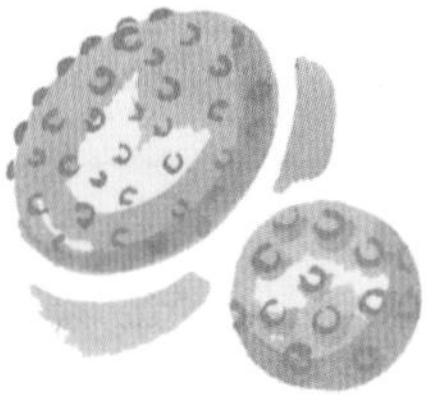

Add a touch of contemporary boho chic to your favourite outfit with this avant-garde, low-slung hipster chain belt – you can also use the same method to make a matching necklace.

Silver Chain Belt

you will need

60cm/24in medium-gauge silver wire
Round-nosed (snub-nosed) pliers
25 15mm/⅝in diameter flat glass beads
6 6mm/¼in diameter silver beads
Wire cutters
75cm/30in silver chain with large links
60 silver jump rings
3 silver head pins
40cm/16in silver chain with small links
Fastening chain
Silver crab-claw fastener

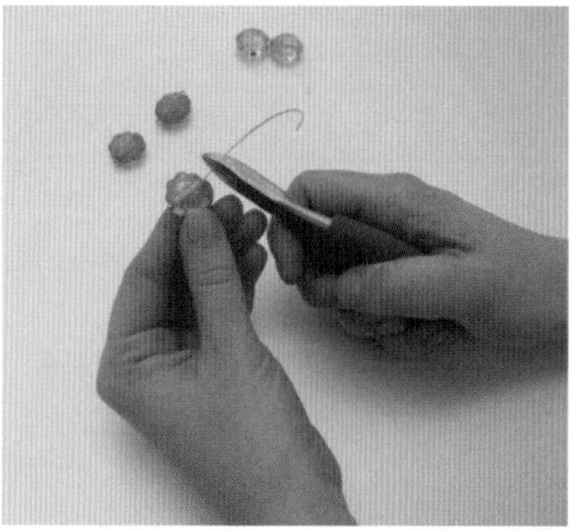

1 Mount each of the beads on silver wire by making a small loop at one end of the wire with round-nosed (snub-nosed) pliers and threading on the bead. Trim the end to 6mm/¼in and bend in another loop in the opposite direction.

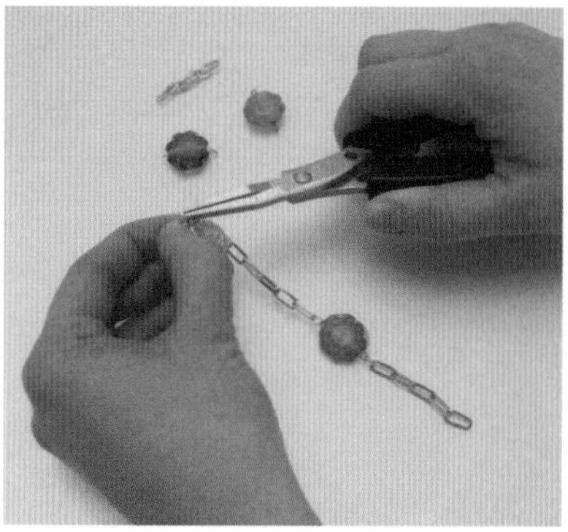

2 Cut the large-link chain into 4cm/1½in sections. Use jump rings to link alternate wired beads and chains, until the belt is the right length.

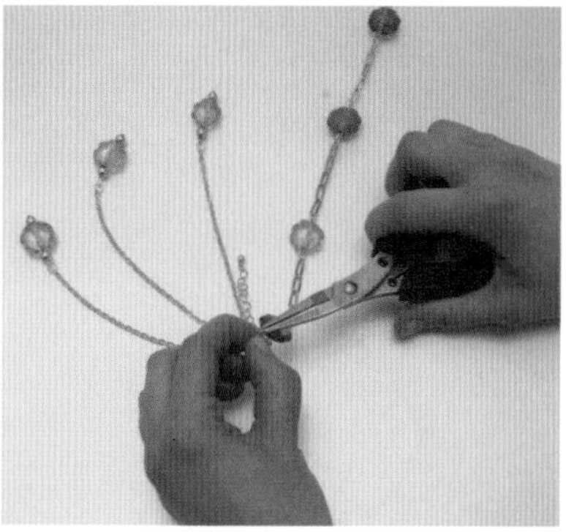

3 For each dropper, thread a silver, a glass and a silver bead on to a head pin. Clip the end and bend it into a loop. Cut the fine chain into three and fix a dropper to each one with a jump ring. Join the three chains and the fastening chain together using a jump ring and fix this to the belt. Fix the fastener to the other end with a jump ring to complete the belt.

These sinuous bracelets are made using a simple off-loom weave known as peyote stitch. Once you have mastered the technique, the creative possibilities and colour variations are endless.

Spiral Bracelets

●●●

you will need

Nymo or quilting thread to match beads
Scissors
Beading needle or size 10 sewing needle
Rocailles in metallic green and red and green stripes
2 bell caps
2 2.5mm/⅛in silver beads
Small jump ring
Crab-claw fastener

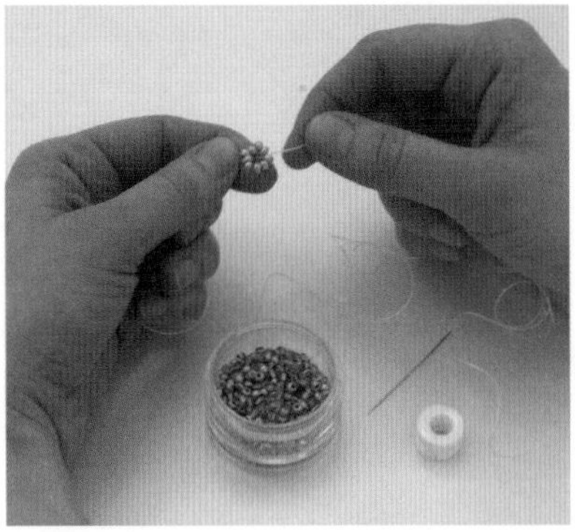

1 Thread a 2m/2yd length of thread through the needle. Thread on nine green beads and tie them into a loop with a reef knot, 25cm/10in from the end. Hold the end of the thread between finger and thumb.

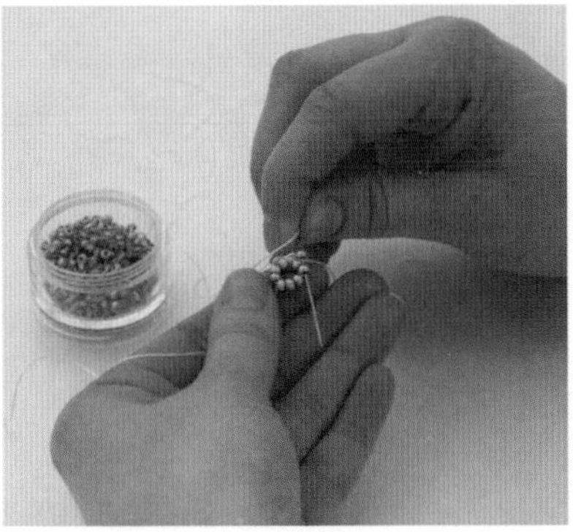

2 To make the first round, add a striped bead, then skip one bead and take the needle through the next bead. Thread on a green bead, skip one bead and pass the needle through the next bead.

3 To complete the round, add a striped bead and pass the needle through the next but one bead, then thread on a green bead, skip one green bead and go through the next bead. You will now have a flat, four-pointed star shape.

4 Start the next round by threading on a striped bead and taking the needle through the next striped bead to the right. Add a green bead and take the needle through the next green bead. Repeat this twice more and pull the thread up tightly so that the beads begin to form a cylinder.

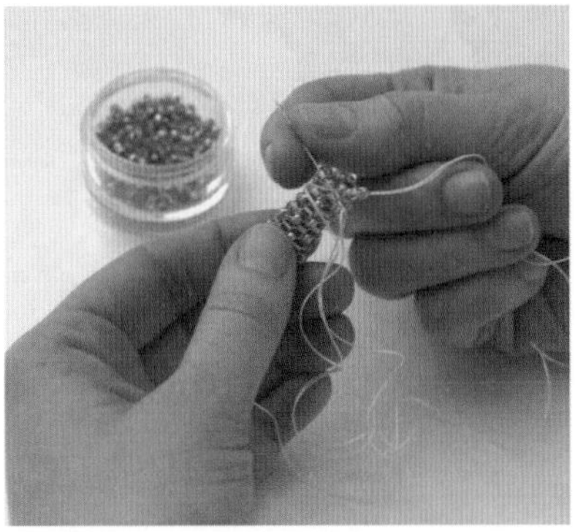

5 When the thread runs out, join on another length with a reef knot. Use the point of the needle to position the knot so that it sits close to the last bead, then continue weaving, leaving the ends trailing on the outside of the cylinder. Taper the end with three beads between the next two beads. Repeat until you reach the required length, with space for the fastening.

6 Thread the needle once again through the last four beads. Bring it out through the centre of the cylinder and add a bell cap, a large silver bead and the jump ring. Go back through the findings five times, then fasten off.

7 Re-thread the needle at the other end, then complete in the same way, adding the fastener after the silver bead. Darn in the loose threads by taking them back through the weave for 2.5cm/1in and trim the ends.

8 To make striped patterns, work rounds of beads in a single contrasting colour or use three colours in one round to vary the width of the stripes. A bracelet made in a single colour is also very effective.

This dramatic scarf is decorated with appliqué and beadwork leaves; some are velvet and others are stitched with tiny sequins. To complete the effect, beaded flowers are dotted among the foliage.

Devoré Scarf

you will need

Dressmaking scissors
28cm/11in x 130cm/52in devoré velvet, with leaf pattern
Iron
20cm/8in square fusible bonding web
Embroidery scissors
20 x 110cm/8 x 45in organza
Sewing-machine, with darning foot
Matching sewing threads
Embroidery hoop
Fabric marker
Sewing needle
Matching embroidery thread
Small silver sequins
Small silver glass beads
6mm/¼in blue oval beads
10 x 110cm/4 x 45in silk, in contrasting colour

1 Cut a square of devoré velvet 20 x 20cm/8 x 8in. Using a hot iron, fuse the bonding web to the wrong side. Cut out individual leaf shapes from the fabric using embroidery scissors.

2 Peel away the backing paper from the leaf shapes. Scatter them on one end of the organza, right sides up, and fuse in place with a hot iron.

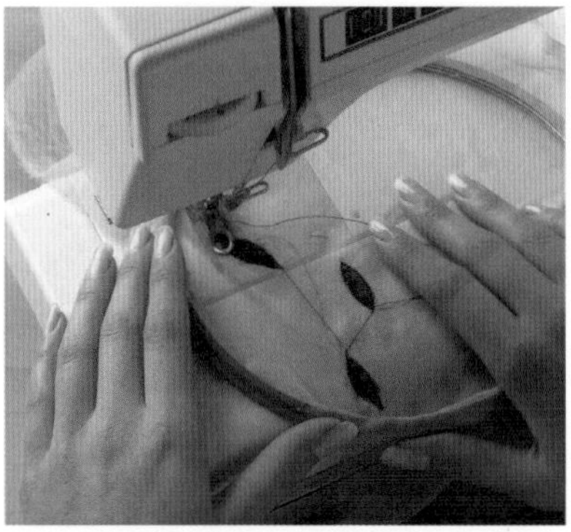

3 Attach a darning foot to the sewing-machine and set to darning mode. Place the organza in an embroidery hoop and zigzag stitch around the edge of each leaf in matching thread.

4 Using a fabric marker, draw extra leaves over the scarf. Place the end with the devoré leaves back into the embroidery hoop.

5 Fill in the outlines of the drawn leaves with overlapping sequins: thread on a sequin then make a stitch in matching embroidery thread at the side of it. Bring the needle up on the other side, thread on another sequin, then insert the needle in the centre of the first sequin. Bring it out on the other side of the second sequin and continue.

6 Fill in some drawn shapes with small silver beads applied by hand. To make the flowers, stitch a small silver bead in the centre of a sequin. Bring the needle out on one side of the sequin, then thread on a silver bead, a blue bead and another silver. Insert the needle in the fabric and bring out on the other side of the sequin. Stitch five more petals around the sequin.

7 Cut a piece of devoré fabric 28 x 110cm/11 x 45in. Wrong sides together, machine stitch to the organza on all four sides. Cut strips of contrasting silk fabric 3cm/1¼in wide, stitch together and press to make a continuous binding. Right sides together, stitch all around the scarf. Fold the binding over the edge of the scarf, tuck under the raw edges and slip stitch in place.

The geometric pattern and pearlized ice-cream colours of this woven bracelet are inspired by the jazz age designs of the Art Deco movement. Each bead is represented by one square on the chart.

Woven Bracelet

●●●

you will need
Bead loom
Beading thread
Scissors
Beading needle
Small glass beads in light green, pink, grey and purple
Adhesive tape
Wool lining fabric
Sewing needle
Sewing thread
3 buttons with shanks

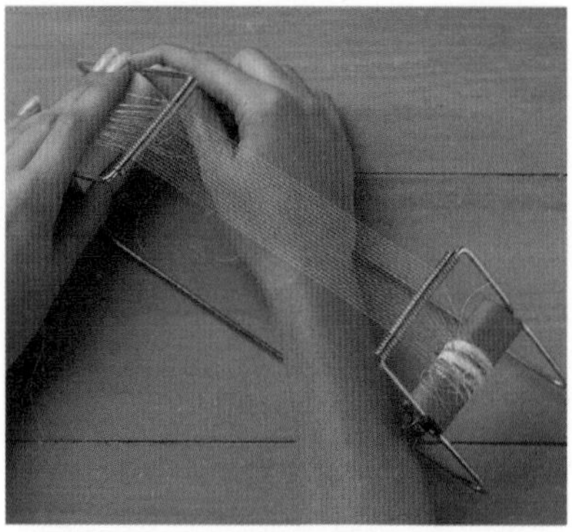

1 Following the instructions on page 29, thread the loom with a 75cm/30in warp of 21 threads. Thread a beading needle with a long thread and tie the end to the far-left warp thread, 2cm/¾in from the rollers. Following the pattern at the back of the book, thread on the first 20 beads.

2 Push them up into the spaces between the warp threads with the forefinger. Pass the needle back through the beads in the opposite direction, above the warp, and pull up. Thread on the next 20 beads and continue weaving to the last row of the chart.

3 Finish by passing the needle back through several rows, knotting and trimming the thread. Stick a length of adhesive tape over the warp threads at each end. Cut the threads.

4 Cut a piece of wool lining to the same size as the weaving. Tuck under the threads and place the weave on top of the lining. Join together with slip stitch.

5 At one end of the bracelet, stitch on three evenly spaced buttons. At the other end, make three beaded loops large enough to fit over the buttons.

We are accustomed to thinking of Victorian colour schemes as dark and sombre, but this jewellery set was reproduced from vivid original pieces, found in a local costume museum.

Victorian Earrings and Brooch

you will need
Thin card (stock)
Pencil
Craft (utility) knife
Fabric marker
30cm/12in square cream cotton fabric
Dressmaking scissors
Embroidery hoop
Needle
Stranded cotton in pink; and green
Tiny crystal beads
30cm/12in square iron-on interfacing
30cm/12in square satin lining
Sewing thread
Beading needle
Brooch pin
2 earring hooks

1 Trace the brooch template on to thin card and cut out. Draw around it on to the centre of the cream fabric and mount in a hoop. Starting at the outer edge and using three strands of green cotton, work four rows of chain stitch. Work the next three rows in pink, then four more in green. Fill in the remaining space with beads.

2 Iron the interfacing on to the lining and draw on the brooch shape. Cut out, leaving a 1cm/½in seam allowance all round. Trim the corners, snip the curves and turn in the edges.

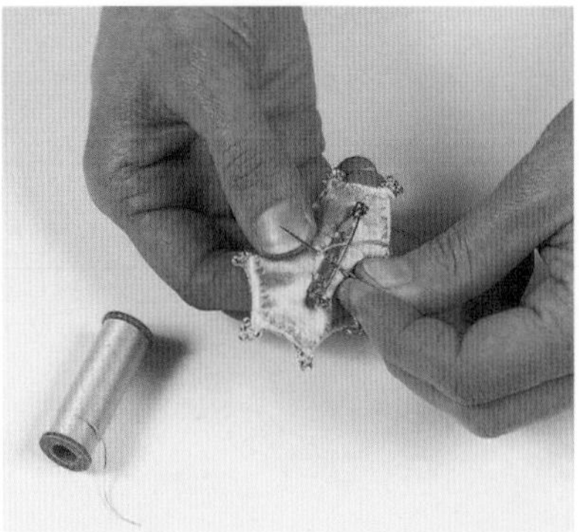

3 Slip stitch the backing in place. Sew a loop of five beads on to each point of the brooch, using a double thread, and finish off securely. Sew on the brooch clip.

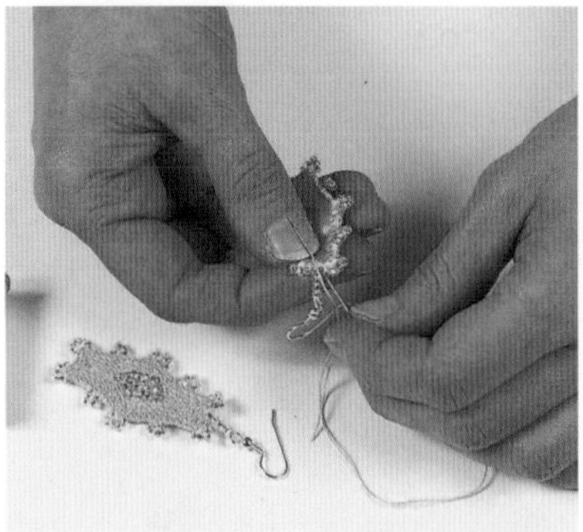

4 Make the earrings in the same way, but add extra loops of beads in between the points. At the top of the earrings, thread on four beads and an earring hook and bring the thread back through the beads before finishing off securely.

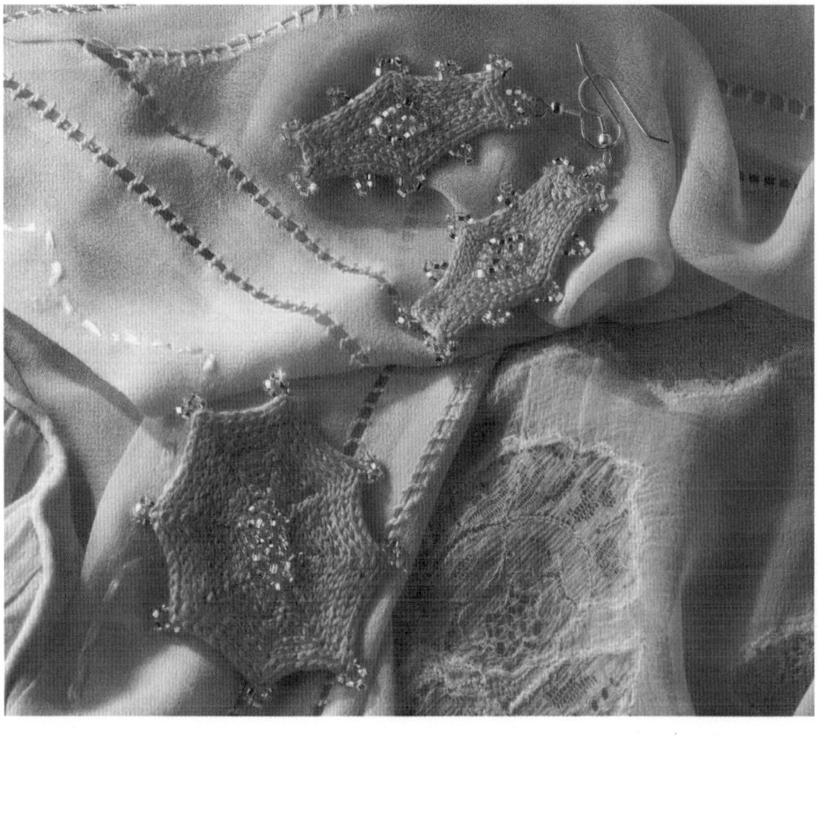

Unmistakeably Victorian in style, this butterfly would look most elegant on a simple evening dress. It could also be pinned to a belt or even adapted as a hair ornament for a special occasion.

Butterfly Brooch

you will need

Thin card (stock)
Pencil
Craft (utility) knife
Fabric marker
20cm/8in square close-woven fabric, black
Embroidery hoop
Beading needle
Black sewing thread
Large round iridescent beads, small long black beads and small round black beads
Scissors
20cm/8in square felt, black
Mounting (mat) board
Metal ruler
Double-sided tape
Brooch fastening

1 Transfer the butterfly template on to card and cut out. Draw round it on the centre of the black fabric and mount in an embroidery hoop. Thread a needle with black thread and knot both ends together to make a double length.

2 Sew on the large iridescent beads individually to make the eyes and wing highlights. Use the small long beads to stitch around the outline and then fill in the background with small round beads.

3 Cut out the butterfly, leaving a 6mm/¼in border. Remember to snip into the curves. Cut the shape of the butterfly from felt and mounting (mat) board. Score down each side of the "body" on the mounting board and turn over. Cut bits of double-sided tape to fit round the edges.

4 Stretch the beaded fabric on to the mounting board shape. Glue the felt shape on to the back of the brooch. Allow to dry before sewing the bead feelers on to the head and the brooch fastening on to the back. Gently bend the wings forward.

This tiny pair of child's slippers is embroidered with a golden stream of bugle beads. The templates at the back of the book are for the right foot: scale them up to size and reverse the pieces for the left foot.

Child's Slippers

●●●

you will need

Tracing paper and pencil
Dressmaking scissors
50cm/20in square pale blue wool fabric
Sewing-machine, with darning foot
Matching sewing threads
30cm/12in square dark grey velvet
Metal ruler
Dressmaker's pins
Sewing needle
Beading needle
Beading thread
Gold bugle beads
20cm/8in square grey wool fabric
20cm/8in square wadding (batting)

1 Enlarge the templates and cut out from paper to the size required. For each slipper, cut four back pieces from blue wool. Machine stitch the back seams together, then assemble each pair, wrong sides together. Work a zigzag stitch along the top and bottom edges. Using a sewing-machine with a darning foot, stitch wavy lines over the pieces to quilt.

2 To make bias binding, fold the velvet square in half diagonally, unfold and mark the line. Mark parallel lines across the cloth 3cm/1¼in apart. Cut along the lines. Match the raw edge of a length of bias binding to the outside top edge of the back piece, right sides together, and pin.

3 Machine stitch the binding 6mm/¼in from the edge of the slipper, fold the binding over to the wrong side and tuck under the raw edges. Slip stitch in place.

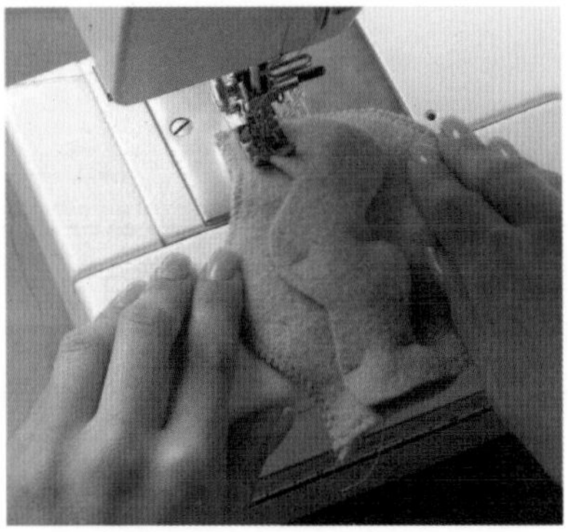

4 Cut one piece of fabric to the size of the template for each toe piece. Machine stitch the dart. Cut out the piece for the beaded appliqué, pin it to the toe as shown. Work a zigzag stitch around the appliqué.

5 Bind the top edge of the toe piece. Fold 30cm/12in of binding in half widthways and pin the fold to the centre front edge, right sides facing. Pin around the front and stitch 6mm/¼in from the edge.

6 At the top edge of the appliquéd piece, make a few fastening-on stitches, then thread enough bugle beads on to a beading needle to follow the line of the piece. Insert the needle at the other side.

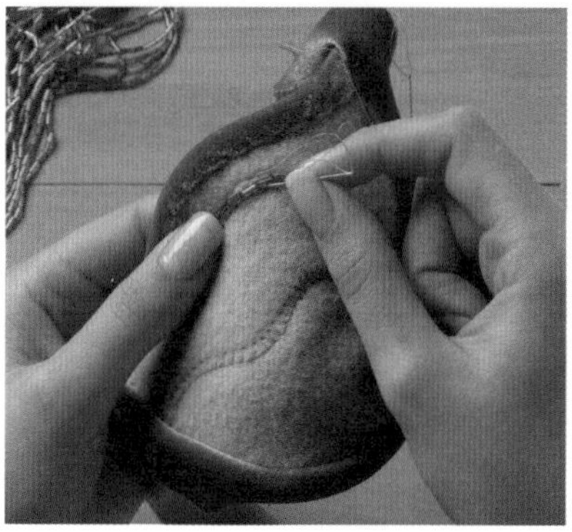

7 Thread a second needle and make a tiny stitch over the laid thread between the first two beads. Push the third bead up close and make another stitch between that and the fourth bead. Make another 12 rows of couching in this way, following the same contours.

8 For each sole, cut two pieces of grey wool fabric and one of wadding to the size of the template. Assemble the wadding between the wool pieces. Set the sewing-machine to darning mode, attach the darning foot, then stitch a wavy line to quilt the layers. Work a wide zigzag stitch round the edge.

9 Pin and stitch the back piece around the sole, matching the centres. Pin and stitch the toe piece over the front and stitch the sides to the back where they meet. Pin and machine stitch the binding round the back base, and neaten the join with slip stitch. Fold it over the edge and slip stitch in place.

An easily learnt off-loom technique has been used to create this pretty diamond-shaped woven bracelet in delicate shades of lilac and purple: use beads with a silver core for a glittering effect.

Off-loom Mesh Bracelet

●●●

you will need

3mm/⅛in lilac bugle beads
2mm/1/12in clear rocailles
3mm/⅛in purple rocailles
Beading needle or size 10 sewing needle
Fine beading thread
2 6mm/½in round beads
Scissors

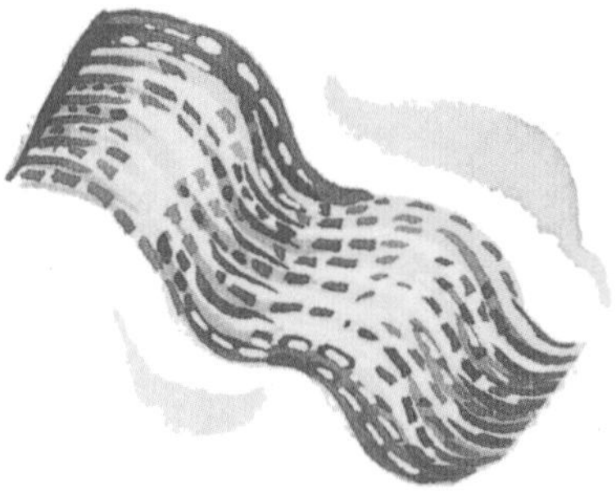

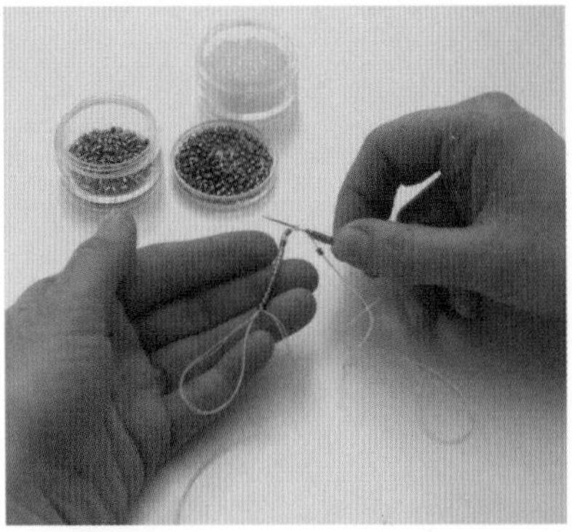

1 Thread the needle with 2m/80in of thread and knot the two ends together. Make a slip knot 15cm/6in from the end. Thread on four large rocailles, then seven bugles with small rocailles between them. Add another four large rocailles and a bugle, and take the needle back through the last small rocaille.

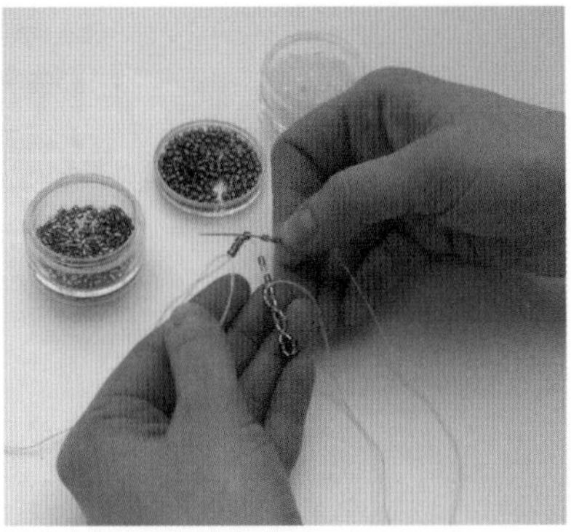

2 Add a bugle bead then go through the second rocaille to the left. Thread on a bugle, a small rocaille and another bugle and take the needle through the second small rocaille to the left. Repeat this sequence twice, taking the needle through the first of the large rocailles on the left, on the second action.

3 Add three large rocailles and a bugle, then go through the first rocaille to the right. Thread on a bugle, a small rocaille and a bugle.

4 Pass the needle through the second rocaille to the right. Repeat this sequence, taking the needle through the first large rocaille at the end of the row. Thread on another three small rocailles and a bugle.

5 Take the needle through the first rocaille to the left. Continue weaving in this way until the cuff fits snugly around your wrist. Tie on additional lengths of thread with a reef knot, positioned close to the last bead of a row. Leave the ends loose.

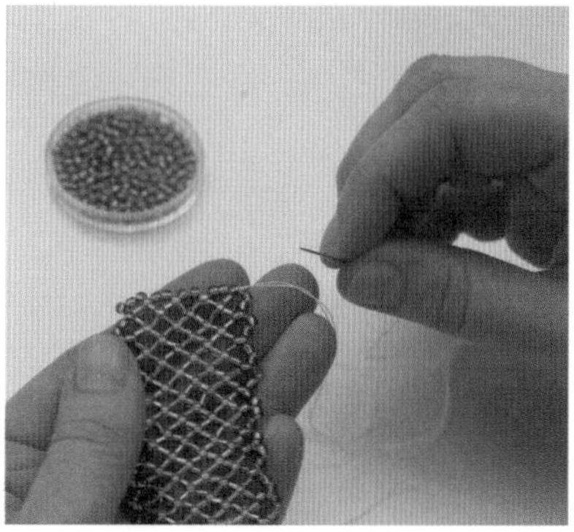

6 To finish off the end, thread on three large rocailles and take the needle through the next small rocaille. Thread on two large rocailles and go through the next small rocaille, Repeat this sequence twice, taking the needle through the first large rocaille at the end of the row.

7 Weave the needle back through the beads so it comes out through the final rocaille bead. Add three large beads, a large round bead and a large rocaille. Take the needle back through the large bead and three rocailles, then weave through to the second small rocaille along. Make another stalk in the same way and finish off securely.

8 At the other end, undo the slip knot and add large rocailles. Weave the needle through to the first rocaille and thread enough rocaille beads to make a loop to slip over the large bead. Add one more rocaille, then go back through the first rocaille and make another loop next to the next but one rocaille. Weave in any loose ends.

An engraving in a vintage department store catalogue provided the inspiration for this heart-shaped bridal bag, which is just big enough to hold a lace handkerchief, lipstick and other essentials.

Heart-shaped Bag

you will need

- 20 x 40cm/8 x 16in heavy interfacing
- 45 x 90cm/18 x 36in cream silk
- Beading needle
- 60 small seed pearls
- 60 small long pearl beads
- 16 1cm/½in pearl drop beads
- mounting (mat) board to size
- PVA (white) glue
- Cream embroidery thread
- 30 x 45cm/12 x 18in cream lining silk
- 15 x 45cm/6 x 18in striped silk
- 45 x 5cm/18 x 2in cream lace
- 1m x 3mm/1yd x ⅛in cream ribbon
- Tapestry needle
- 2 large pearl drop beads

1 Using the template, cut two heart shapes from the interfacing. Cut two more hearts from the cream silk, allowing 18mm/¾in extra all around. Tack (baste) an interfacing heart to each silk heart. Embroider one heart with pearls, as shown, with a beading needle and sewing thread.

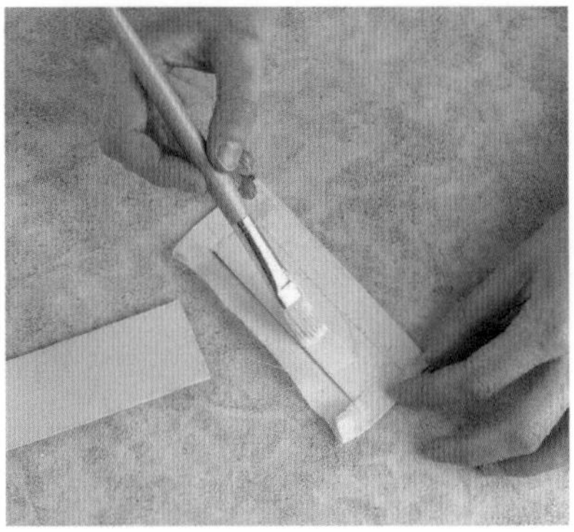

2 From the mounting (mat) board, cut two rectangles, 12 x 5cm/4½ x 2in, for the side. From the silk, cut two 18 x 10cm/7 x 4in rectangles, to cover. Place the board centrally on the silk and spread a thin layer of PVA (white) glue around the outer edges of the fabric. Fold over the corners, and glue.

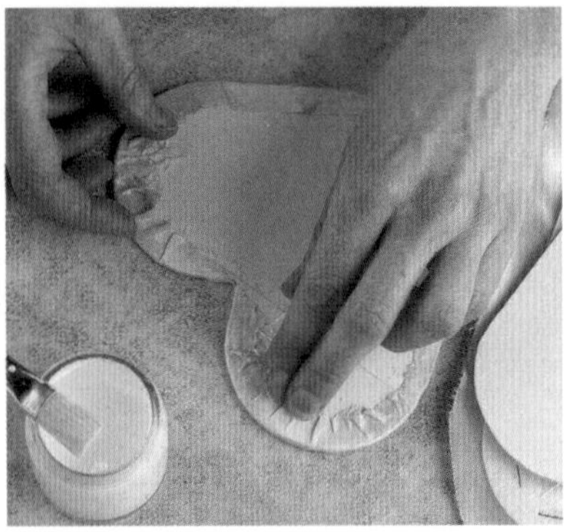

3 Cut two hearts from the mounting board. Lay the beaded heart face-down and place a board heart on top, matching it to the interfacing. Spread glue thinly around the edge and gently stretch over the surplus silk, easing and clipping as necessary. Repeat for the second heart.

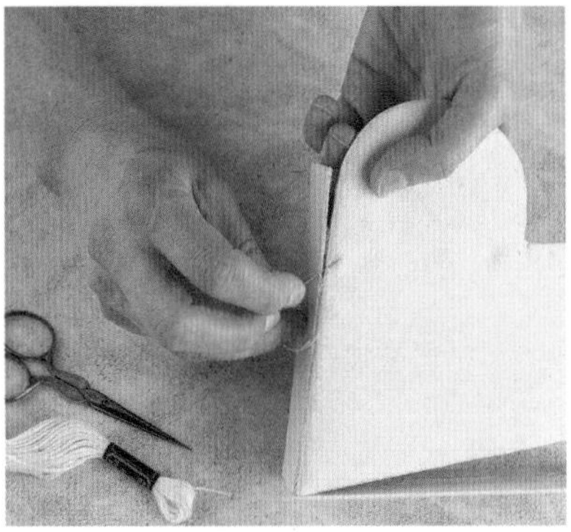

4 Use embroidery thread (floss) to slip stitch the sides together at one short end. Slip stitch the two hearts to the sides. With right sides together, hand stitch the lining and striped silk along one long edge and then the side seam. Run a gathering thread round the lower edge and draw it up.

5 Fold the lining to the inside along the seam and hand stitch the lace to the seam. Sew a row of straight stitch 6mm/¼in below the fold for a gathering channel. Pin lining in place, and slip stitch striped fabric around top of the bag. Thread ribbon through the channel; add a large pearl at each end.

A delicate butterfly made entirely of wired beads, to perch on a favourite hat, a hair clip or a bag – just make sure that there are no projecting wire ends before you wear it.

Crystal Butterfly

you will need

30cm/12in medium-gauge silver wire
3mm/1/8in faceted pale lilac oval beads
6mm/1/4in faceted oval beads in blue and lilac
Flat-nosed pliers
Reel of floristry wire
Wire cutters
Silver rocailles
2 15mm/5/8in heart-shaped blue beads
2 8mm/1/3in heart-shaped blue beads
4 4mm/1/5in round green beads
8mm/1/3in round green bead
4 8mm/1/3in bicone green beads
Round-nosed (snub-nosed) pliers

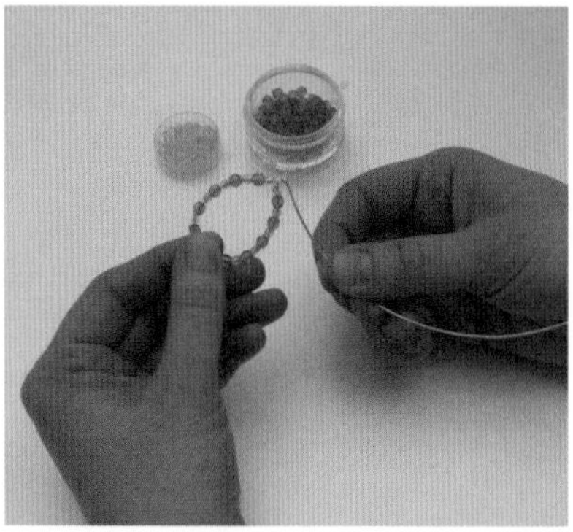

1 Make a small loop at one end of the silver wire, then thread on 12 small pale lilac beads interspersed with 11 large blue faceted beads. Pass the loose end of the wire through the loop, pull it up tightly to make the butterfly's upper wing shape and then bend it outwards.

2 Thread on eight more small beads interspersed with seven large lilac beads. Bend the wire into a loop for the lower wing and pass the end through the loop. Wrap the wire tightly once more through the loop, clip the end and bend it over with the flat-nosed pliers.

3 Fix a 30cm/6in length of floristry wire to the wire frame of the upper wing, just above the fifth large blue bead. Thread on a large lilac, a silver rocaille, a large heart, another rocaille, a large lilac bead and another rocaille. Finish off the wire at the bottom edge, just above the first large blue bead.

4 Thread on another rocaille, a large lilac bead and a rocaille, then twist the wire around the opposite side of the wire frame, just above the top of the final large blue bead. Add a rocaille, a large lilac bead and another rocaille, then pass the wire back up through the heart bead.

5 Add a rocaille, a large lilac bead and a rocaille, then fasten off three beads along from the start. Re-fasten it one bead along, add a rocaille and a small lilac bead, then twist the wire around the top of the heart. Add another small lilac and a rocaille, then fasten off two beads before the start point.

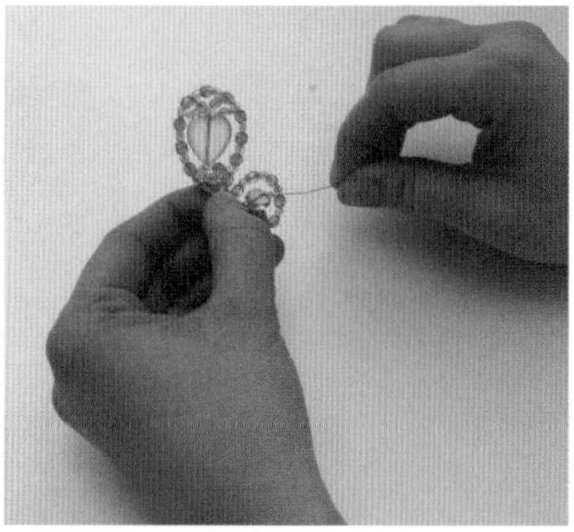

6 Fasten another 30cm/6in length of wire close to the original loop. Thread on a small lilac bead, a large lilac bead, a rocaille, a small heart, a rocaille and a small lilac bead. Secure the other end of the wire to the opposite side of the lower wing just below the seventh bead of the original round.

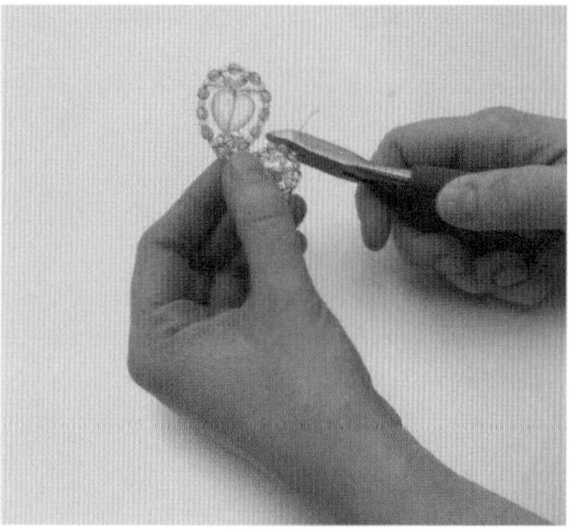

7 Fix the wire to the frame one bead to the right, and add a small lilac and a rocaille. Twist the wire around the bottom of the heart and add a rocaille and a small lilac. Twist the wire twice around the frame, two beads to the left, add a rocaille, a lilac bead and a rocaille. Twist around the frame, three beads along, then fill the remaining space in the same way. Make the second wing as a mirror image.

8 Bind the wings together along the centre with floristry wire. Make a loop in the end of the remaining silver wire and thread on the green beads to make the head and body. Clip the wire to 6mm/¼ in to complete the body. Twist the rest of the wire to make the antennae and slip them through the top loop. Wire the body over the join. Wire a brooch backing to the wrong side if you wish.

This pretty hair comb, heavily encrusted with spirals of faux pearls, would make a perfect tiara type hair adornment for a bride, to hold her veil in place. For bridesmaids, choose pearlized colours instead of ivory.

Pearl Hair Comb

you will need

- Thin card (stock)
- Pencil
- Craft (utility) knife
- Heavyweight interfacing
- Fabric marker
- Embroidery scissors
- 18cm/7in millinery wire
- Jeweller's pliers
- Sewing needle
- Matching sewing thread
- Beading needle
- Matching beading thread
- 1cm/½in pearl bead
- 6mm/¼in pearl beads
- 4mm/⅕in pearl beads
- 4 8mm/⅓in pearl beads
- Four drop beads
- Plastic hair comb

1 Trace the template from the back of the book on to card and cut out. Mark around the template twice on the heavyweight interfacing and cut out.

2 Bend a loop at each end of the millinery wire. Stitch the wire to one piece of the interfacing 2cm/¾in from the straight edge.

3 Mark the centre of each scallop on the right side. Stitch the largest bead to the middle one. Come out at the front and thread eight 6mm/¼in and enough 4mm/⅕in beads to spiral out to fill the circle. Fasten off. Couch down the pearls using sewing thread. Fill the other scallops, using 8mm/⅓in beads in the centres and filling in the remaining spaces with small pearls.

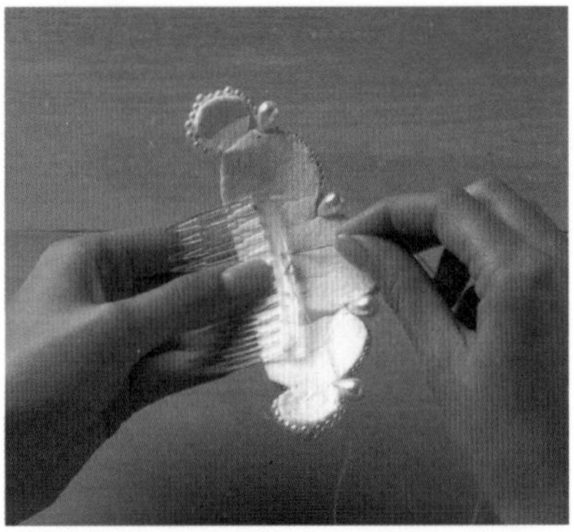

4 Slip stitch the second piece of interfacing to the back of the beaded tiara to conceal the stitches. Stitch the four drop beads between the scallops so they point upwards. Stitch the comb securely to the bottom edge of the beaded piece, on the wrong side.

These richly decorative earrings are made of rolled tubes of card covered with velvet ribbon, wrapped with metallic thread and gold wire, then studded with beads. They are deceptively simple to make.

Wrapped Earrings

●●●●

you will need

Thin card (stock)
Ruler and pencil
Scissors
12 x 5cm/4½ x 2in wide velvet ribbon
Sewing needle
Sewing thread to match ribbon
Red metallic embroidery thread (floss)
Textured gold wire
Wire cutters
Beading needle
Matching beading thread
Small green glass beads
4 hatpins
8 4mm/3/5in flower brass beads
8 6mm/¼in red glass beads
12 4mm/⅕in red glass beads
Round-nosed (snub-nosed) pliers
4 8mm/⅓in hexagonal brass beads
2 silver earring wires

1 Cut two rectangles of card, each 4 x 7cm/1½ x 2¾in. Starting from the short side, roll into narrow tubes 15mm/⅝in in diameter.

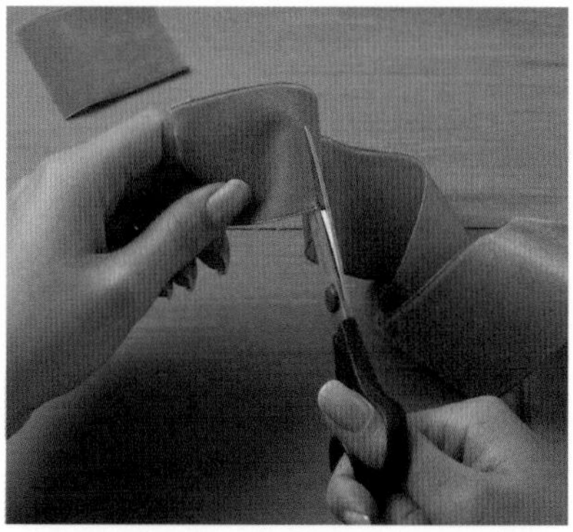

2 Cut the velvet ribbon into two pieces, each 6cm/2½in long. Roll a piece of ribbon around each card tube, right side out.

3 Fold under a narrow hem along the overlapping raw edge of the ribbon and slip stitch it down to neaten. Do the same with the other tube. Thread a needle with a double length of red metallic embroidery thread and knot the ends. Fasten to the edge of a tube, wrap evenly down in a spiral and fasten off.

4 Cut 40 pieces of gold wire, each 15mm/⅝in long. Thread a needle with beading thread and fasten on. Thread on alternate gold wires and green beads. Wrap the thread around the tube and fasten off.

5 Push a hatpin through each tube, 6mm/¼in from the top. Snip the ends, leaving an equal length on each side. Thread a flower bead, large red bead and three small red beads on each side. Twist the pin ends into a spiral with the pliers.

6 Take a hatpin for each tube, thread on a brass bead, large red bead, hexagonal bead, wrapped tube, then the same beads in reverse. Trim each hatpin end, bending it into a loop. Attach the earring wires.

This stylish and contemporary choker is woven in shades of peacock green and silver beads. Once finished, it is mounted on a strip of soft suede and can be tied loosely around the neck.

Loom-Woven Choker

you will need
Bead loom
Black nymo thread
Beading needle
2mm/$^{1}/_{12}$in rocailles in three shades of green
2mm/$^{1}/_{12}$in silver rocailles
2 6mm/$^{1}/_{4}$in beads in a contrasting colour
Soft dark blue suede
Tape measure
Dressmaking scissors
PVA (white) glue
Sewing needle
Matching sewing thread

1 Following the instructions on page 29, thread up a 50cm/20in warp of 11 threads. Knot a 1m/40in length of nymo to the first thread on the left and, using the chart at the back of the book as a guide, thread on the first row of beads. Take the needle from left to right under the warp.

2 Gently lift the beads upwards with the tip of a finger and push them so that one sits in each gap between the warp threads. Slide the needle back through the beads, keeping it above the threads without piercing them. Continue to follow the chart.

3 To make a fringe strand, add on extra beads. Go back through the last but one bead to form a stopper, then pass the needle through the remaining beads and complete the row as usual. Do the same for each strand, adding large beads as indicated.

4 When finished, remove the weaving from the loom. Cut off the knots and knot the remaining threads together securely in pairs.

5 Cut a strip of suede the same width and 50cm/20in longer than the choker. Glue the weaving to the centre, tucking under the threads. When dry, slip stitch the edges neatly to the suede.

An elegant decoration for any lapel, this sumptuous floral spray is made from wired rocaille beads using a technique that dates back centuries. Vary the colours to make a corsage to match a favourite jacket.

French Beading Corsage

you will need

Dark gold metallic rocailles
Bronze metallic rocailles
Fine craft wire in green and bronze
Artificial stamens
Green metallic rocailles
4 18cm/7in florist's wires
Florist's tape (stem wrap)
Brooch fastening
Sewing needle and thread

1 Thread the bronze beads on to the bronze wire. Bend back the last 15cm/6in and twist the bottom 7cm/2¾in for the stalk. Slip down nine beads to make the central core. Take the working wire behind and around the loose wire from left to right and pull it up. Slide down 13 beads to the left. Wrap the wire once around the top of the stem.

2 Count off another 13 beads and take them up to the right. Wrap the wire once around the loose wire, just above the top bead. Make another round in the same way with 17 beads on each side, and one more round with 23 beads on each side.

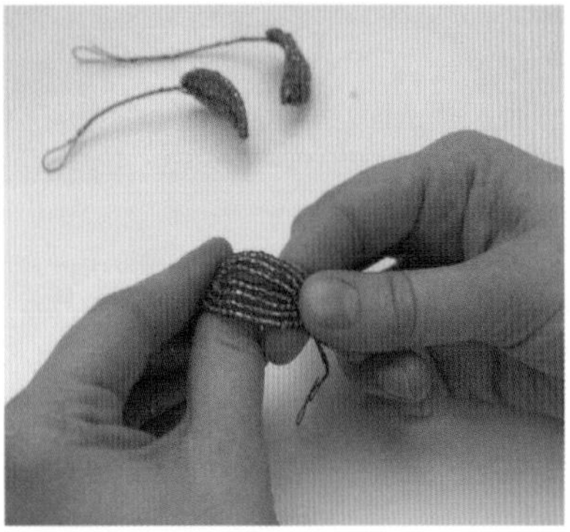

3 The final two rounds have 27 and 31 beads on each side respectively. Make five more petals in the same way. Make three small petals, of three rounds each.

4 Fold 20 artificial stamens in half and wire together. Gently curve the three small petals, then position them around the stamens. Bind them tightly in place with fine wire.

5 Curve the large petals in the same way and bind them, one at a time, around the smaller petals, placing the first three in the spaces between them.

6 Make five small petals with a centre core of five beads and two rounds of eight and thirteen beads. Bind them around a core of stamens. Make a second bronze flower in the same way.

7 Thread the green beads on to green wire. Make nine leaves from 2cm/¾in to 4cm/1½in. The central core can be from four to eleven beads. Add four beads to a round to increase the size.

8 Hold a small flower at the end of the florist's wires and bind all the wires with florist's tape, adding flowers and leaves as you go and covering sharp ends. Sew on a brooch backing.

Decorative Beading Projects

Some of the most desirable home accessories are now adorned with, or constructed from, a glittering array of beads. Bead curtains, crystal-decked wall sconces, candle holders and fringed lampshades all make the most of their light-enhancing qualities, whilst traditional favourite beadwork techniques, including wiring and embroidery, are still used to embellish fashionable cushion covers, bolsters and picture frames.

There's nothing difficult about the method used to decorate these sparkly picture frames: simply treat small beads like glitter and sprinkle them generously across a glued surface.

Bead-encrusted Frames

you will need

Flat wooden picture frames
Medium-grade abrasive paper
Emulsion (latex) or acrylic paints
Medium paintbrushes
Saucer or palette
PVA (white) glue
Small glass rocailles in a variety of colours
Large sheet of paper
Glitter
Bugle beads in a variety of colours

1 Prepare the frames by rubbing them down with medium-grade abrasive paper to remove any existing paint or varnish. Paint each one in a different flat, bright colour and set aside until completely dry. Add a second coat of paint, if necessary, for even coverage.

2 Paint a heart shape in each corner of a square frame, using PVA (white) glue. Sprinkle rocailles generously over the glue, using a different colour for each heart, and press them down lightly. After the beads have settled for a minute or two, lightly tap the frame to remove any that may remain loose.

3 Paint the rest of the frame with PVA glue. With the frame on a large sheet of paper, sprinkle on the glitter. Tap off the excess glitter and return it to the container.

4 Spread glue around the centre of the round frame and sprinkle with bugle beads. Continue working out to the edge, using darker or lighter beads of the same colour for a shaded effect.

5 To decorate the edge of a small block frame simply glue the sides, one by one, and then press down on to a selection of assorted beads lying on a piece of paper.

Twisted silver wire, sparingly threaded with beads, has a delicate yet sculptural quality. An assortment of toning glass beads attracts the light and looks wonderful entwining a pair of glass candlesticks.

Beaded Wire Candlesticks

you will need
Tape meaure
Wire cutters
Medium-gauge silver wire
Round-nosed (snub-nosed) pliers
Medium decorative glass beads in yellow, green, silver and clear
Pen or pencil
Small glass rocailles and square beads in complementary shades
Pair of glass candlesticks

1 Cut four 1m/40in lengths of medium-gauge silver wire for each candlestick. Use the pliers to make a small loop at the end of the first length and thread on a decorative bead. Wind the end of the wire around a pen or pencil six times to form a spiral.

2 Thread on about eight small rocailles and divide them among the loops. Thread on another medium-sized bead and repeat, forming spirals and threading beads until you reach the end of the wire.

3 Thread on the final decorative bead. Using the pliers, twist the final 8mm/⅓in of wire into a loop to keep the beads in place.

4 Make up the other three spirals in the same way, distributing the coloured beads evenly among the loops.

5 Wrap two spiral lengths around the stem of each candlestick to form an interesting shape. Secure the spirals in place by binding them gently to the stem with more wire.

No Victorian tea tray was complete without a dainty beaded cover to protect the contents of the milk jug (pitcher). Here is an updated, version of this traditional idea, which is now making a come-back.

Bead-trimmed Voile Jug Covers

you will need
Dressmaking scissors
Tape measure
Checked and plain orange voile
Sewing needle and tacking (basting) thread
Sewing-machine
Matching sewing thread
Iron
Dressmaker's pins
Large orange plastic beads
Medium pink frosted glass beads
Small frosted glass beads in red and pink
Small orange opaque glass rocailles
Small square orange frosted glass beads

Checked cover

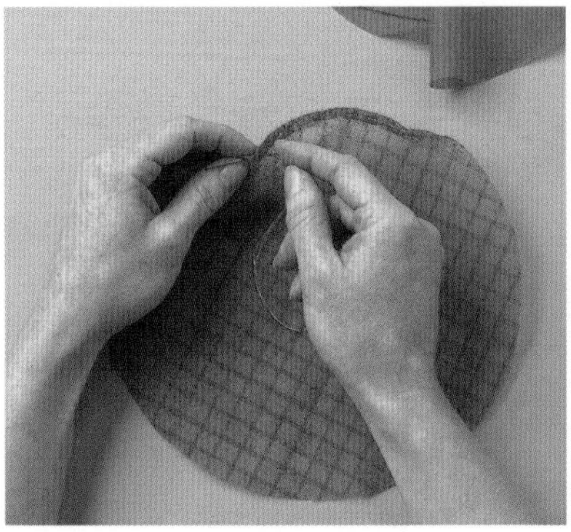

1 Cut out a 20cm/8in diameter circle of checked fabric. Turn under and tack (baste) a narrow double hem around the curved edge. Machine or hand stitch the hem, close to the inner fold, with matching thread.

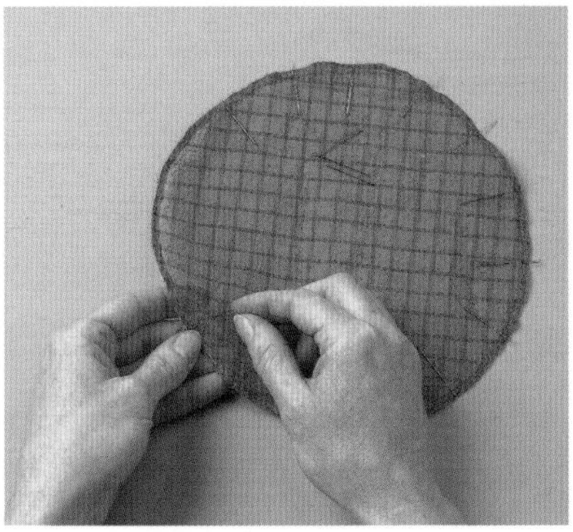

2 Fold the hemmed circle into quarters, then eighths, then sixteenths. Press the folds lightly with an iron to divide the circle into 16 equal sections. Mark each of the creases with a pin.

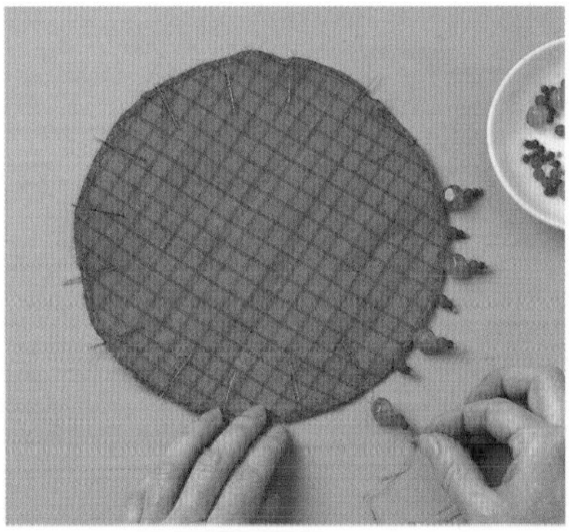

3 Secure a length of matching thread to the hem at a pin marker, then thread on one large orange plastic bead, one medium pink frosted, one red frosted and one orange rocaille. Pass the thread back through the first three beads and make a double stitch at the hem to secure.

4 Feed the thread along the hem halfway to the next pin marker and thread on one medium pink frosted bead, one red frosted and one orange rocaille. Pass the thread back through the first two beads and make a double stitch at the hem. Repeat the pattern all around the hem to complete.

Plain cover

1 Prepare the plain voile as before and fasten on. Add a square bead, a small pink, a square, a small pink, a square, a large pink and a rocaille. Go back through the large pink and last square beads. Repeat for the other side.

2 Secure at the hem with a double stitch. Add one square, one red, one square, one small pink and a rocaille. Go back through the pink and repeat.

3 Double stitch at the hem to secure. Continue round the hem to complete.

Perfect for a small window, multicoloured beads will dress your window without blocking the light. Nylon line supports the beads, and large crystal drops at the end of each strand define the shape.

Glittering Window Decoration

you will need

Pencil
Ruler
Length of 4 x 4cm/1½ x 1½in wooden batten (furring strip) to fit outside window frame
Drill and drill bit
Scissors
Nylon fishing line
Selection of plastic beads, including drops, pendants and long or bugle beads, in various colours and sizes
4cm/1½in wide ribbon
Staple gun
2 screw-in hooks

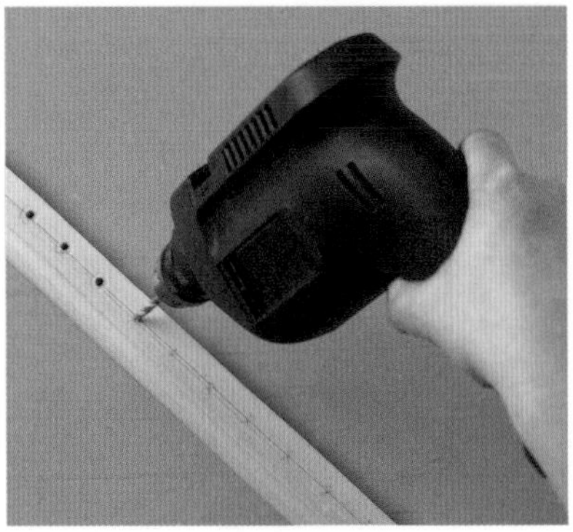

1 Using a pencil and ruler, mark points 2.5cm/1in apart all along the wooden batten (furring strip), 2.5cm/1in from one edge. Allow enough space between the first and second holes at each end for the window frame. Drill a hole at each point.

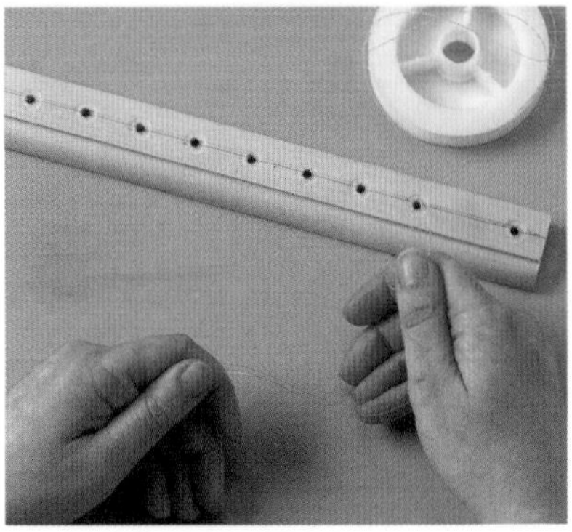

2 Cut a length of fishing line twice the length of the window plus 50cm/20in. Thread both ends through the second hole, then through the loop formed by the doubled thread.

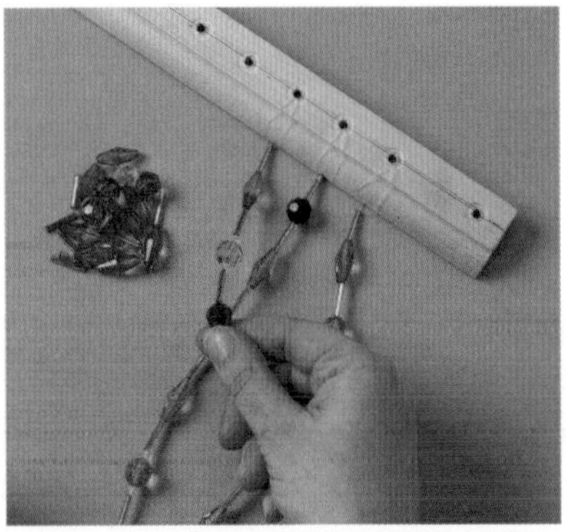

3 Pull the fishing line taut. Thread on the beads in a random manner, using bugle or long beads to space out the round beads.

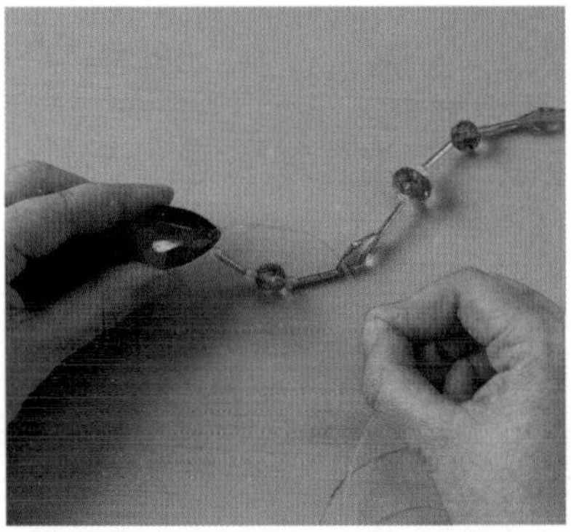

4 When you reach the desired length, thread on a large pendant bead, pass the fishing line back through the last few beads and make a knot. Thread the fishing line back up the length of the strand, knotting the ends twice more, and trim the ends.

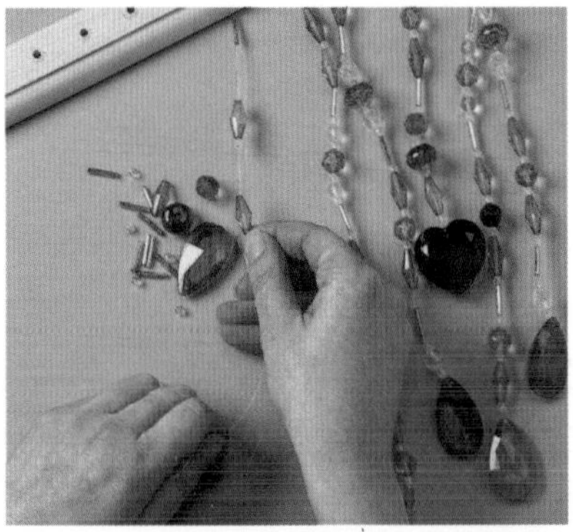

5 Repeat the process for the other strands, making them shorter towards the centre of the window. Cut a length of ribbon to the length of the batten plus 2cm/¾in. Staple it in position at either end. Attach a screw-in hook at either end of the batten from which to hang the curtain.

A bead curtain hung across the kitchen door is a tried and tested way to deter insects on a hot, sunny day. Make this jaunty, striped version from coloured drinking straws, and wooden and plastic beads.

Simple Door Curtain

you will need
Tape measure
2–3 large spools of plastic-coated jewellery wire
Wire cutters
Large, flat glass beads with central hole
Large plastic beads
Medium and small wooden beads
Scissors
Coloured and striped plastic drinking straws
Pencil
Length of 2.5 x 2.5cm/1 x 1in wooden batten (furring strip) to fit inside door frame
Drill bit
Staple gun

1 Cut a length of wire to fit the door length plus 25cm/10in, and tie one end to a large glass bead, which will act as a weight at the bottom.

2 Thread on a large plastic bead between two medium wooden beads to cover the knot.

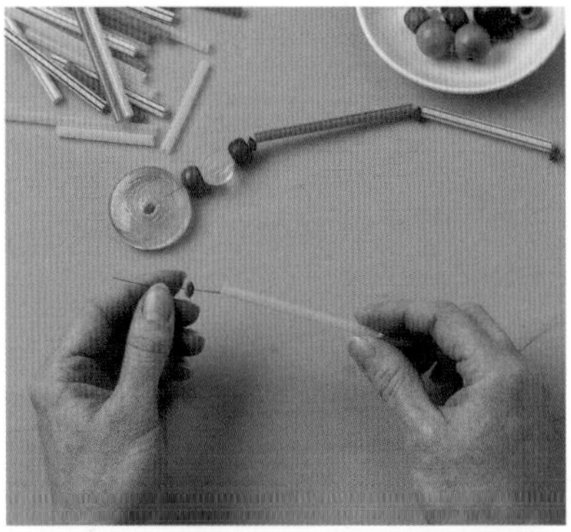

3 Snip the drinking straws into 7.5cm/3in lengths. Thread on three straws, alternating plain and striped, and threading a small wooden bead in between each.

4 Thread on a group of medium and large beads and repeat the sequence, using assorted colours, to fill the wire. Make more strands to complete the curtain: you will need one strand for each 2.5cm/1in of the width.

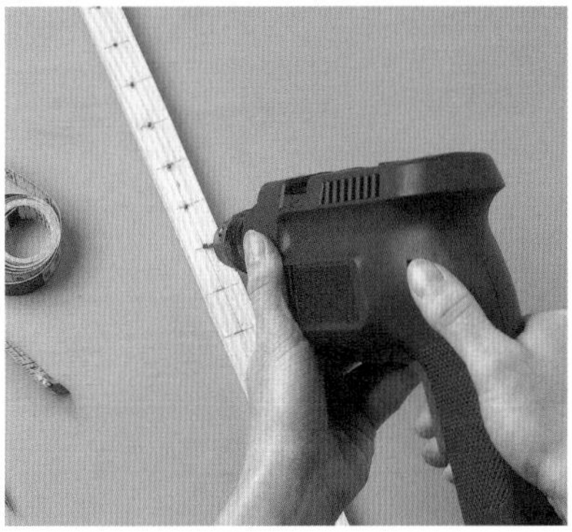

5 Mark and drill holes at 2.5cm/1in intervals all along the batten, plus a screw hole at each end.

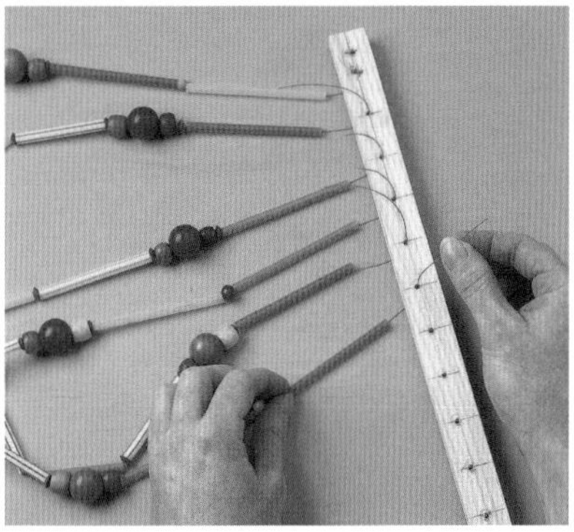

6 Thread the end of each wire through one of the holes in the batten. Hold the batten in place to check for length.

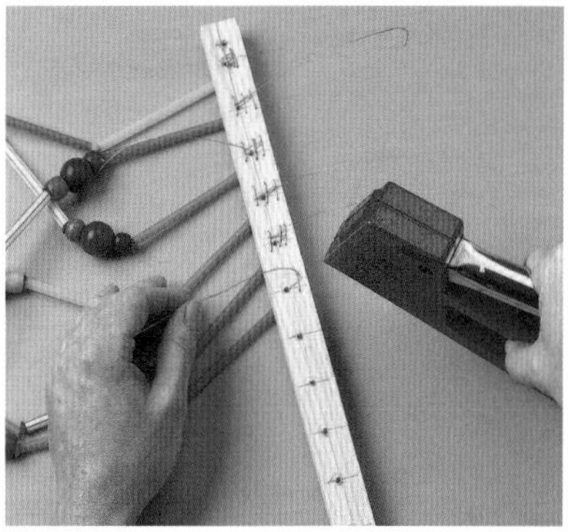

7 Use a staple gun to secure the ends of the beaded thread in place.

Brightly painted wooden beads are ideal for fringing a plain cotton throw, as they are light in weight and easily threaded. Combine them with the occasional metallic bead to catch the light.

Beaded Throw

you will need
Florist's wire
Wire cutters
Ready-made throw with fringe
1 medium, 1 small and 1 large wooden bead and 2 brass beads for each strand to be beaded

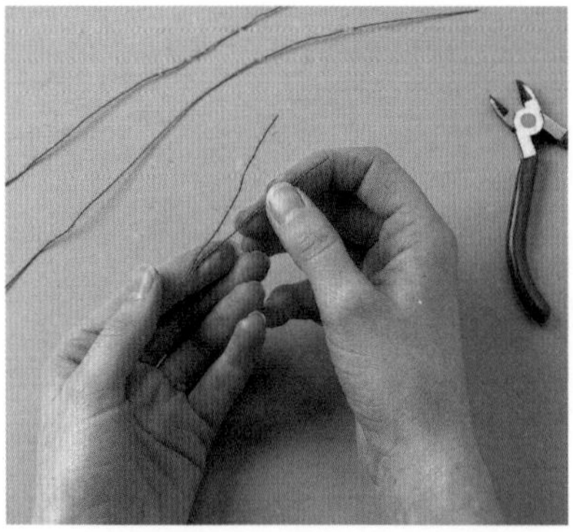

1 Make a threader from 20cm/8in of wire bent into a 'U'. To use, wrap the loop around a single strand. Slide the required beads over both ends of the wire and on to the threads.

2 Every alternate strand of the fringe is beaded. Prepare the strand by untying the existing knot at the top end and threading on a brass bead using the wire threader.

3 Twist the strand of fringe together to secure any stray thread, and make a new knot, just below the brass bead.

4 Add one small, one large and one medium bead. Finish off with a knot as before. Repeat for every other strand to the end.

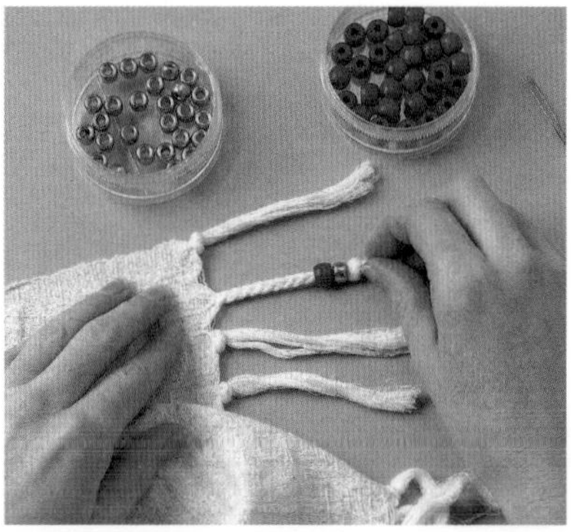

5 As a variation, try plaiting the strands of the fringe together and adding a coloured bead and a brass bead before knotting the end.

A bead curtain (drape) lets in and prettily reflects all available light. This one is made from transparent nylon line threaded with glass and silver beads, which will glitter prettily in the sunlight.

Bead Window Hanging

you will need

- Length of 2.5 x 2.5cm/1 x 1in wooden batten (furring strip) to fit inside window frame
- Pencil
- Ruler
- Tape measure
- Nylon fishing line
- Scissors
- Large, flat glass beads with central hole, in two colours
- Strong glue
- Silver bugle beads
- Silver rocailles
- Silver square beads
- Assorted large glass beads
- Staple gun
- 2.5cm/1in wide ribbon
- Beading needle and matching thread

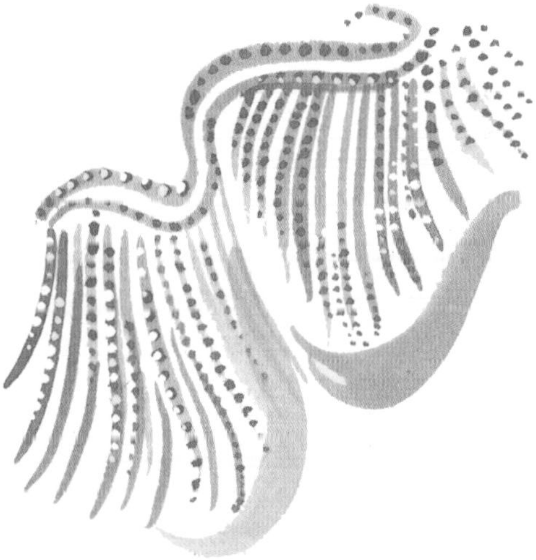

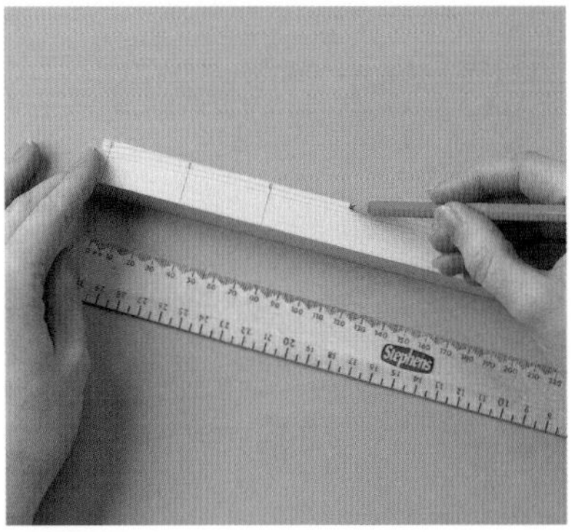

1 Using a pencil and ruler, mark equidistant points about 4cm/1½in apart along the length of the batten.

2 Measure the window from top to bottom and cut lengths of nylon fishing line to this measurement plus 20cm/8in to allow for knotting. You will need one length of fishing line for each mark on the batten.

3 Prepare the strands of the curtain one at a time. Thread on a large, flat glass bead and tie a knot. Trim the excess line and then apply a blob of glue to the knot for extra security.

4 Add on a 5cm/2in length of silver bugles, rocailles and square beads, then a large glass bead. Make a knot 4–8cm/1½–3¼in along the line (vary this distance as you go). Thread on 4–8cm/1½–3¼in of beads arranged symmetrically on either side of a large centre bead. Continue to the end.

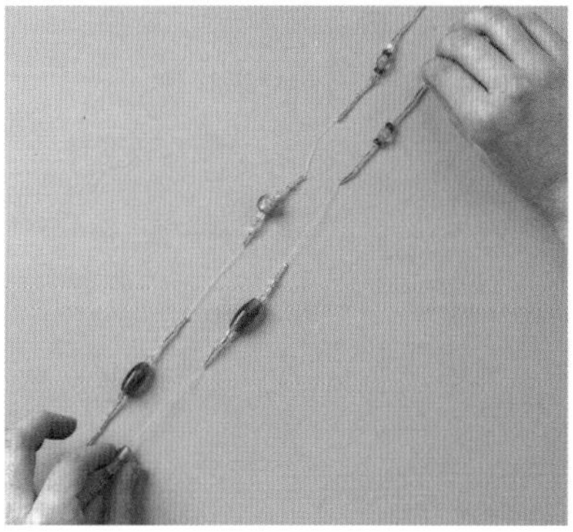

5 The next length will be slightly shorter than the first to create a staggered line at the bottom of the curtain. Lay the second length of nylon alongside the completed first length and, when threading this length, position the beads so that they roughly correspond with the beadless gaps on the first length.

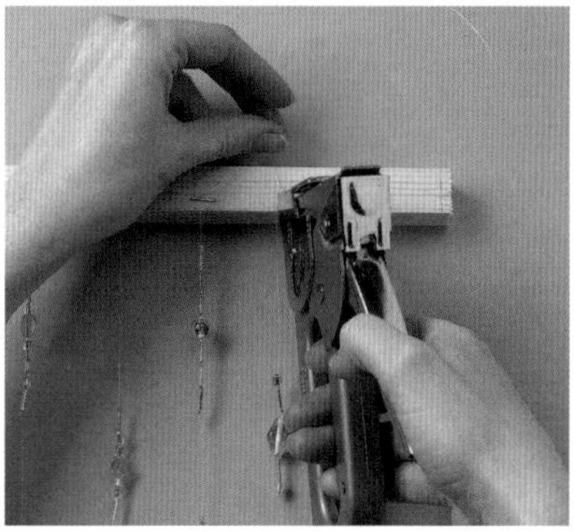

6 As you complete each length, tie a double knot at the top. Staple the lengths at the marked positions on the batten; the knot will act as an anchor above the staple. It's easier to do this in a hanging position to make sure the bottom of the curtain is level.

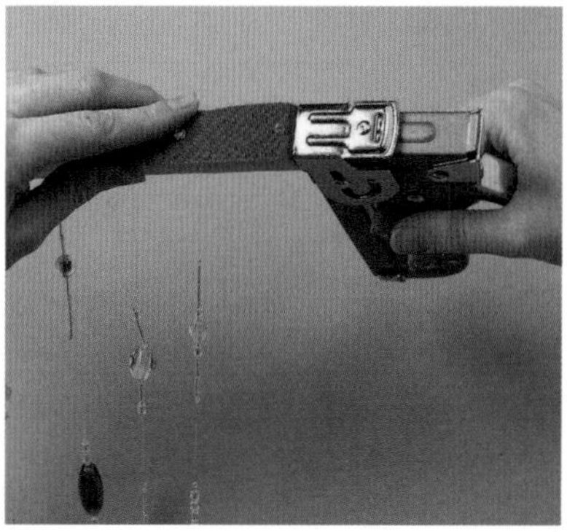

7 Cut a length of ribbon to the length of the batten, plus 6cm/2½in. Stitch a single row of beads along the centre, then glue to the front of the batten to conceal the staples. Secure the ends with staples.

Sequins make wonderful decorations, twinkling and sparkling as they catch the light. Use concave sequins to give the finished baubles a smooth surface and pin them in place with short lil pins.

Christmas Beadwork Decorations

●●●

you will need
2 compressed cotton spheres, 6cm/2½in diameter
Felt-tipped pen
6mm/¼in diameter round concave sequins in a variety of colours, including metallic
Lil pins
Beading needle
Beading thread
Small bronze glass beads
Fluted metal beads
Dressmaker's pins
Silver pointed oval sequins
Ribbon

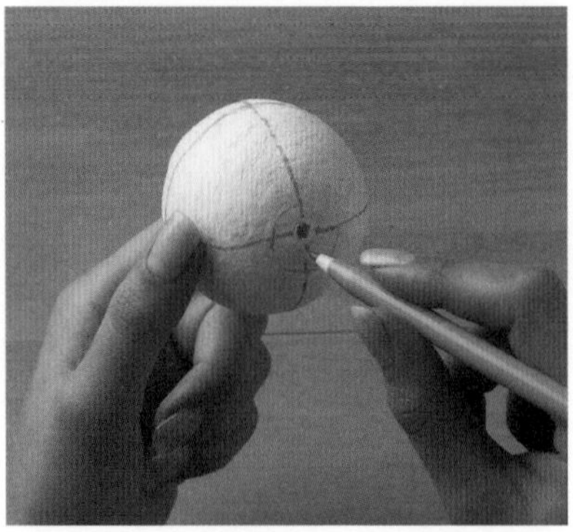

1 To make a block-coloured bauble, using a felt-tipped pen, divide the surface of one of the cotton spheres into four segments, as shown. Mark around the middle of the sphere to divide it into eight sections.

2 Outline the eight sections of the cotton sphere with round concave sequins, using different colours. Use lil pins to attach the sequins and overlap them slightly. Fill in each of the sections, again overlapping the sequins slightly.

3 To make the hanging loop, thread a fine needle with beading thread and secure to the top of the ball with a few stitches. Add 8cm/3in of small bronze beads and sew down the other end. Thread a metal bead on a lil pin and press into the sphere to secure the loop.

4 To make the star bauble, mark several horizontal stripes on the other sphere. Press in a sequin at the top and bottom. Working outwards from these points, press in silver pointed oval sequins to form a star shape.

5 Fill in the rest of sphere with round sequins, as in step 2. As an alternative hanging loop, attach a 10cm/4in piece of ribbon to the top, using a dressmaker's pin and metal bead as in step 3.

These pulls are an ideal way to make the most of your larger beads: just one or two favourite examples can deliver real impact, and you can have the added satisfaction of using them every day.

Giant Bead Cord-pulls

you will need

Extra-long head pins
Small silver rocailles
5 coloured resin beads
2 metal cones
Wire cutters
Round-nosed (snub-nosed) pliers
Medium- and fine-gauge silver wire
2 small round metal beads
Extra-large metal bead
Coloured leather thongs
Ready-made tassel
2 large handmade foil-and-glass beads
Tape measure
Silk cord
Stranded embroidery thread (floss)
2 large, dyed bone beads
Strong non-stretch beading thread
4 long, bleached bone beads
8 small bone beads
Satin ribbon
Large, flat handmade glass bead with large hole
Sewing needle and sewing thread

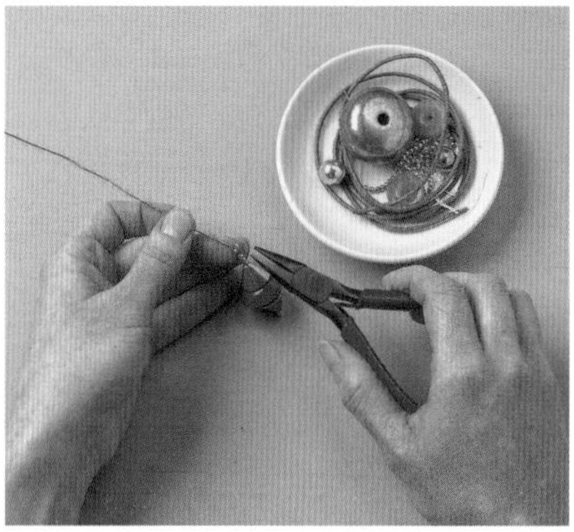

1 For the metal cord-pull, take an extra-long head pin and thread with small silver rocailles and a large resin bead between two metal cones. Snip off the excess wire and bend the end into a small loop at the top. Take a length of medium-gauge silver wire, bend the end into a small loop and attach it to the top loop of the pendant.

2 Thread on two small silver rocailles, a small round metal bead, a resin bead, an extra-large metal bead, another resin bead, another small metal bead and two more silver rocailles. Snip off the excess wire and bend into a loop at the top with the round-nosed pliers.

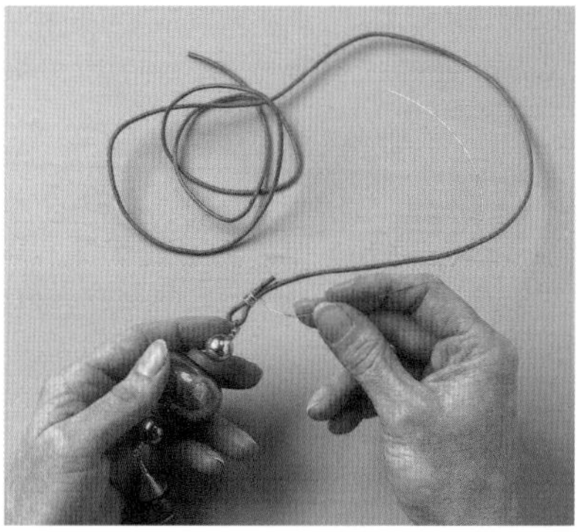

3 Thread one end of a coloured leather thong through the wire loop. Fold the last 2.5cm/1in back on itself and bind the end to the thong with fine-gauge silver wire. Ensure the ends are securely tucked under the coiled wire.

4 To make the tassel cord-pull, bend one end of a length of medium-gauge silver wire around the loop at the top of a tassel. Pass the wire through two large foil-and-glass beads, snip the wire about 15mm/$\frac{5}{8}$in above the top bead. Use pliers to bend it into a small loop.

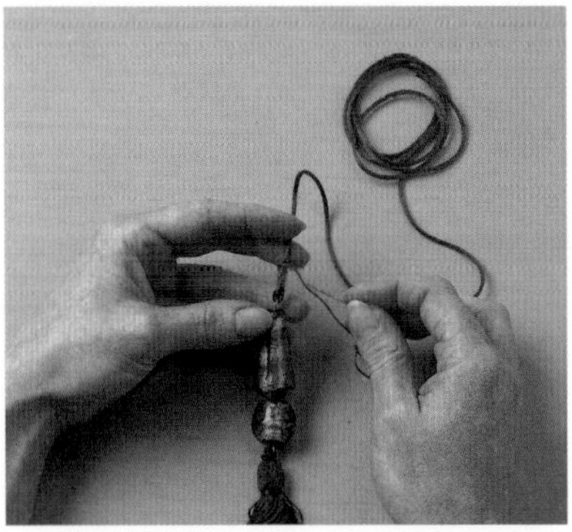

5 Pass the end of a length of matching silk cord through the loop, fold it back on itself and bind securely with embroidery thread (floss).

6 For the decorative bone cord-pull, thread a large bone bead on to an extra-long pin between two coloured resin beads. Use pliers to bend the end of the pin into a small loop.

7 Take a short piece of medium-gauge silver wire, bend a small loop in one end and pass through a second large bone bead. Snip off the wire and bend it into a loop at the top.

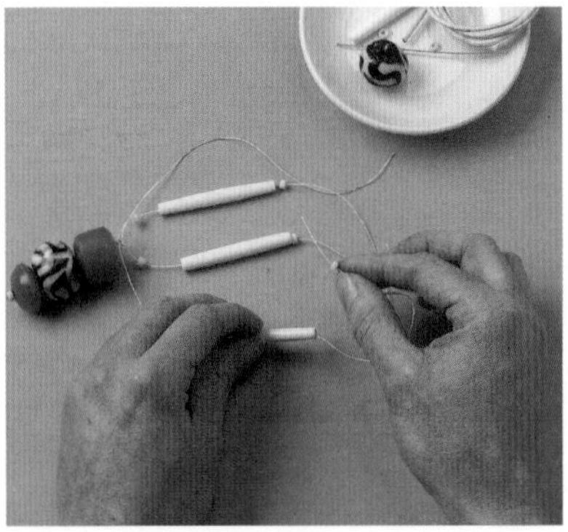

8 Tie two strands of strong non-stretch bead thread to the wire loop at the top of the group of beads, leaving four long ends. Thread each through a small bone bead followed by a long bleached bone bead and finally another small bone bead.

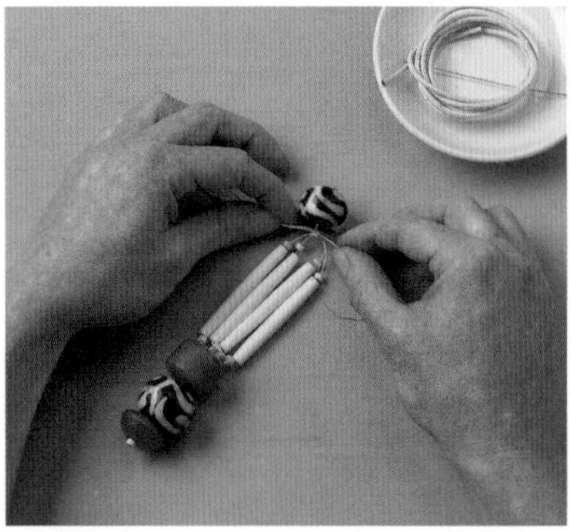

9 Tie the threads securely to the wire loop under the top bead and thread the ends back through the bone beads to conceal them. Pass a leather thong through the topmost wire loop, fold it back on itself and bind it with wire as in step 3.

10 For a simple ribbon-pull, thread the end of a satin ribbon through a large, flat handmade bead. Fold back the short end and stitch in place, close to the top of the bead. Use pliers to bend the end of a short length of medium-gauge silver wire into a spiral, then use the rest to bind around the ribbon.

Glass rocailles, wired into simple stripes, make a lovely napkin holder, and adding a matching night-light holder makes a complete personalized table decoration that will shimmer in candlelight.

Table Decoration Set

you will need
Fine-gauge galvanized wire
Ruler or tape measure
Wire cutters
Round-nosed (snub-nosed) pliers
Plastic bottle and beaker, to use as formers
Glass rocailles in pink, red and orange
Fine-gauge silver wire
Adhesive pads

1 For the napkin ring, take about 1.75m/2yd of galvanized wire and bend a small loop in one end using round-nosed pliers. Wind the wire about ten times around the bottle.

2 Thread enough pink glass rocailles on to the wire to fit around the bottle once, then change to red and thread another round of beads.

3 Go on threading red and pink beads in this sequence until the wire is full, then use the pliers to bend another small loop in the end to prevent the beads falling off.

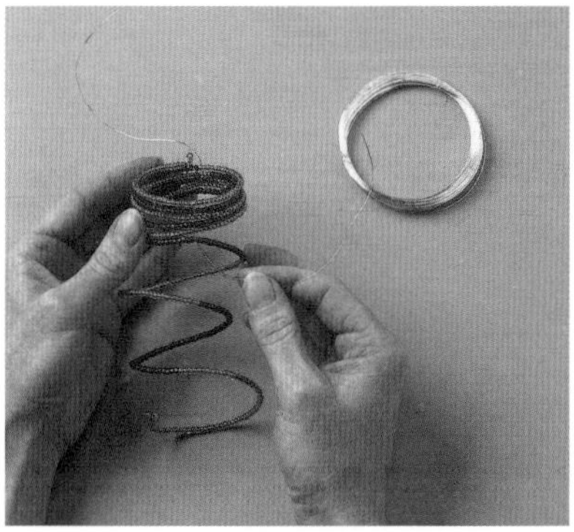

4 Bend the beaded wire around the bottle to restore its shape. Secure a length of fine wire to the first row, then bind it around the others. Do this at three other points around the ring.

5 When the ring is complete, wind the ends of the silver wire back around the previous rows to neaten, and snip off the excess.

▶

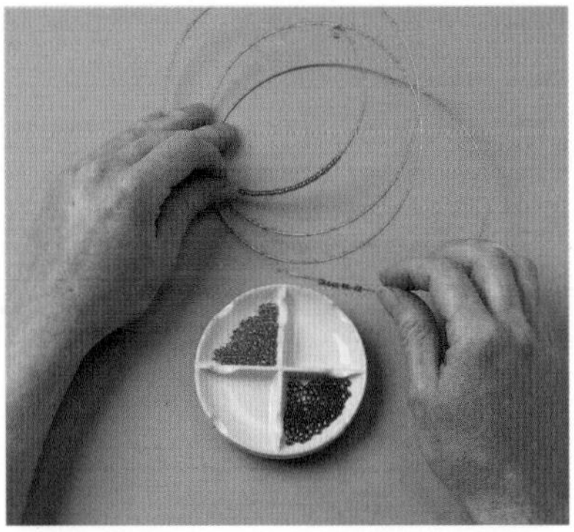

6 To make the night-light holder, bend one end of a long piece of galvanized wire into a small loop as before. Thread the first part of the wire with orange glass rocailles.

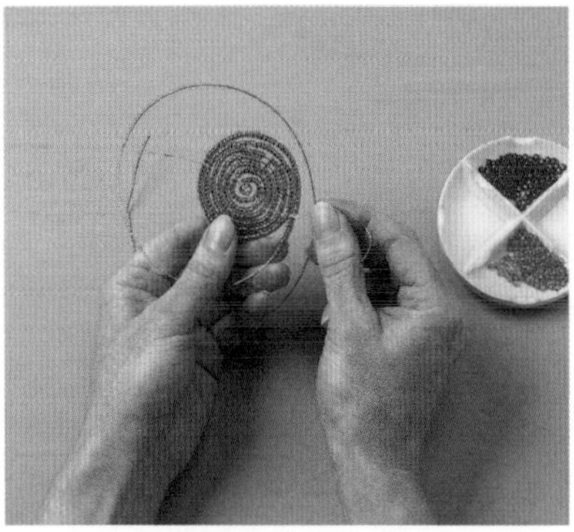

7 Bend the beaded wire into a small spiral to form the base of the night-light holder. Attach two lengths of silver wire to the centre of the spiral and bind each row to the previous one to secure the shape. Thread on more beads until the base fits that of the beaker.

8 Use adhesive pads to attach the beaded spiral base temporarily to the base of the beaker. They will hold it in place while you construct the sides, and can then be removed.

9 Join on more wire, if necessary, by twisting the ends together with pliers. Then thread on enough orange rocailles to wind around the beaker about four or five times.

10 Wind the beaded wire around the beaker, binding each row to the last using the silver wire. Pull the wire quite tight to hold the shape.

11 Change to the red beads and repeat until the holder reaches the height you want. To finish, bind the silver wire a few times tightly around the beaded wire and back around the previous rows. Snip off the ends.

Beads add detail to this stylized flower decoration for a loose chair cover. With a design of strong shapes and contrasts, created in sturdy fabrics, the beads add a delicacy that creates a delightful surprise.

Bead-encrusted Appliqué Flower

you will need
Scissors
Fusible bonding web
Cotton fabrics in three colours
Iron
Thin card (stock)
Pencil
Sewing-machine, with zip foot
Matching sewing threads
Beading needle
Beading thread
Small glass rocailles
Bugle beads
Assorted round glass beads
Dressmaker's pins
Sewing needle and tacking (basting) thread

1 Cut a piece of fusible bonding web, the same size as each of the fabric pieces you have chosen for the flower appliqué. Following the manufacturer's instructions, iron them to the wrong side of the fabric. Copy the templates at the back of the book for the petals and the flower centre on to card, and cut out.

2 Draw around the petal template on the backing paper and cut out 12 shapes. Cut out the circular centre for the flower from a contrasting fabric.

3 Arrange the petals on a square of the background fabric, peel off the backing paper and iron them in place. Iron on the flower centre.

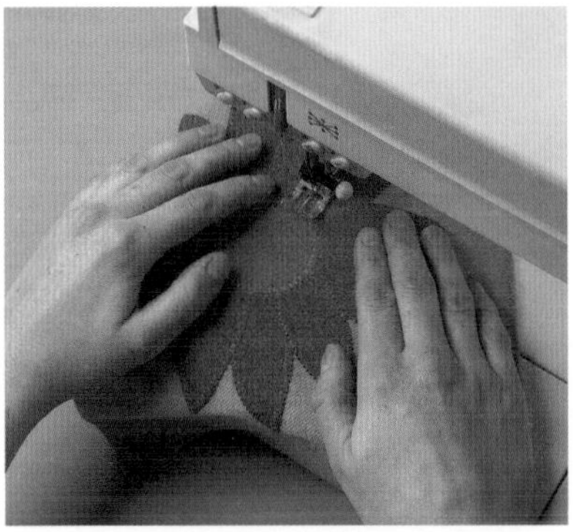

4 Stitch around the shapes using a decorative stitch, such as zigzag stitch or satin stitch, and matching threads.

5 Decorate the flower centre and petals with an assortment of evenly spaced glass rocaille and bugle beads.

6 Fold under a 1cm/½in hem along each raw edge of the background square and press in place.

7 Following the folded seam line, sew on an assortment of small and medium round glass beads in various assorted colours, stitching them about 1cm/½in apart.

8 Pin the panel on the chair cover, and tack (baste) in position. Thread the sewing-machine with matching thread and fit a zip foot so that the beads will not get damaged. Stitch the panel in place close to the edge.

In this exquisite modern interpretation of a traditional glass chandelier, droplets of coloured glass hang and quiver from a simple structure of spiralled wire. Suspend it with a loop of clear monofilament.

Spiralled Chandelier

you will need

Wire cutters

2.5m/2$\frac{3}{4}$yd of 2mm/$\frac{1}{12}$in wire

Round-nosed (snub-nosed) pliers

0.2mm/$\frac{1}{120}$in wire

Selection of spherical and faceted glass and plastic beads

Small glass beads

4mm/$\frac{1}{5}$in bugle beads

1 Use wire cutters to snip two 120cm/4ft lengths of thick wire and bend each one into a spiral. Use round-nosed pliers to make a small loop at each of the four ends.

2 Hold one end of each wire together, and carefully arrange the coils so that the two spirals run alongside each other.

3 To make the droplets, thread a piece of thin wire through a large glass spherical bead and a small bead – the small bead will act as an anchor. Pass the wire back through the beads and twist the ends together.

4 Thread on some bugle beads, then twist the wires to make a stem. Make about 30 droplets, using different beads in different arrangements.

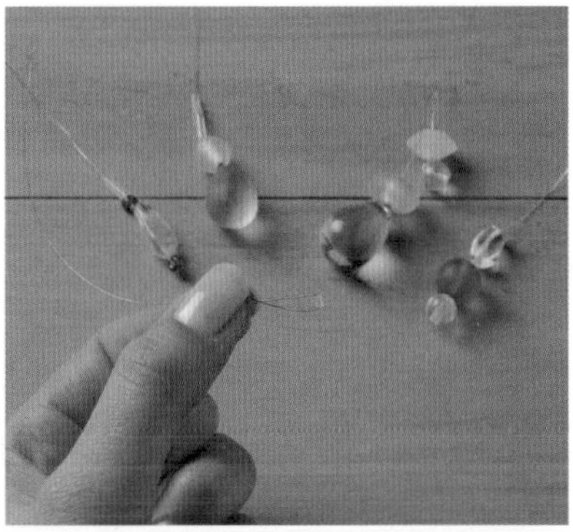

5 Make a hanging hook for each droplet by winding a short piece of thin wire on to each stem. Use the round-nosed pliers to bend the wire back into a hook.

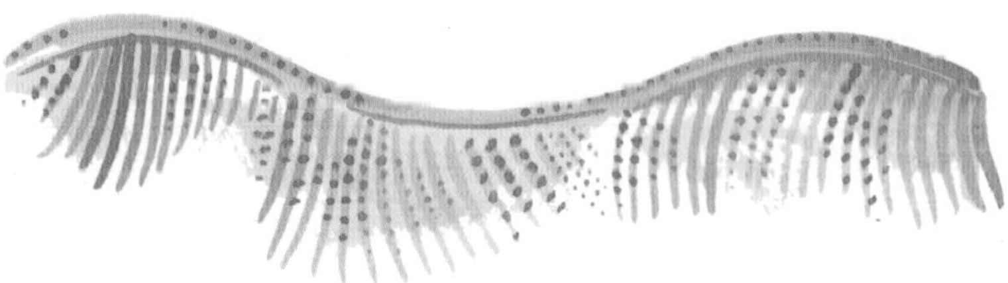

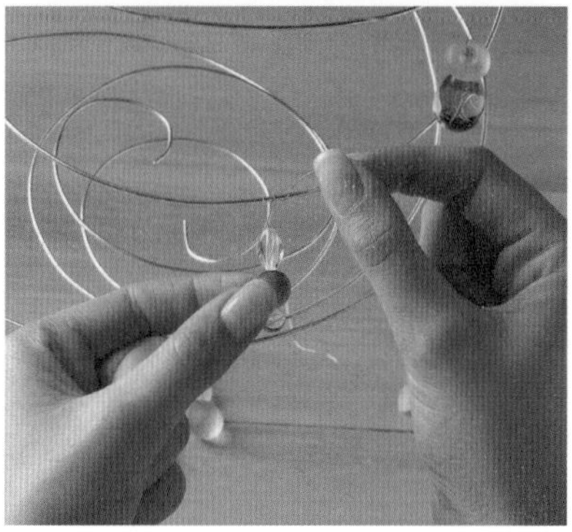

6 Suspend the droplets at intervals on the frame, alternating shapes and colours for a varied arrangement.

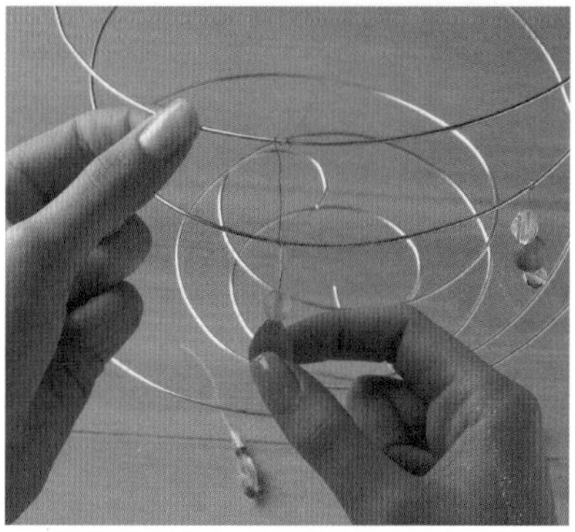

7 To hold the spiral shape in place, some of the droplets should be twisted over two rounds of the spiral.

8 As a finishing touch, add glass beads on to the bottom ends of the spiral wire frame.

Rocailles in restrained shades of grey, white and gold are used to make this sophisticated container, and the colours come to life in the flickering light. For safety, always use a candle in a metal holder.

Bead Candle-holder

you will need
Wire cutters
Tape measure
0.6mm/1/40in gold wire
Glass tumbler
Adhesive tape
Large rubber band
0.2mm/1/120in gold wire
Round-nosed (snub-nosed) pliers
4mm/1/5in grey glass beads
4mm/1/5in white glass beads
4mm/1/5in gold glass beads

1 Cut two pieces of thick gold wire twice the height and diameter of the glass plus 10cm/4in. Twist the wires together at their halfway points, then tape the knot to the centre of the glass base. Slip a rubber band over the glass to hold the wire in place. Fold the wire ends over the lip of the glass.

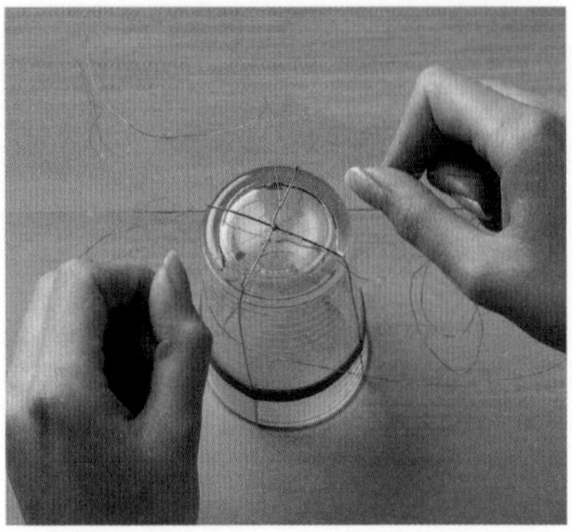

2 Cut two pieces of fine gold wire approximately 1m/40in long. Find their halfway points, then twist both pieces around the knot on the base of the glass. Wrap each wire around your hand first to stop it becoming tangled.

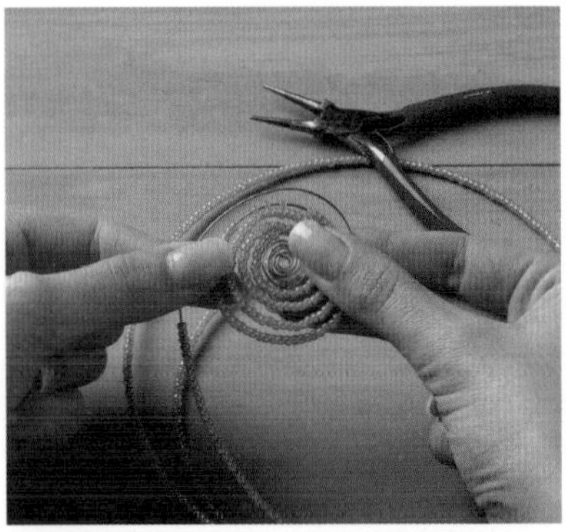

3 Thread the grey beads on to the thick wire. To begin the winding wire, bend one end of the thick wire into a 2cm/3/4in flat spiral with pliers. Secure at the centre of the base by weaving the thin wire over and under the frame of thick wire and the spiralled wire.

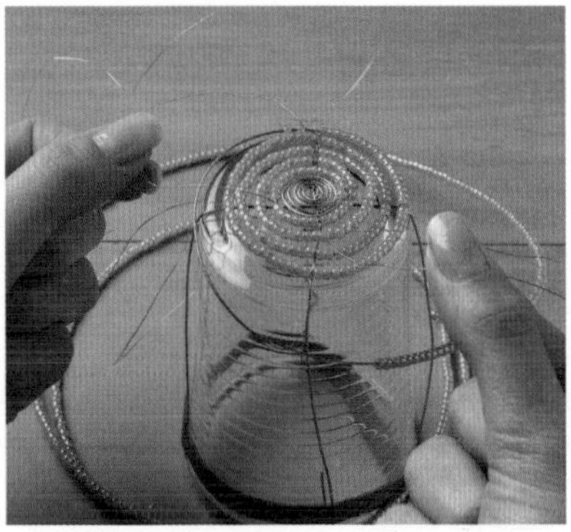

4 Thread more grey beads on to the winding wire and continue to wind it into a spiral, weaving the thinner wire under and over the frame. Continue up the sides of the glass to within 1cm/1/2in of the top. Remove the rubber band.

5 To make a lip, ease the top of the frame outwards and thread on some white beads. Continue to weave the thinner wire under and over the winding wire and the frame. Thread on small gold beads. Open out ends of frame, remove glass, trim ends and fold over. Secure the ends to frame.

Use large glass beads in strong colours to make tie-backs that will become the focal points of your window. Before you begin, gather up the curtain (drape) in a tape measure to calculate the length.

Chunky Bead Tie-backs

you will need
For each tie-back:
2 split rings
2 decorative dividers with attachments for three strings
Glue gun and glue sticks
2 flat-backed blue glass nuggets
Scissors
Pencil
Paper for template
Tape measure
Strong non-stretch beading thread
Clear nail polish
Cylindrical orange handmade glass and ceramic beads
Round blue glass beads
Large blue glass beads

1 Attach one of the split rings to the loop at the top of each triangular divider. These will be slipped over the wall hooks. Using a glue gun, attach a flat-backed blue glass nugget to the centre of each divider.

2 Cut a curved, symmetrical paper template to the required shape of the finished tie-back. Make sure it is wide enough to hold all the folds of the curtain (drape) and deep enough to accommodate all three rows of beads.

3 Cut a length of strong thread, 30cm/12in longer than the width of the template. Knot one end securely to the top loop of the first divider. Dab the knot with clear nail polish to keep it in place.

4 Thread on the large and small beads in a symmetrical pattern, using the main picture as a guide to the sequence. Pass both the main length of thread and the spare end through the first few beads to secure them.

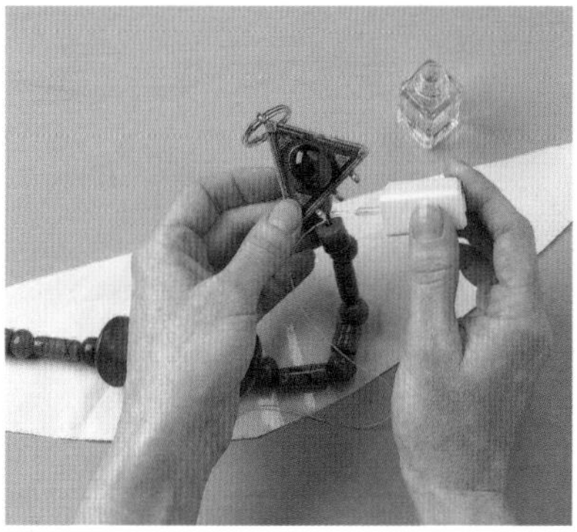

5 Thread on enough beads for the first row to fit across the top of the template and knot the loose end of thread firmly to the second divider. Trim the end and secure the knot with a blob of nail polish as before.

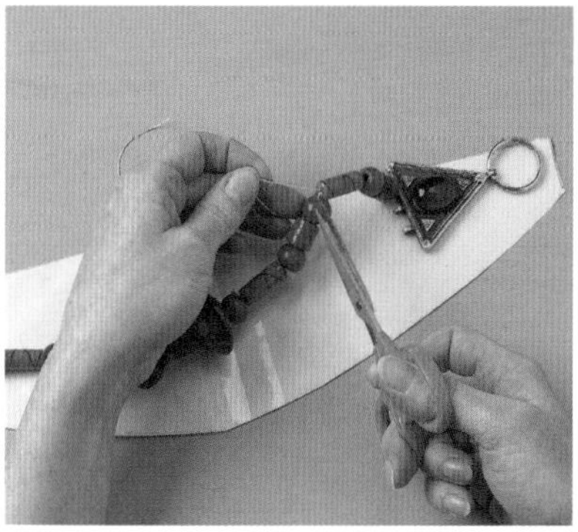

6 Pass the spare tail of beading thread back through the last few beads on the strand and snip off the remainder.

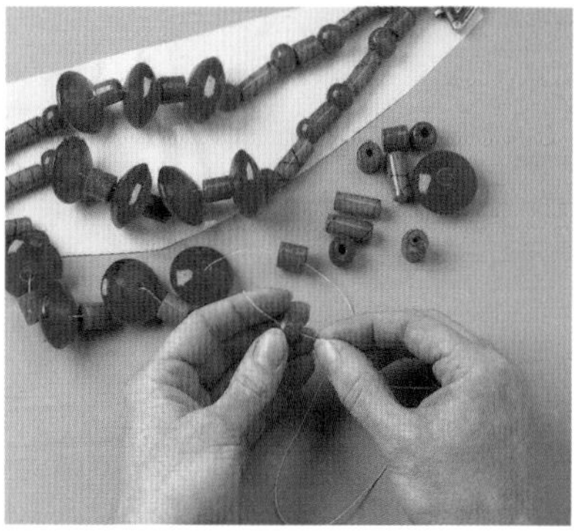

7 Thread up the second and third rows following the same sequence, adding extra beads to make each row a little longer than the previous one. Repeat for the other tie-back.

French-style beaded light fittings are beautiful but expensive. However, you can easily create your own by adding gold paint and swags of cheap plastic crystal beads to a junk-shop or flea-market find.

Beaded Wall Sconce

●●●

you will need
Wall sconce
Stiff card (stock)
Pair of compasses and pencil
Scissors
Metallic gold paint
Medium paintbrush
Thick sewing needle
Wire cutters
Fine brass wire
Medium-sized transparent plastic crystal drop beads
Round-nosed (snub-nosed) pliers
Transparent plastic crystal beads
Large and small coloured beads

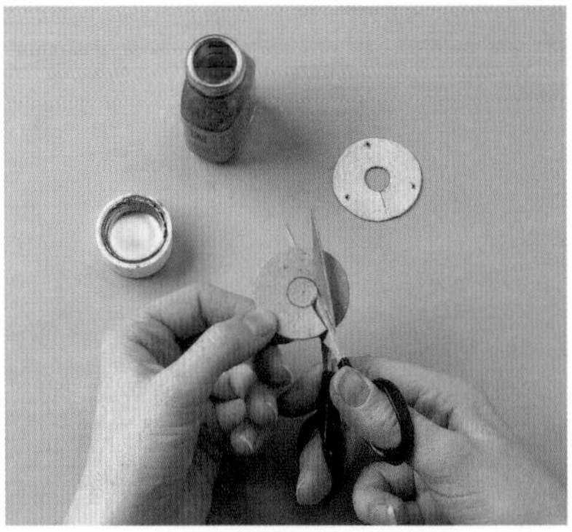

1 Cut two circles of stiff card and paint them gold. These will be inserted in the joints where the arms unscrew, so should be a little wider than the arms at this point. Cut out the centres to fit around the flex and snip across. Pierce three equidistant holes around the edge with a thick needle.

2 Three bead drops are needed for each disc. The links are made with individual lengths of wire to give flexibility. Using the wire cutters, cut a piece of brass wire about 3cm/1¼in long. Thread on the base crystal drop bead and use the pliers to twist the wire once. Leave the ends open.

3 Take a second length of wire of about the same length and make a small closed loop at one end using the pliers. Slip this loop over one of the open ends of the previous wire and twist the open ends together to secure the link. Trim the excess wire.

4 Thread on a medium-sized crystal bead. Cut the wire to 8mm/⅓in and make a closed loop. Cut a length of wire, thread it through and make another closed loop. Thread on a small coloured bead. Repeat this process to add another medium-sized crystal bead. Add the final length of wire.

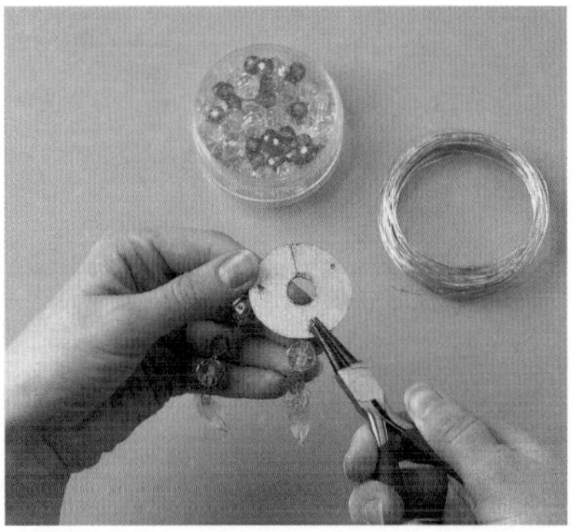

5 Repeat steps 3–5 for the remaining drops. Attach the drops to the gold-painted discs, looping the wires through the punched holes.

6 Make the swags using looped wires: use small and medium beads with a large coloured bead in the centre.

7 Paint the sconce with one or two coats of gold paint and leave to dry.

8 Twist the ends of the wire around the sconce arms to attach the swags. Fit the discs in the joints of the arms.

Easy and satisfying to make, these spheres look rich and exotic massed together. You could add ribbon loops to make opulent Christmas decorations, but they are too pretty to be put away for the rest of the year.

Glittering Bead Spheres

you will need

Polystyrene (styrofoam) balls, 5cm/2in, 7cm/2¾in and 10cm/4in diameter
Skewer
Acrylic paints in blue and green
Artist's paintbrushes
Lil pins
Silver-lined glass rocailles
Round frosted glass beads in assorted sizes in shades of blue and green
Pen or pencil
Large faceted sequins in blue and green
Small glass rocailles in blue and green
Round metallic embroidery beads in blue and green

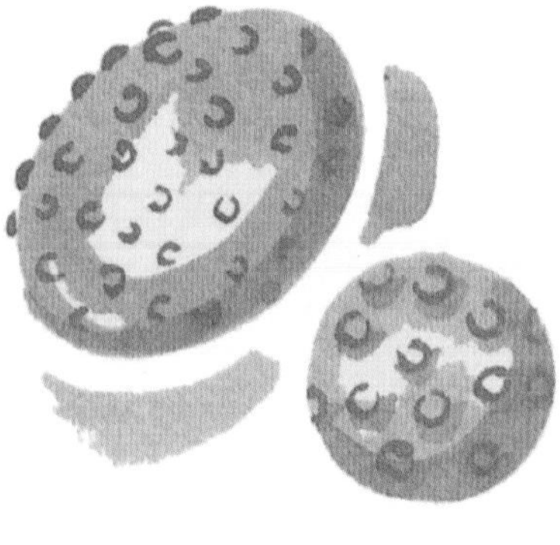

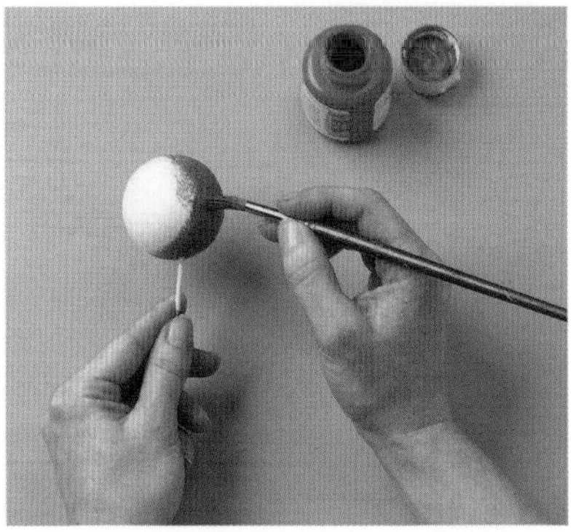

1 Stick the small polystyrene (styrofoam) ball on a skewer to hold it steady while painting. Paint it with a coat of blue acrylic paint and allow to dry. Apply another coat if necessary.

2 With a lil pin, pick up a small silver-lined rocaille and a larger blue frosted bead and insert them in the ball. Repeat, pinning the beads close together all over the ball.

3 Paint the 7cm/2¾in ball with green acrylic and allow to dry. Then use a pen or pencil to mark out a grid pattern as shown: divide it into halves, then quarters, both vertically and horizontally.

4 Pin a large green sequin, a large frosted bead and a green rocaille at each intersection. Fill in the design with small rocailles and tiny embroidery bead.

5 To make the panelled design, paint the large ball blue, allow to dry and mark out into six equal sections.

6 Pin groups of large sequins, large frosted beads and small rocailles in a row along each line.

7 Fill in each panel with small glass rocailles, positioned as closely together as possible.

Elaborate pincushions were popular among Victorian women, and are simple yet effective to make. Other shapes can be used, and for a gift the beads can mark out the recipient's initials.

Strawberry Pincushion

you will need

Thin card (stock)
Pencil
Craft (utility) knife
Fabric marker
Small piece of red velvet
Dressmaking scissors
Tape measure
Needle and matching sewing thread
Sawdust or bran, for stuffing
Small glass rocailles in green and red
White pearlized beads
Green sequins
Dressmaker's pins
Scrap of green ribbon

1 Trace the strawberry shape template from the back of the book, increase in size by around 140 per cent, cut it out, and trace around it on to the wrong side of the piece of velvet, using the fabric marker.

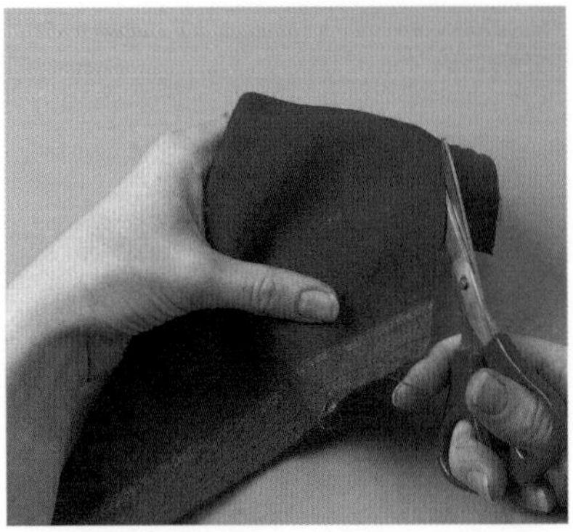

2 Cut out the two strawberry shapes. Cut a strip of velvet for the gusset measuring 21 x 2.5cm/8½ x 1in.

3 Join the two ends of the gusset strip, right sides together, stitching the seam in back stitch and leaving a seam allowance of a scant 3mm/⅛in.

4 With right sides together, hand stitch the two strawberry shapes to the gusset, leaving a small gap on one side.

5 Carefully turn right-side out and stuff with sawdust or bran. Add the filling a pinch at a time until the shape is firm and full.

6 Tuck in the raw edges of the opening. Slip stitch neatly to close, using a double length of matching sewing thread.

7 Decorate the strawberry shape with beads and sequins. Start at the top by threading a green bead and sequin on to a pin, then fixing it into the pincushion. Work the beads and sequins in a leaf shape.

8 Continue decorating the pincushion with red rocailles interspersed with white pearlized beads to represent seeds. Finish the pincushion by pinning or stitching a loop of green ribbon to the top.

Hang these pretty tassels from keys in the bedroom or bathroom. Worked in colours that co-ordinate with the rest of the room's decor, they make charming decorative details.

Silken Key Tassels

you will need

- 2 skeins stranded embroidery thread (floss) for each tassel, plus extra for loops and ties
- Stiff card (stock)
- Scissors
- Tape measure
- Sewing needle and matching thread
- 2 large ceramic beads
- Beading needle
- Small glass rocailles in red, orange and turquoise
- Large glass rocailles in red and turquoise
- Medium red glass crystals
- Small red opaque rocailles

1 To make a plaited tassel, wind two skeins of stranded embroidery thread around a piece of stiff card. Cut a 20cm/8in length of thread and tie it into a hanging loop, then tie the ends tightly around the top loop of the wound thread. Carefully slip the tied bundle of thread from the card.

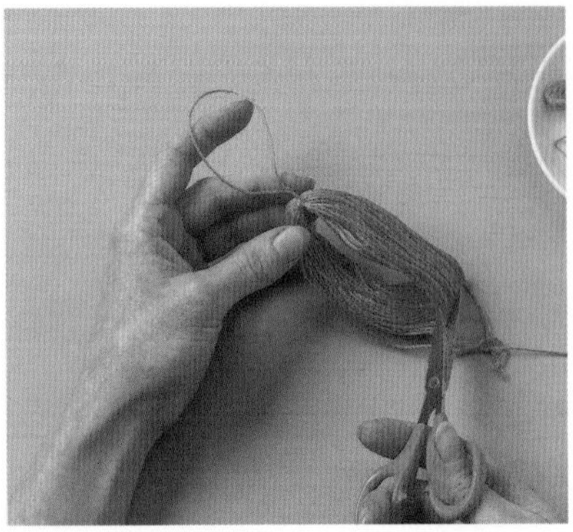

2 Holding the knot in one hand, cut through the other end of the loop to form the tassel. Separate six threads into three pairs and make a tight plait. Use a needle and matching thread to secure the end. Make another three plaits in the same way around the tassel.

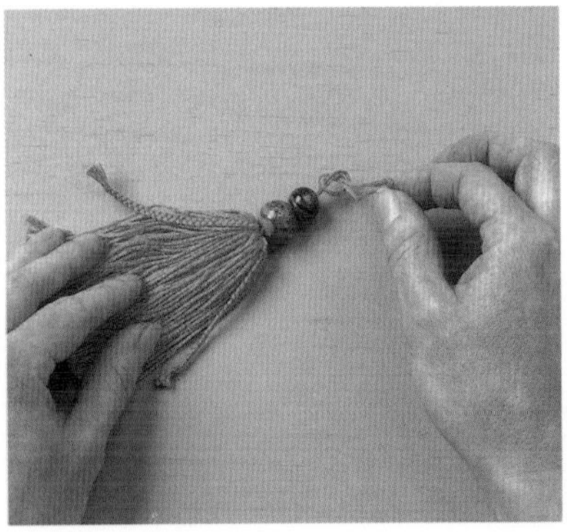

3 Trim the ends so they are level. Thread the hanging loop through the two ceramic beads, then tie the loop in a small knot to secure.

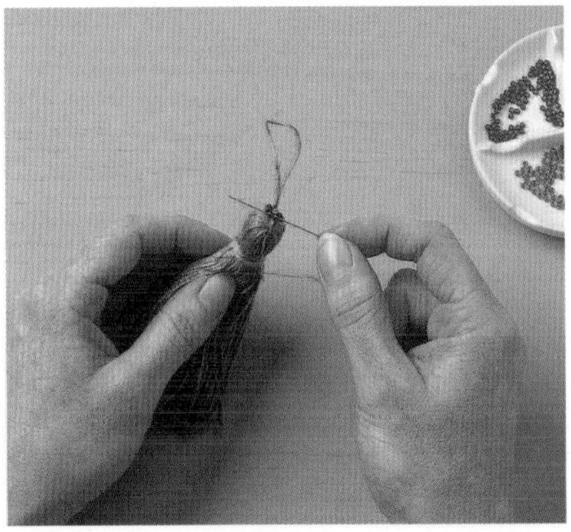

4 To make a beaded tassel, repeat steps 1–3, then tie a length of thread around the bundle about 2cm/¾in down from the top. Stitch a length of thread to the top of the tassel and thread on eight small red rocailles. Tie off with a double knot to make a ring around the hanging loop.

5 Passing the thread through alternate rocailles in the previous round, make three loops of two orange, two turquoise, two red and one large red rocailles, reversing the sequence to complete the loop. Make three more similar loops, passing the thread through the large red rocailles.

6 Link the large red beads from step 5 with a round of six red rocailles between each, then add a round of six orange rocailles. Link the large beads again with six turquoise rocailles. Suspend a pendant loop from each large red bead: thread three red, three turquoise, thee orange and one red rocaille, then one medium red glass crystal and one small red opaque. Go back through the last two beads and reverse for the other side.

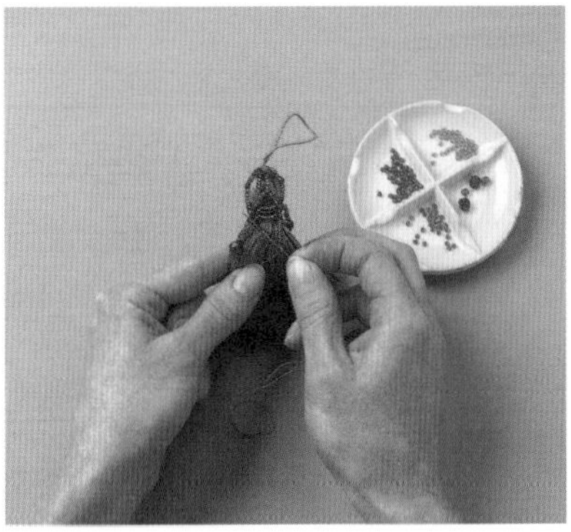

7 Again passing the thread through the large red rocailles to link them, make three loops of three red, three turquoise and three orange rocailles, one red rocaille, then one large turquoise rocaille and one small red opaque. Go back through the last two beads and reverse for the other side. Finish off with a knot.

This sumptuous and eleborate bead-fringed pincushion, with its four embellished velvet hearts, typifies the nineteenth-century passion for ornament and home decoration.

Edwardian-style Pincushion

you will need

2 12cm/ 5in squares taffeta
Matching sewing thread
Sewing needle
Sawdust or bran, for stuffing
Fine sewing needle
Rocailles in gold, pink and green
4 pink crystal beads
Scraps of velvet
Brass dressmaker's pins
An assortment of glass beads in different colours and sizes
Sequins
5 rose-shaped buttons

1 Join the taffeta squares with a 1cm/½in seam, leaving a 5cm/2in gap at one side. Trim the corners, turn inside out and stuff firmly with sawdust or bran. Slip stitch the gap to close. Thread a fine needle with a double thread and fix to one corner.

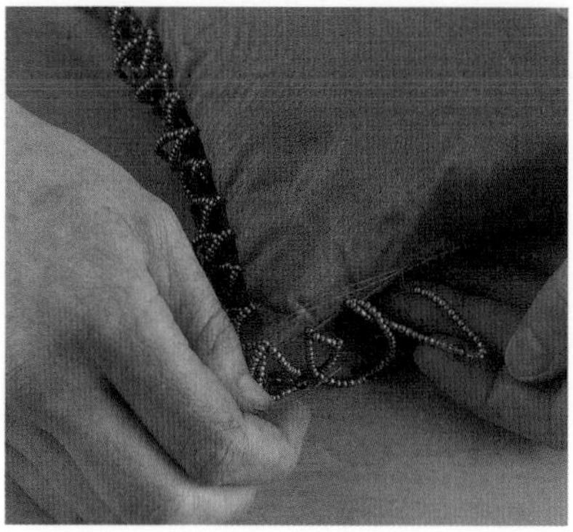

2 Thread on 35 rocailles and secure the loop with a few stitches 1cm/½in along. Make a second loop, passing the needle through the first loop before securing. Continue all around the cushion, adding a pink crystal to each corner loop.

3 Conceal the seam with green rocailles. Cut a velvet heart for each corner. Hold in place with pins threaded with a small and a large bead: use a different colour for each heart.

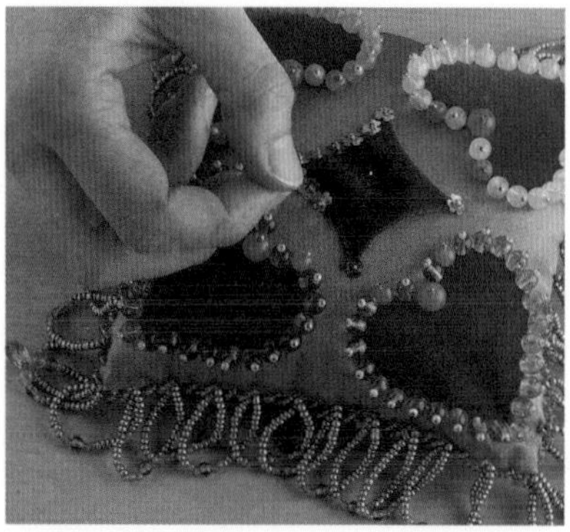

4 Cut a diamond from velvet and position in the centre. Fix in place around the outside edge with pins threaded with a rocaille and a sequin.

5 Sew a rose-shaped button or a ribbon rose (see technique on page 176) to each corner and to the centre of the velvet diamond.

The beads on this dramatic bolster are attached with fine wire, which creates three-dimensional, curling tendrils. The beading wire acts as a needle and thread to 'stitch' through the fabric.

Velvet Bolster Cushion

you will need

Bolster cushion pad
Tape measure
Pair of compasses
Pencil and paper
Dressmaking scissors
50 x 100cm/20 x 40in blue-black embossed velvet
Fine beading wire
Small red glass beads
Sewing needle
Matching sewing thread
Sewing-machine
Dressmaker's pins

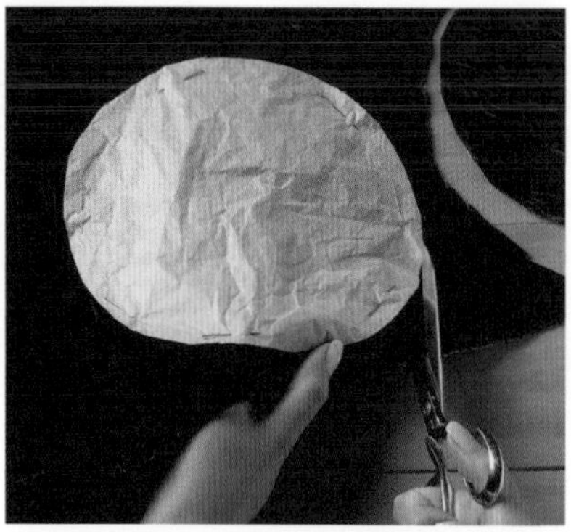

1 Measure the diameter of the end of the bolster cushion pad and divide in half to find the radius. Draw a circle to this size on paper, using a pair of compasses, then redraw, adding a 1.5cm/⅝in seam allowance. Cut two circles of embossed velvet.

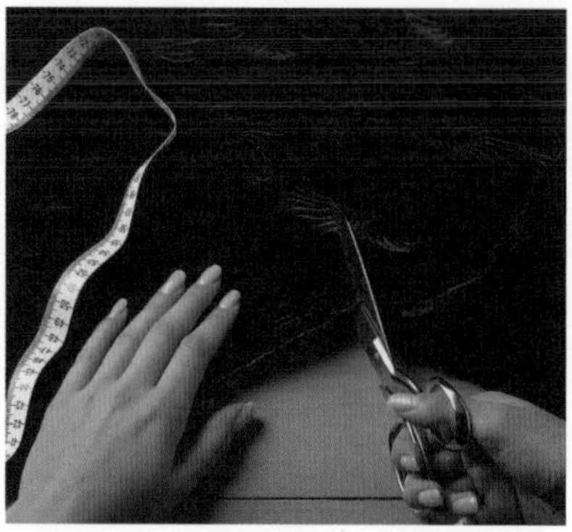

2 Measure the length and circumference of the bolster pad. Cut a piece of embossed velvet to this size plus a 3cm/1¼in seam allowance all around.

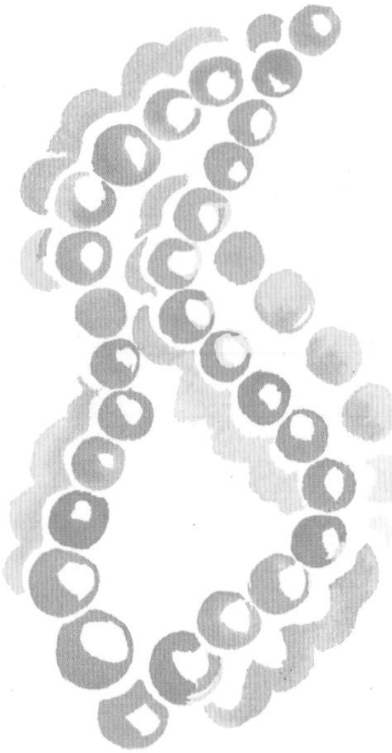

3 Tie one end of a piece of beading wire in a knot and pass the other end through the centre of a velvet circle to the right side. Thread on red beads for 10cm/4in. Insert the end of the wire back into the velvet 4cm/1½in from the knot to make a loop.

4 Thread the wire through the fabric again 5cm/2in from the first loop. Make a second loop as before. Repeat until there are about 20 loops, using extra wire as needed. Fasten the wire off. Repeat for the second circle.

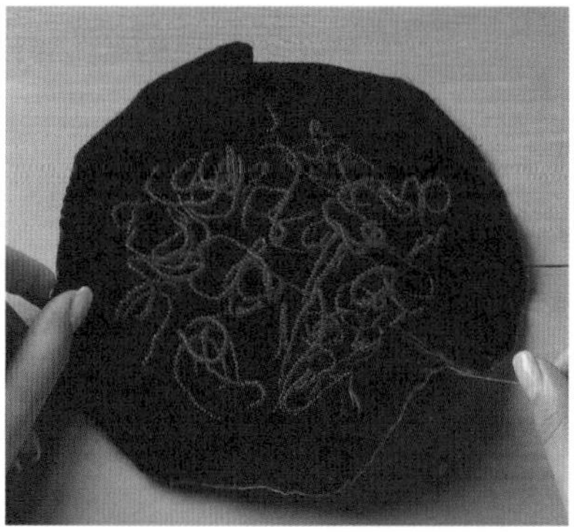

5 Run a gathering stitch around each circle, using a double length of matching sewing thread. With right sides facing, fold the embossed velvet in half across the centre.

6 Machine stitch the short ends, 1.5cm/⅝in from the edge, leaving a gap for the pad. Machine stitch both circles in place, adjusting the gathering stitch to fit each end. Turn the cover right-side out through the gap.

7 Insert the cushion pad and ease it into place. Pin and slip stitch the opening to close.

All types of needlework can be further embellished with beadwork: here tiny glass beads have been used to add highlights to a charming folk-art needlepoint of a boat at sea.

Beaded Boat Tapestry

you will need

- 10-count tapestry canvas
- Tapestry frame
- Drawing pins (thumb tacks) or staple gun
- Ruler
- Pencil
- Tapestry needle
- Tapestry wool (yarn) in white, red, very pale blue, pale blue, royal blue, jade green, green, yellow, grey, brown and black
- Glass embroidery beads in five colours to co-ordinate with the wool
- Fine needle and matching sewing thread
- Scissors
- Towel
- Iron
- Backing card (stock)
- Stapler
- Picture frame

1 Fix the canvas to the frame with drawing pins or the staple gun. Mark the centre of the canvas with a ruler and pencil: use this as a starting point to work the design from the chart at the back of the book.

2 Thread the needle with one strand of tapestry yarn and fasten it on at the centre of the frame. Begin to work the design using tent stitch, following the chart, in which one square represents one stitch.

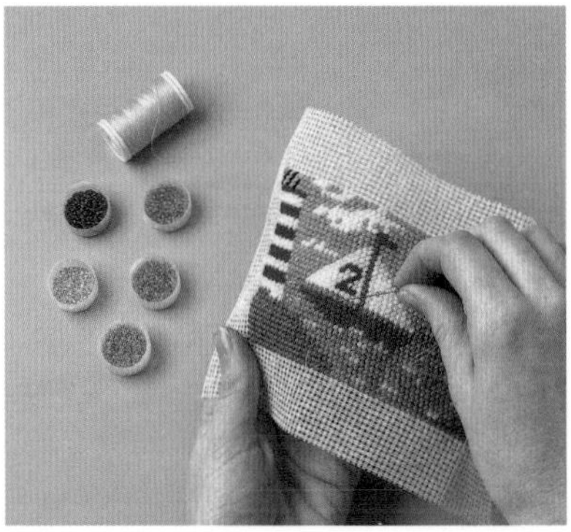

3 Remove the canvas from the frame when the design is complete. Add the beads with a fine needle, using them as highlights on the waves and details.

4 Continue sewing on beads in complementary colours to provide points of contrast in the sky, clouds and sea.

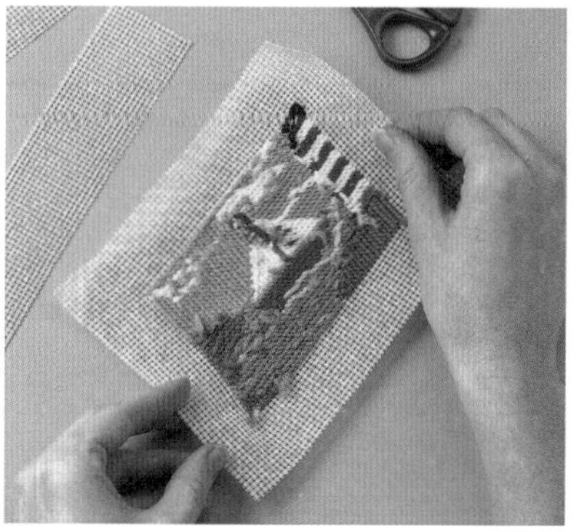

5 Measure a 3cm/1¼in border all around the design, and cut away any excess canvas. Gently stretch the canvas to regain its shape.

6 Using a towel to protect the stitches, press the tapestry from the back, using an iron on a low heat.

7 Cut a piece of backing card 1cm/½in larger all around than the tapestry. Staple the tapestry to the backing, trim away any excess canvas, and fit into the frame.

A bead loom will enable you to weave fabulous patterns, reminiscent of the traditional decorative art of Native Americans. Make the beadwork as long as you need, winding it around the spool as it grows.

Woven Bead Trim

you will need
Bead loom
Strong, non-stretch beading thread
Tape measure
Scissors
Fine beading needle
Small opaque rocailles in four colours
Adhesive tape (optional)

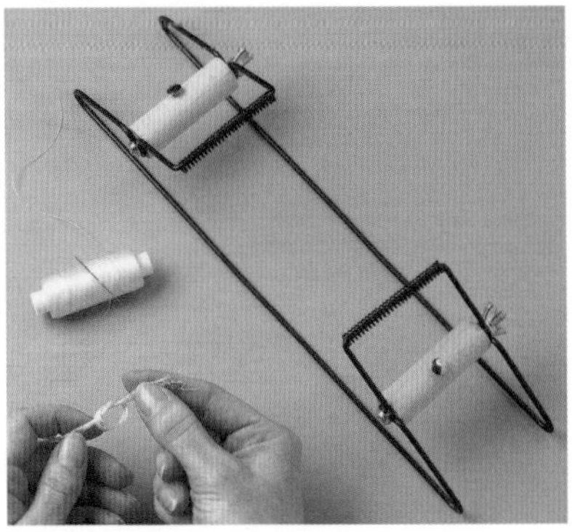

1 To make the warp, cut 19 strands of beading thread, each the desired length of the finished panel, plus 40cm/16in. Tie the ends together in a knot.

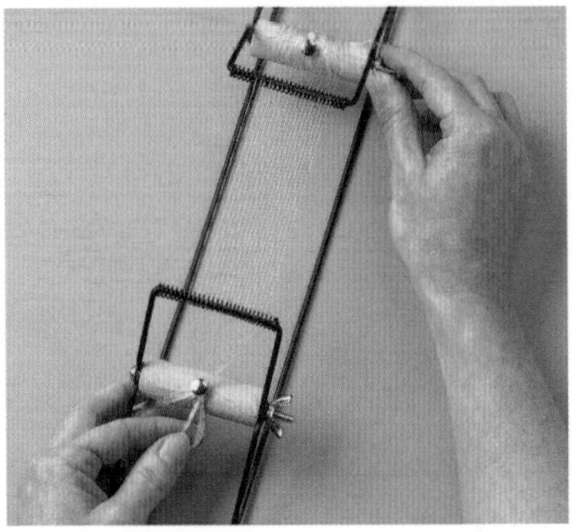

2 Prepare the warp following the instructions on how to set up a bead loom and how to weave on page 29.

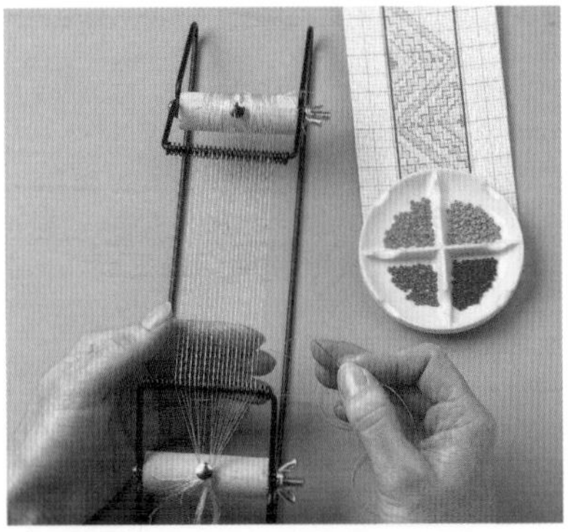

3 Thread the beading needle and tie the end of the thread in a double knot to the right-hand warp (lengthways) thread on the loom.

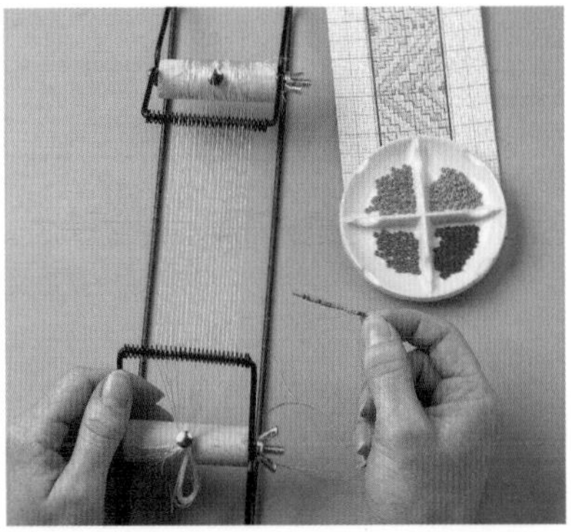

4 Following the chart at the back of the book, pick up coloured rocailles on the needle to correspond with the first row of the pattern. Place the beads under the warp threads and, using your finger, press a bead between each of the warp threads.

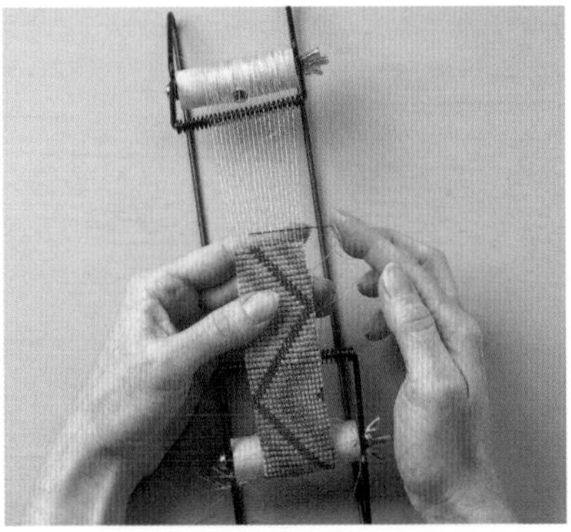

5 Pass the needle back through the beads, being sure to pass over the warp threads. Continue following the chart row by row until you have the desired length of trim. To finish, weave the beading thread under and over the warp threads for a short distance to secure the beads. Tape or stitch this woven part behind the trim before attaching it.

Glass beads are at their most beautiful and magical when lit from behind, or in this case from within: even a plain paper lampshade can be transformed with the addition of a long bead fringe.

Fringed Lampshade

you will need

Yellow oil-based marker pen
Tubular white paper lampshade
Tape measure
Sharp sewing needle
Scissors
Yellow and white beading thread
Beading needle
Pencil
Graph paper
Small yellow glass beads
Small purple glass beads
4cm/1 3/2in purple bugle beads
Purple teardrop beads
Small transparent glass beads

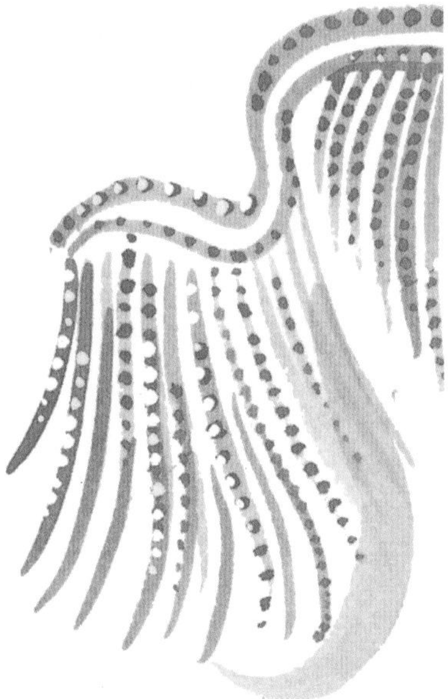

1 Draw freehand stripes of varying widths down the length of the lampshade using the oil-based marker pen. Leave until dry.

2 Using a sharp needle, pierce a row of holes 6mm/¼in apart just above the bottom rim.

3 Cut a piece of yellow beading thread twice the desired length of the fringe plus 25cm/10in and double through the beading needle. Knot the ends together and pass the needle through a hole on a yellow stripe, then loop through and pull taut.

4 Mark the bead sequence on graph paper. Thread on small beads: 12cm/4½in of yellow, one purple, one yellow, one purple and one yellow. Add a bugle, then alternate five small yellow and four purple. (On alternate strands, add an extra two of each colour.) Add three yellow.

5 Add one purple teardrop and three yellow beads. Insert the needle just below the purple teardrop and make a fastening-off stitch, checking that no thread is showing. Pass the needle back up the strand.

6 Make a fastening-off stitch below the bugle then pass it up through the bugle and make another fastening-off stitch. Pull gently on the strand to remove kinks. Continue around the shade. For the white stripes, use white thread and substitute transparent beads for yellow ones.

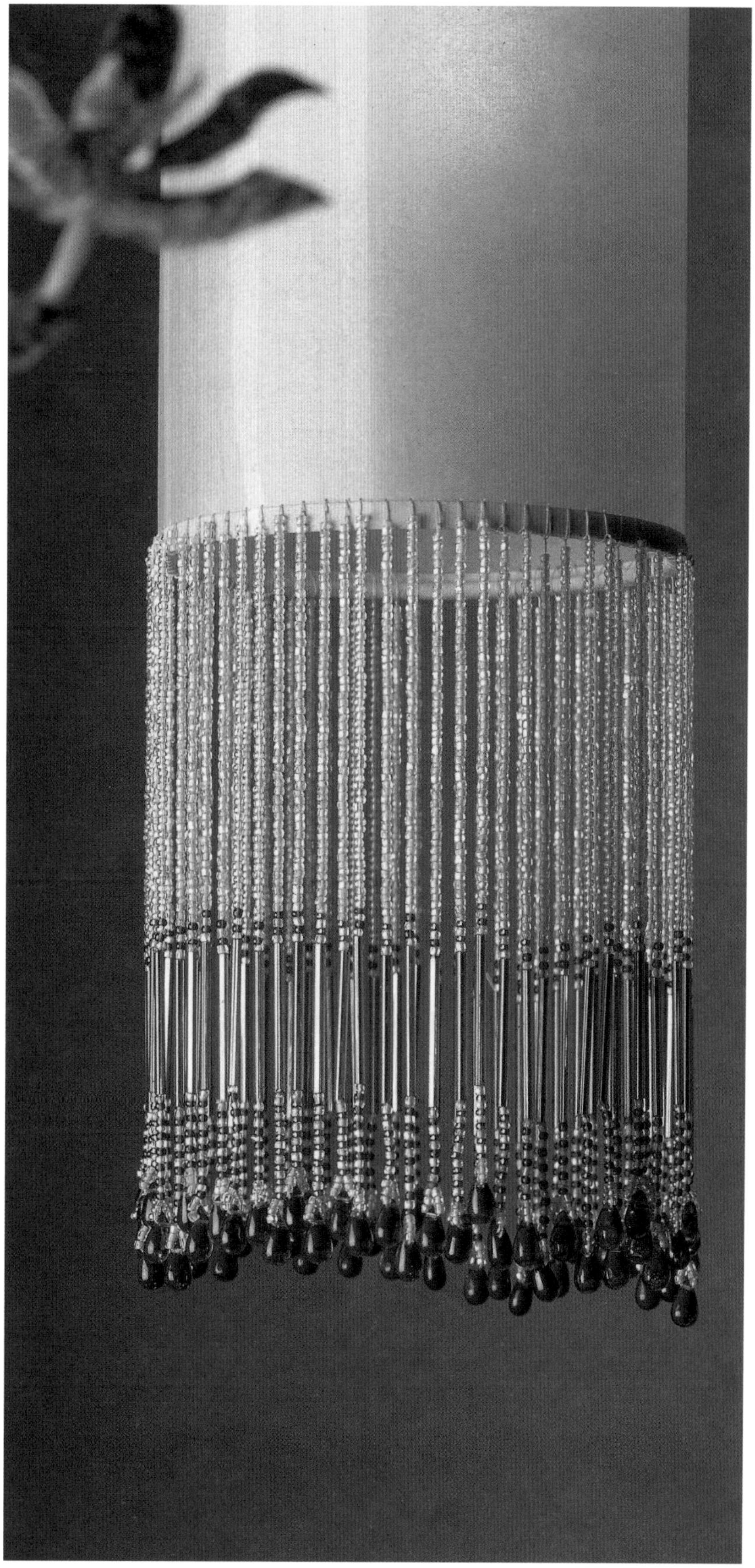

Clusters of beads make an original addition to mosaics, and are perfect for creating intricate shapes. Mix sizes and colours for the fish, but stick to just one type of bead for the starfish for a contrasting effect.

Fish Mosaic Splashback

●●●●

you will need

Pencil
Paper
Piece of plywood to fit splashback area
Carbon paper
Coloured glass mosaic tiles
Wood glue
Interior filler
Mixing container
Spoon
Acrylic paints in a variety of colours
Selection of beads including metallic bugle beads, frosted and metallic square beads, large round beads and mixed beads
Mosaic clippers
Tile grout

1 Following the picture opposite as a guide, sketch the design to fit the required size of the splashback on a large sheet of paper. Keep the shapes simple and bold. Use a sheet of carbon paper to transfer the design on to the plywood by drawing firmly over all the lines using a sharp pencil.

2 Begin by adding the mosaic squares on to the border, which uses complete square tiles. Lay them out around the top and side edges in two rows, alternating the colours to give a chequered effect. Then apply a thin layer of wood glue to the border, a small section at a time, positioning the tiles textured side down as you go.

3 Following the manufacturer's instructions, mix up a small amount of interior filler, then add some acrylic paint to colour it to match the beads.

4 Spread green filler thickly over the seaweed fronds, then carefully press in metallic green bugle beads. Fill in the fish fins using green filler and metallic green square beads.

5 Make sure all the beads are on their sides so that the holes don't show. Spread orange filler thickly over the starfish and press in square frosted beads. Use some darker beads for shading.

6 Glue on a large bead for the fish eye using wood glue. Thickly spread white filler on to a 5cm/2in square section of the fish body and press in mixed beads. Repeat, working in small sections, until the fish is complete. Glue on large beads for bubbles.

7 For the background and rocks, use mosaic clippers to cut the mosaic tiles into 1cm/½in squares. Clip the edges where necessary to fit closely around the curves.

8 Stick the clipped tiles down with wood glue in the marked areas. When the design is complete, Mix the tile grout and spread over. Spread very lightly and carefully over the beaded areas. Wipe off the grout with a damp cloth and leave to dry.

These brightly coloured tassels are inspired by ethnic beadwork. Stitched to either end of a bolster or to a cushion, they would certainly add a note of drama to an interior design scheme.

Beaded Tassels

●●●●

you will need
Tape measure
Scissors
Fabric tape
Beading needle
Beading thread
Small turquoise and red glass beads
Large turquoise glass beads
Sewing needle and matching thread
Turquoise embroidery thread (floss)
Medium red crystal bead
Small white and light green glass beads
2 large orange glass beads
Small dark green glass beads

1 For the turquoise and red tassel, cut 25cm/10in of fabric tape. Thread the needle with beading thread and fasten on to one end of the tape. To make the first strand, thread on 18 small turquoise, eight small red, one large and one small turquoise beads. Take the needle back through the large bead and the strand. Make two stitches to one side, then continue making strands along the tape.

2 Roll up the tape tightly to make the head of the tassel. Sew the loose end of the tape down with several stitches to keep it in place. Fasten on the turquoise embroidery thread and wind it firmly around the head to form a rounded shape. Finish off securely.

3 Fasten on to the top of the fringe. Add on 15 small beads and pass the needle down through the head. Go through the first bead, add 13, go through the final bead and down the head. Repeat to cover. Make a loop of 20 beads.

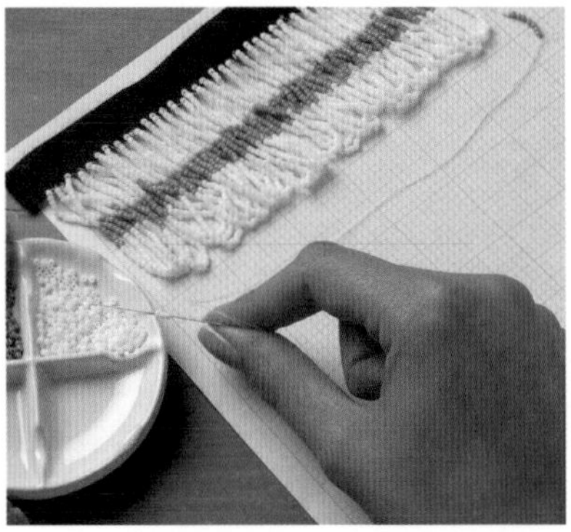

4 For the head of the looped green and white tassel, cut a 25cm/10in length of tape. Fasten on at the bottom left corner with beading thread, then add 13 white, 7 green, 24 white, 7 green and 13 white small beads.

5 Insert the needle back into the tape at the same point to make a loop. Make a stitch to secure, then make a stitch to one side. Repeat along the length of the tape.

6 Bind the head as in step 2, then cover it with turquoise, green and white beads as for step 3. Add a large red bead and a small turquoise bead at the top and a ring of turquoise beads around the base of the head.

7 For each of the eight strands of the green and orange tassel, cut a long length of thread. Thread on 20 light green, 40 dark green and 24 light green small beads. Pass the needle through the last-but-one bead, and make fastening-off stitches along the entire strand. Do the same at the other end.

8 Fold the strands in half and tie a length of thread around the centre. Thread on a needle and add an orange bead. Add a green glass bead, 17 small light green beads, another crystal and a small light green bead. Go through the crystal, add 17 more small light green beads, go back through the first two beads, then fasten off securely.

Use an assortment of large glass beads, interspersed with smaller gold ones, for a jewel-encrusted, sparkling shade. Space the large beads randomly along the wires so that each one is framed by small beads.

Chunky Beaded Lampshade

●●●●

you will need

Drum-shaped lampshade frame with reversible gimbal, top diameter 20cm/8in, bottom diameter 25cm/10in, height 25cm/10in
Gold spray paint and face mask
Scrap paper
Fine brass wire
Jeweller's pliers and wire cutters
0.6mm/$^{1}/_{40}$in gold-plated jewellery wire
Small flat round gold crystal beads
Selection of chunky glass beads
Ceramic lamp base
Brown acrylic paint
Dish
Kitchen sponge
Clean cotton rag
Picture framer's wax gilt

1 Spray the frame on some scrap paper with gold paint. Wear a face mask and work in a well-ventilated area.

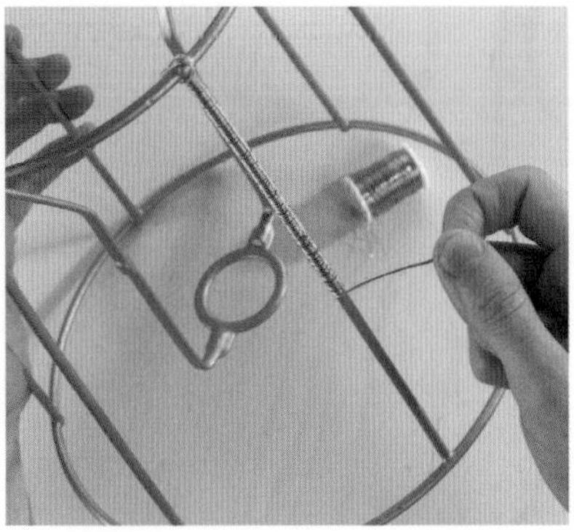

2 For each upright strut, cut a piece of fine brass wire approximately 3m/10ft long. When the frame is dry, fold the wire in half and in half again, loop it over the top ring and wind the strands down each strut. Finish at the base of the strut with a small knot.

3 Cut a piece of the thicker jewellery wire approximately 70cm/28in long and spiral one end about five times around the top ring next to a strut. Thread enough beads on to the wire to fit between the top and bottom rings, including a few large ones.

4 Spiral the long end around the bottom ring about five times and pull up tightly. Thread on the same number of beads, then spiral the long end around the top ring. Snip the end with the cutters. Continue back and forth in this way all around the shade.

5 Cut a piece of the fine wire approximately 3m/10ft long, fold in half and in half again. Loop the wire around an upright strut and spiral the strands closely around the bottom ring, finishing with a small knot. Wrap the top ring in the same way.

6 To decorate the base, squeeze some brown acrylic paint into a dish, dab a sponge in the paint and wipe it over the base in an uneven criss-cross manner, avoiding the brass fitting. Leave to dry completely.

7 Using a clean cotton rag, wipe gilt wax over the paint, rubbing harder in some areas to give an uneven finish. Leave to dry completely before attaching the shade.

This lampshade gives you the perfect opportunity to sort out your bead collection and use all your prettiest shapes in rainbow colours. A large crystal drop at the bottom of each strand gives weight to the fringe.

Bead Pendant Light

you will need

Enamel spray paint
Face mask
Scrap paper
Flush pendant lamp ring
Fine jewellery wire (this design used about 20m/22yd)
Scissors
Large crystal drop beads
Medium round and shaped beads
Bugle beads

1 Spray-paint the lamp ring on a piece of scrap paper in a well-ventilated area and leave it to dry.

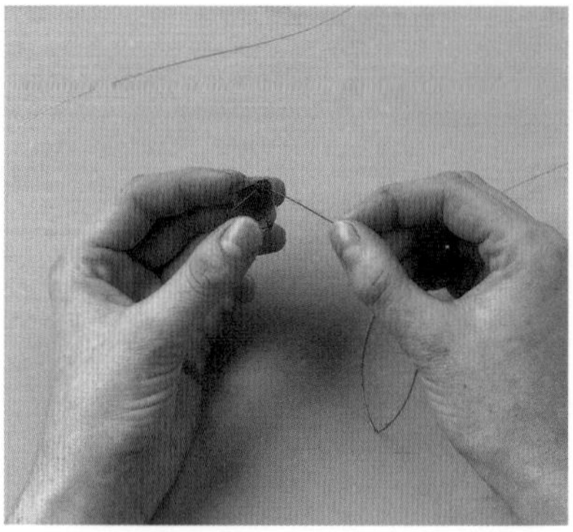

2 Cut a piece of jewellery wire a little more than twice the length you want the finished fringe to be and thread on a large crystal drop bead.

3 Take the bead to the centre of the length of wire and hold the two ends together. Thread on an assortment of beads in different sizes and colours, spacing them with bugle beads.

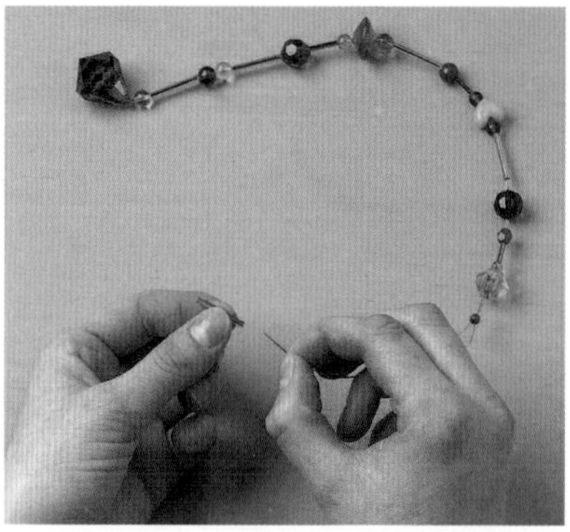

4 Complete the strand with a long bugle bead, making sure you have left enough wire to tie on to the lamp ring. Attach the strand of beads on to the metal ring by tying the two ends of the wire together.

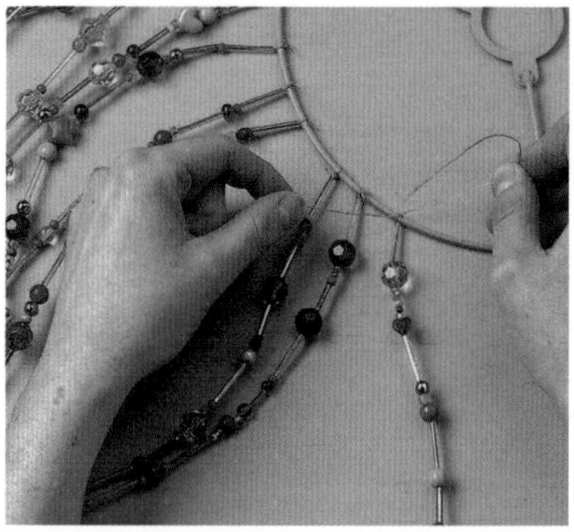

5 Continue making beaded strands to tie evenly all around the ring. Thread the two wire ends back through the beads on each strand to conceal them.

This delicate and nostalgic picture frame, made from satin ribbon encrusted with beads, will suit a special family photograph and is bound to become a family heirloom.

Sequin and Bead Frame

you will need
Pencil
Metal ruler
Mounting (mat) board
Self-healing cutting mat
Craft (utility) knife
White calico
Scissors
Sewing needle and thread
Matching embroidery threads (floss)
6cm/2½in wide satin-backed velvet ribbon
15mm/⅝in wide green ribbon
Translucent sequins
Small gold glass beads
Clear crystals

1 Draw the frame outline on to mounting board: it measures 18 x 13cm/7 x 5in with 4cm/1½in wide borders. Using the frame as a template, cut two white calico frames 6mm/¼in larger all around. Turn under the raw edges and oversew the pieces together to cover the back and front of the frame.

2 Measure the outer edge of the frame and cut a length of wide satin-backed velvet ribbon slightly longer. Fold the ribbon so that it is 4cm/1½in wide and tack the fold. Using the frame as a guide, fit the ribbon to the frame shape, mitring the corners. Pin. Remove the ribbon. Stitch the mitres.

3 Sew the green ribbon over the seam with matching embroidery thread. Thread five small gold glass beads on to a needle and stitch across the green ribbon. Continue stitching until all the ribbon is covered, spacing the beads closely together. Stitch the ribbon frame to the calico-covered frame.

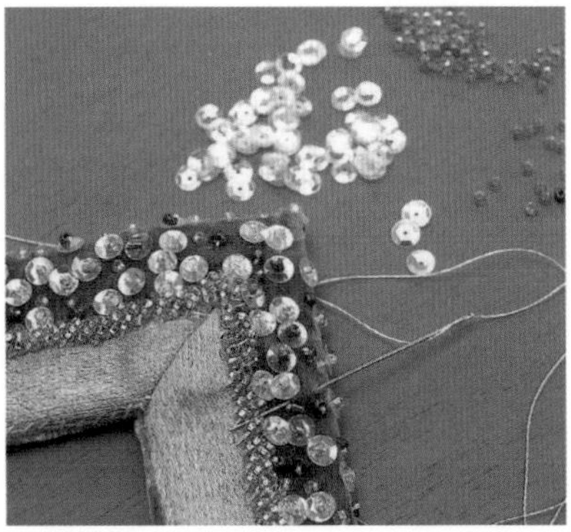

4 Stitch a random selection of translucent sequins and glass beads over the velvet border.

5 Sew clear crystals and small glass beads on to the grey satin part of the ribbon, spacing them closely together. Stitch a strip of the wider ribbon to the back to hold the photograph. Leave the top edge unstitched so that the photograph can be changed.

You can turn plain glass bottles into jewelled treasures with these exquisite beaded collars. Fill them with anything from bath salts to scented oils to make wonderful gifts.

Lacy Bottle Collars

●●●●

you will need

Strong, non-stretch beading thread
Beading needle
Small glass rocailles in dark green, lilac and lime
Glass bottles
Glass bugle beads in green and lilac
Small pearlized embroidery beads in green
Small, medium and large faceted glass crystals in green and lilac

Large Bottle

1 Thread a row of alternate small dark green and lilac rocailles on to a long length of thread and tie it securely around the bottle neck. Pass the thread through the beads once again, then thread on a green bugle and a lilac rocaille.

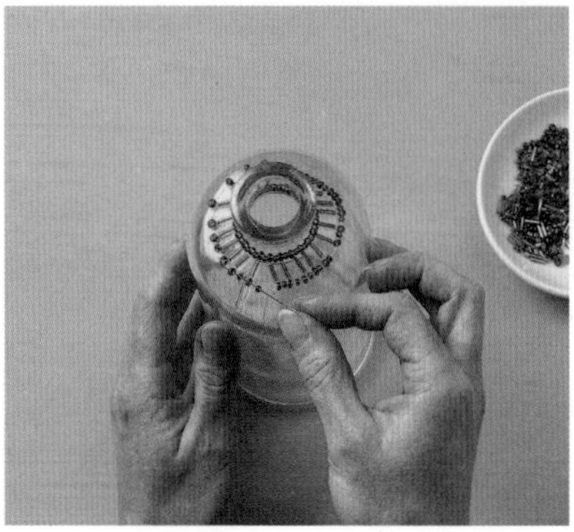

2 Go back through the bugle and the next green rocaille, and continue around the neck. Pass the thread through each lilac rocaille, adding a small dark green rocaille between each. Pull the thread up tightly to form the neck collar and tie securely.

3 Passing the thread through alternate lilac rocailles, add pendant loops consisting of three lime rocailles, a small dark green rocaille, then three more lime rocailles.

4 Passing the thread between each dark green rocaille of the last round, make a round of loops, consisting of a lilac bugle, a green embroidery bead, a small green crystal, a green embroidery bead and a lilac bugle.

Small Bottle

1 Follow steps 1 to 3, using lime and dark green rocailles and alternate lilac and green bugles to make the collar. Bring the thread out through a green rocaille.

2 For each point, thread on a green bugle, a lilac rocaille, a green bugle, a lilac crystal and a green embroidery bead. Pass the thread back through the crystal and repeat the sequence on the other side. Go through the second green rocaille, and continue all around the collar.

The plainest cushion cover can be dramatically transformed with a fringe of beads: these three designs show how beads of different sizes and colours produce different effects.

Bead-fringed Cushions

you will need

Tape measure
Square cushion pad
Dressmaking scissors
Yellow velvet
Iron
Sewing-machine and matching thread
Dressmaker's pins
Beading needle
Matching beading thread
6mm/¼in white glass beads
7mm/⅜in opaque yellow beads
Small copper glass beads
7mm/⅜in opaque white beads
7mm/⅜in opaque blue beads
Rectangular cushion pad
Striped fabric
Fabric marker
Graph paper
Pencil
Small glass beads in pink and yellow
7mm/⅜in yellow disc-shaped beads
Rectangular cushion pad
Pink velvet
Small glass beads yellow and pink
6mm/¼in white glass beads
6mm/¼in turquoise glass beads

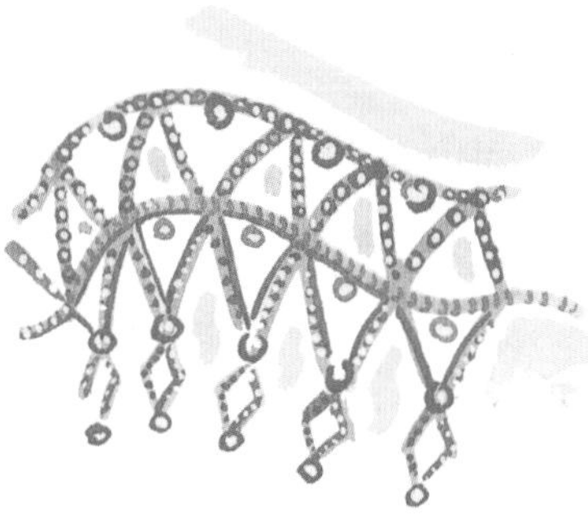

Yellow cushion

1 Cut a piece of yellow velvet the size of the pad and two back panels the same depth and two-thirds the length. Hem one short side of each panel. With right sides facing and hems overlapping, join with a 1cm/½in seam. Clip the corners and turn through.

2 Thread a beading needle with double beading thread and fasten to one corner. Thread on two white glass beads, a yellow and a copper bead. Go back through the yellow bead and thread on two white glass beads. Insert the needle 2cm/¾in to the right.

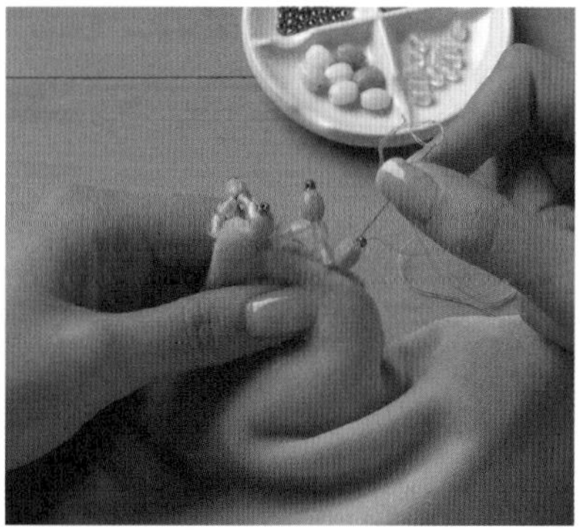

3 Make a tiny stitch, then thread on a blue or white opaque bead and a copper bead. Pass the needle back through the blue or white bead, then insert the needle 2cm/¾in farther on. Repeat the sequence of steps 2 and 3 along each side of the cover.

Striped cushion

1 Cut a piece of fabric the size of the cushion pad plus 2cm/¾in on the width and 20cm/8in on the length. Cut two back panels the same depth and two-thirds the length.

2 Hem one short side of each. Then, right sides facing and hems overlapping, sew 1cm/½in from each long edge. Turn through. Stitch a line 10cm/4in from each raw edge and fringe the fabric to this line.

▶

3 Mark the length of fringe, 10cm/4in, on graph paper. Cut thread four times this measurement and double through the needle. Insert the needle at the inner edge of the first stripe of the fabric and secure with a knot, pass the needle through the loop and pull taut.

4 Mix a few pink with the yellow beads. Thread on 9.5cm/$3\frac{3}{4}$in of beads, using the graph paper as a guide. Thread on a disc and a small yellow bead. Pass the needle back through the disc, make a finishing stitch, pass the needle up the strand and make another finishing stitch. Pull gently on the strand to remove any kinks. Trim the thread. Repeat with the other stripes.

Pink cushion

1 Make up the pink velvet cover as in step 1 (yellow cushion). Mark points 15mm/$\frac{5}{8}$in apart along two opposite sides. Fasten a double length of thread on to one corner.

2 Mix a few yellow with the pink beads, and thread on 2cm/$\frac{3}{4}$in. Add a white bead, 2cm/$\frac{3}{4}$in of pink or yellow and one turquoise and one copper bead. Go back through the turquoise bead, thread on 2cm/$\frac{3}{4}$in pink or yellow, a large white, then more pink or yellow. Insert the needle at the third point.

3 Make a back stitch to bring the needle out at the second marked point. Thread on 2cm/$\frac{3}{4}$in of pink or yellow beads, then pass the needle through the large white bead already in place, on the strand to the right.

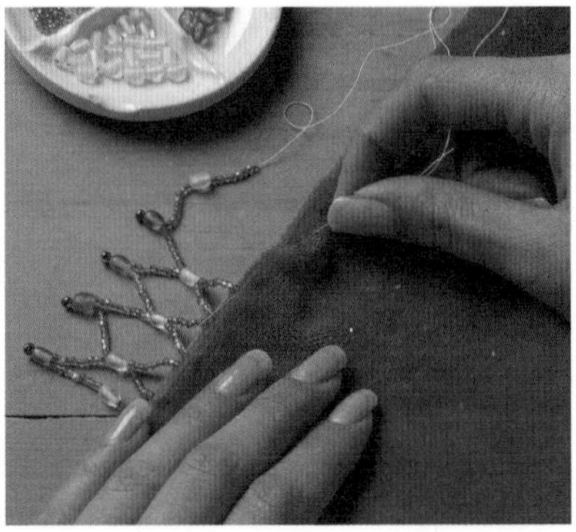

4 Thread on another 2cm/$\frac{3}{4}$in of pink or yellow beads, one turquoise and one copper bead. Repeat this three-step sequence along each side of the cushion, to make the lattice edge.

These more intricate bead edgings, made from rocaille, bugle, pearl and crystal beads, have a delicate appearance, but they are stitched along the seams with strong thread and are unlikely to break.

Beaded Cushion Trims

you will need

50cm/20in each purple and green linen
Dressmaking scissors
Tape measure
Dressmaker's pins
Sewing-machine
Matching sewing thread
2 cushion pads, measuring 35cm/14in square and 30cm/12in square
Beading needle
Strong non-stretch beading thread
Iridescent beads in pink and green
Rocailles in gold, silver and red
Frosted bugle beads in pink, blue and green
Green metallic bugle beads
Small crystal beads in pink, blue and yellow

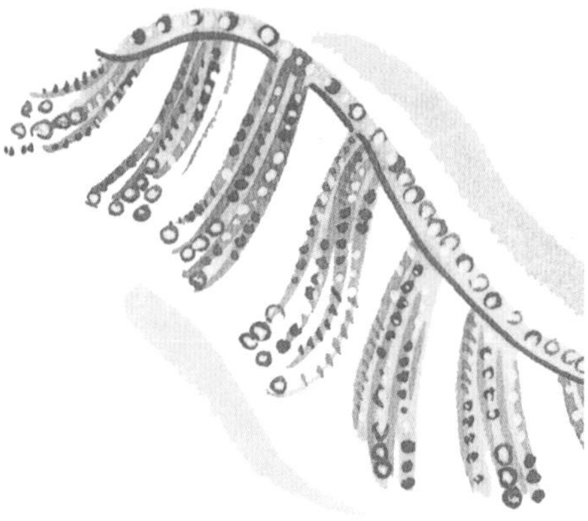

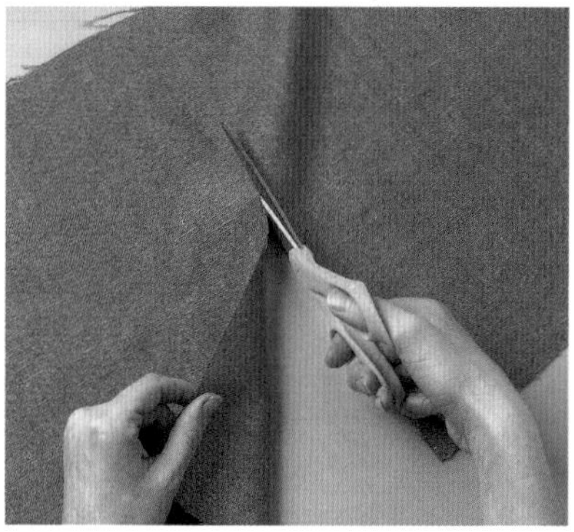

1 First make up the covers. Cut a 38cm/15in purple square for the front of the large cushion, and two back panels measuring 38 x 28cm/15 x 11in. For the small cushion, cut a 33cm/13in square and two 33 x 23cm/13 x 9in panels.

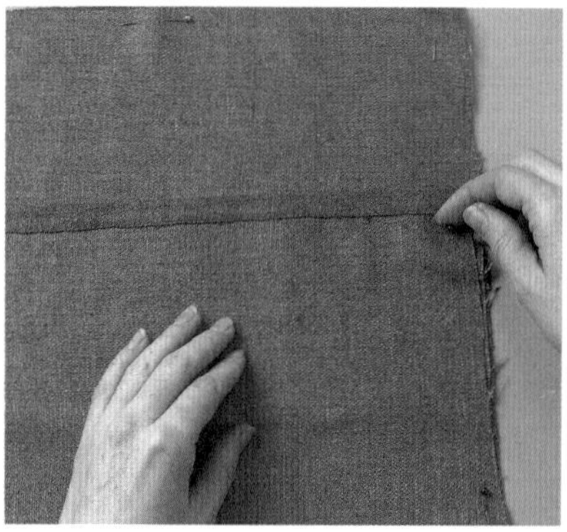

2 Hem one long edge of each back panel. Place them on top of the front, with right sides facing and hems overlapping at the centre. Machine stitch around all four sides of both cushion covers with a 12mm/½in seam. Turn right-side out and insert the pads.

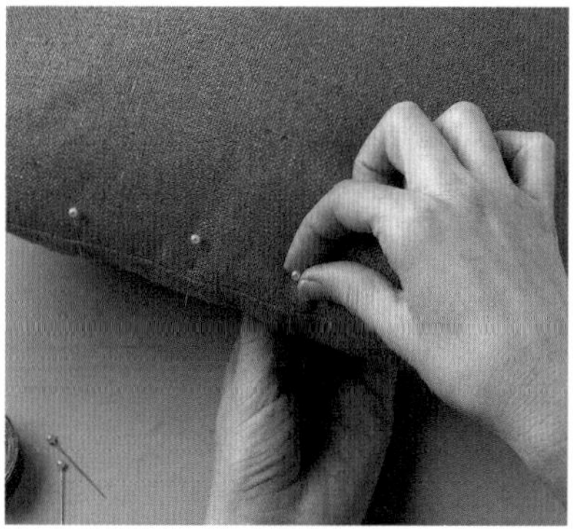

3 The trim for the purple cushion is made up of alternate swags and drops and is stitched along two opposite edges of the cushion. Measure one edge of the cushion and divide it at equidistant points approximately 5cm/2in apart. Mark each point vertically with a pin.

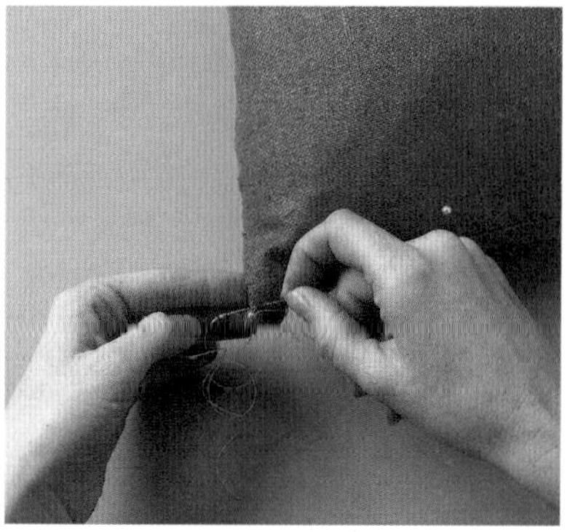

4 The first row of beads is worked along the seam line. Fasten on at the bottom left corner and thread on an iridescent pink bead followed by a gold rocaille. Take the needle back through the pink bead, into the seam and back out along the stitching, beside the pink bead.

5 Thread on 2.5cm/1in of alternate pink bugles and gold rocailles. Make a small stitch through the seam to secure, then repeat until the first marker pin. Secure the thread. Attach a green iridescent bead with a gold rocaille as for the pink bead. Repeat to the second corner.

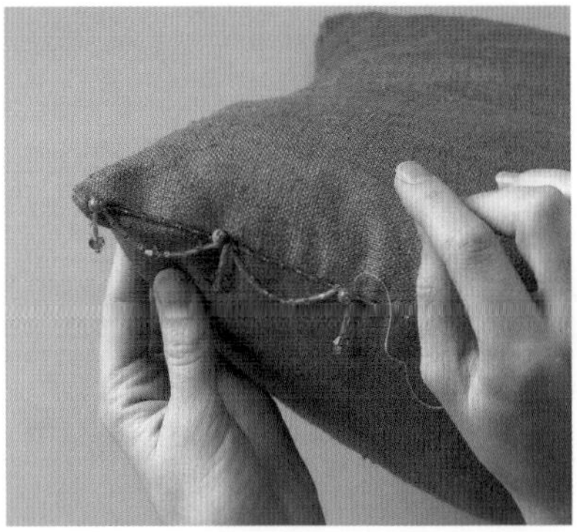

6 Starting again at the corner, make the drop from a silver rocaille, a blue bugle, a silver rocaille, a blue bugle, a silver rocaille, a pink crystal and another silver rocaille. Take the needle back through the crystal and the rest of the strand. Secure with a small stitch in the seam and come out one bead to the right.

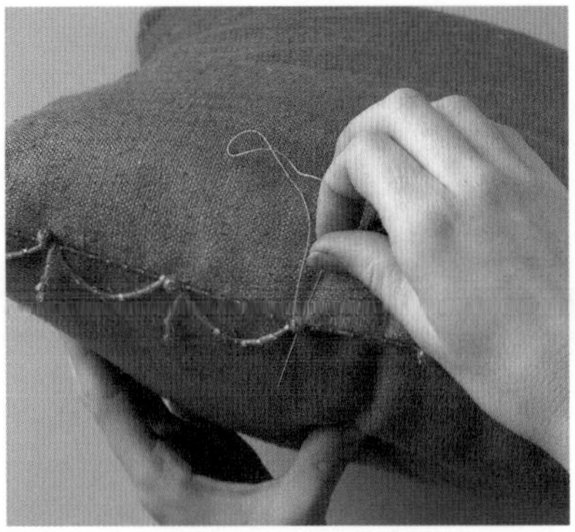

7 For the swag, thread a silver rocaille and a frosted bugle. Repeat twice, then add a silver rocaille, a gold rocaille and a pink crystal. Thread the beads on the other side of the crystal as a mirror image. Secure at the seam, just under the iridescent bead. Continue making drops and swags to the end of the row.

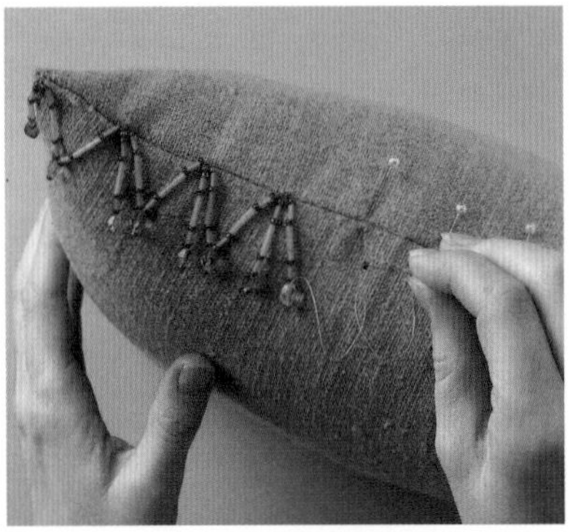

8 Pin at 3cm/1¼in intervals along the green cushion. For the drop, thread two red rocailles, a blue bugle, a red rocaille, a green bugle, a red rocaille, a blue bugle, a red rocaille, a blue crystal and a red rocaille. Go back through the crystal and the strand. Secure, then come out one bead along. Starting with a single red rocaille, thread the same sequence but using a yellow crystal and a rocaille. Go back through the crystal.

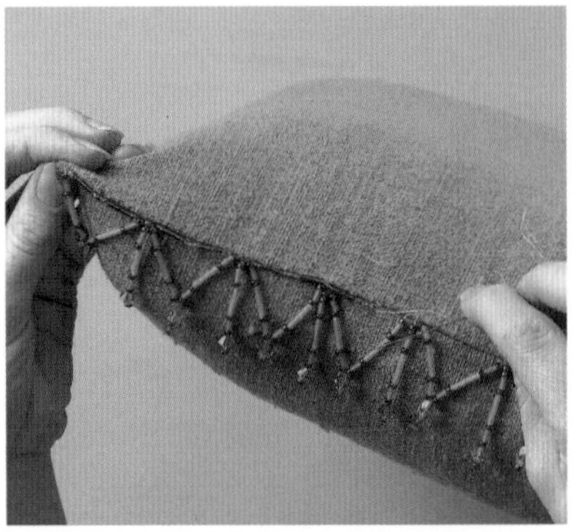

9 Thread the second side of the triangle as a mirror image of the first. Secure to the seam just to the left of the next pin and secure. Continue making alternate drops and triangles to the end. Starting again at the corner, conceal the seam as before with a line made up of a gold rocaille, a green metallic bugle, three gold rocailles, a green bugle and a gold rocaille.

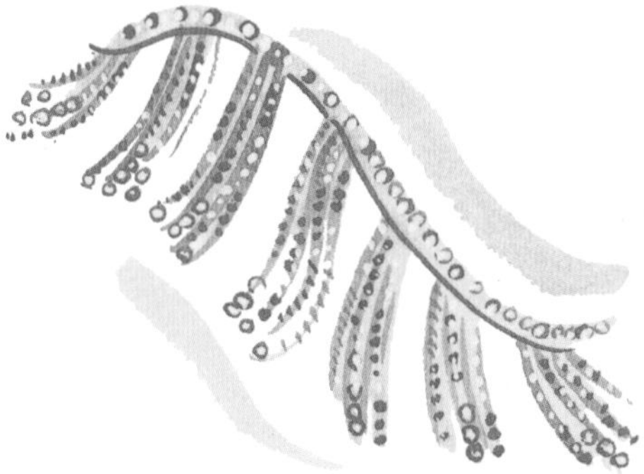

Here a Victorian craft – stitchery embellished with beads – has been brought up to date with a striking modern design. The glossy beadwork contrasts beautifully with the background of matt (flat) woollen yarns.

Needlepoint Photograph Album

you will need

Tapestry wool (yarn), in shades of green
Tapestry needle
48 x 34cm/19 x 13½in tapestry canvas, 10 holes to 2.5cm/1in
Embroidery scissors
Beading needle
Matching fine beading thread
Small glass rocailles in copper, light blue, gold, silver and black
Craft (utility) knife and ruler
Card (stock)
Bookbinding fabric
PVA (white) glue
Adhesive tape
Black or white paper
Hole punch
2 brass screw binders

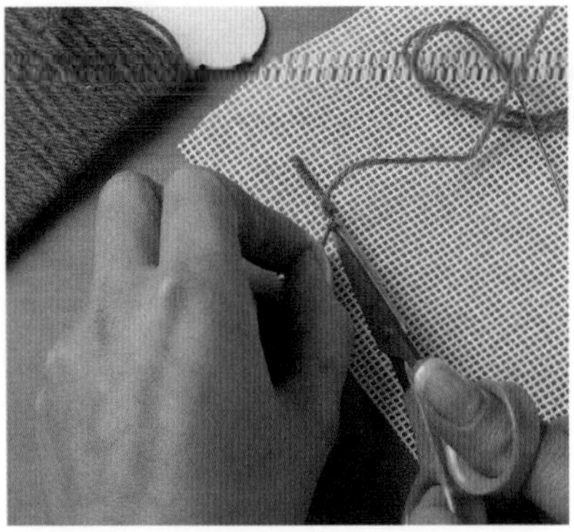

1 Work the background in tent stitch, following the chart at the back of the book. Bring up the needle and go down one space diagonally below to the left. Come up through the space immediately to the right.

2 Continue stitching in vertical rows, leaving the beadwork motifs unstitched. One square of the chart represents one stitch: merge the shades of green as shown. Leave a border all around.

3 Add the beadwork using the different coloured beads. Thread a beading needle with fine thread and stitch them on singly, making a tent stitch in the opposite direction to the wool stitches, so they lie flat. Make an extra stitch for security every four stitches.

4 Cut two pieces of card, the same depth as the embroidery and 10cm/4in wider. Score a line 10cm/4in from one side of each piece to enable the covers to fold. Cut a piece of bookbinding fabric 2cm/¾in larger all round. Glue to the card, clip the corners, fold and stick the edges. Line with a second piece of fabric.

5 Lay the embroidery on the other card, lining up the right edge. Tape the right, top and bottom borders to the back and the left one to the front. Cut a piece of fabric 12cm/4½in x the card's depth plus 4cm/1½in. Match one edge to the edge of the embroidery and glue down. Glue back the edges, then line.

6 Cut 40 pieces of paper 1cm/½in less all the way around than the card. Mark the position of the holes on the back and front covers and the paper, then use the hole punch to make them. Place the paper between the two covers, thread the screw binders through the layers and secure.

These beautiful flowers and leaves are easily made by threading glass beads on to wire and twisting them into shape. Once you've mastered the technique, they can be used for decorating all kinds of projects.

Flowered Frame

●●●●

you will need
Wire cutters
0.4mm/$^{1}/_{80}$in beading wire
Round-nosed (snub-nosed) pliers
Small glass beads in white, pink and yellow
Floss thread
Wooden frame
Drill and small drill bit
Protective goggles
0.2mm/$^{1}/_{120}$in beading wire

1 To make the leaves, cut 23cm/9in of thick wire. Twist a small knot in one end to stop the beads falling off. Mix up a few pink beads with the yellow. Bend the wire in half, thread on 18 beads, push up to the bend, then twist the wire together to form a beaded loop.

2 Wind the working part of the wire around and down the stem part by 6mm/¼in. Make another loop and thread on 18 more beads. Wrap the working wire around the stem once more. Make another loop at the same level. Make two more pairs of loops along the stem. Twist the wire around the stem.

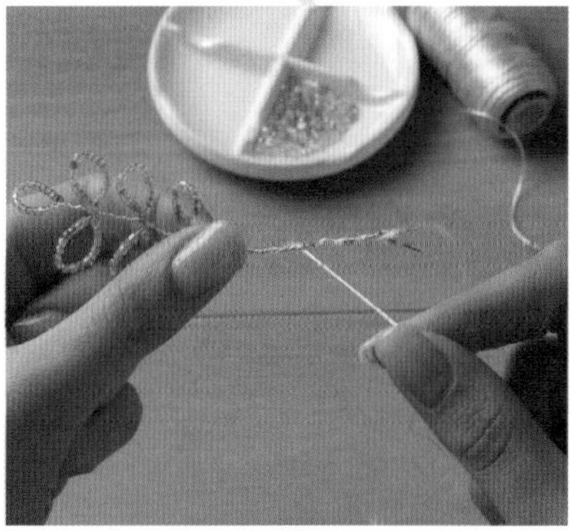

3 To cover the twisted stem, fasten some floss thread to one end, then wrap it around the wire in a tight spiral. Secure at the other end with a few stitches or a dab of glue.

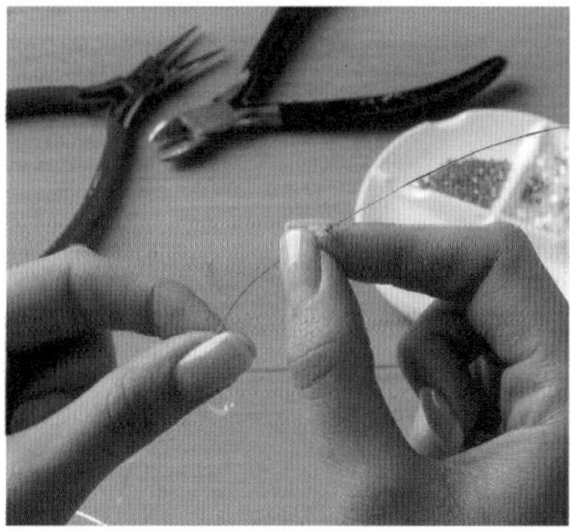

4 Cut 40cm/16in of wire for a small flower and 50cm/20in for the large. Bend each into a circle 10cm/4in from one end. Twist to form a frame. Mix a few pink beads in with the white. Thread on 24 beads for the small flower, 30 for the large.

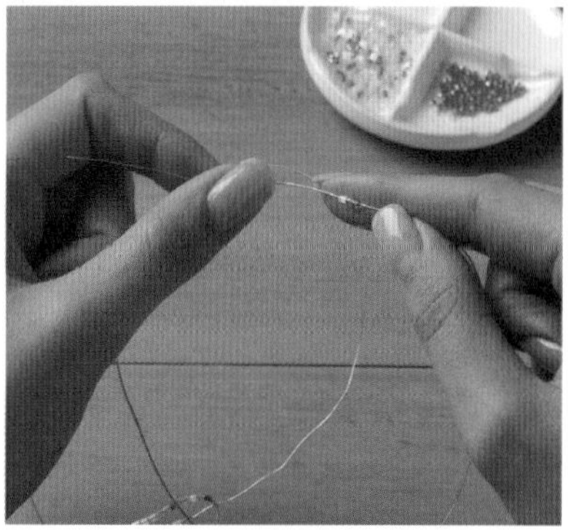

5 Twist the working wire around the circle to make a loop.

▶

6 To fill in the centre of the petal, thread on 16 more beads for the small flower, 24 for the large. Bend the working wire upwards and twist it around the top of the loop.

7 Add on more beads for the next petal and twist the working wire around the spiral frame. To make the remaining petals, make four more loops positioned around the spiral frame.

8 To make the flower centre, thread on 12 yellow beads and twist the wire into a half spiral. Push the working wire through the centre and twist it around the stem to finish off.

9 Make enough leaves and flowers to go round the frame and decide where they are to go. Mark the positions with pencil, then drill a small hole at each point, using a fine bit.

10 Push the stems of the beaded flowers and leaves through the holes. Keep them in place by twisting the wire into a knot on the wrong side of the frame.

11 Trim the ends of the wire using wire cutters. Secure the knots by twisting lengths of the thinner wire around them, making sure that no sharp ends are left projecting.

Shimmering droplets of water appear to cascade down this stunning three-panelled screen: the effect is created by transparent plastic crystals that have been suspended on fine silver thread.

Waterfall Screen

●●●●●

you will need

Saw
11m/11yd of 5 x 5cm/2 x 2in wooden batten (furring strip)
medium-grade abrasive paper and sanding block
12 right-angled brackets and screws
Pencil
Drill and drill bits
Screwdriver
Paintbrush
White emulsion (latex) paint
12 wood spheres, 7.5cm/3in diameter
Silver paint
Hammer
Long nails
1cm/½in diameter plastic tubing
6 hinges
12 screws
Dowelling
Transparent plastic crystal beads in various sizes
2 reels silver machine embroidery thread (floss)
Small silver glass beads
Scissors

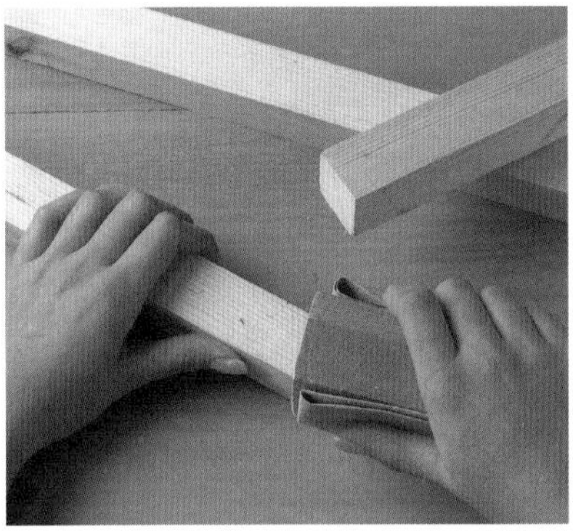

1 For each of the panels, cut two pieces of wood 140cm/55in long for the sides and two pieces 40cm/16in long for the top and bottom. Sand the wood thoroughly to remove any rough edges.

2 Place the two short pieces across either end of the long pieces. Position the brackets on the inside of each corner and mark the position of the screws. Using a drill bit to match, make holes at these points. Screw the brackets in place.

3 Paint the panel with two coats of white emulsion and leave to dry. Paint the spheres with two coats of silver paint and leave to dry.

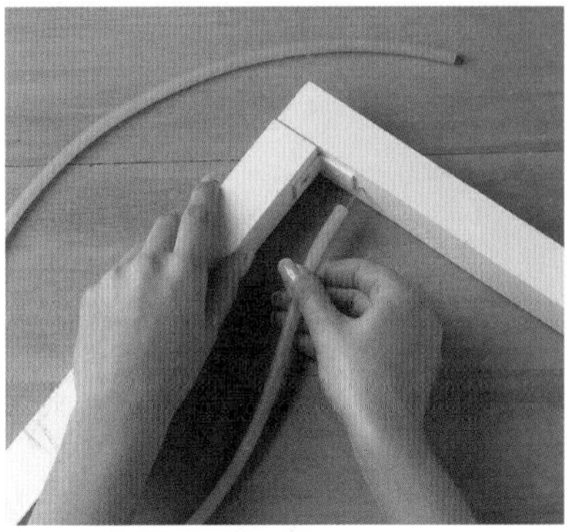

4 Hammer in a long nail 3cm/1¼in from the top and bottom on the inside of each side edge. For each panel, cut two pieces of plastic tubing 45cm/18in long and push over the nail heads.

▶

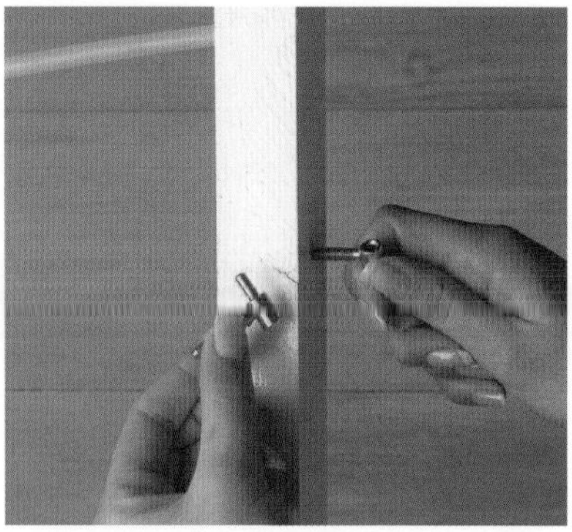

5 Mark the position of the two hinges on the side edges of the panels, 30cm/12in from top and bottom. Check that the screen will fold and unfold properly, then screw the hinges in place.

6 Mark the position of the spheres at the four corners. Cut four pieces of dowelling 5cm/2in long. Drill holes in the frame and the spheres with a drill bit the same size as the dowelling. Push the dowelling into the spheres, then into the frame.

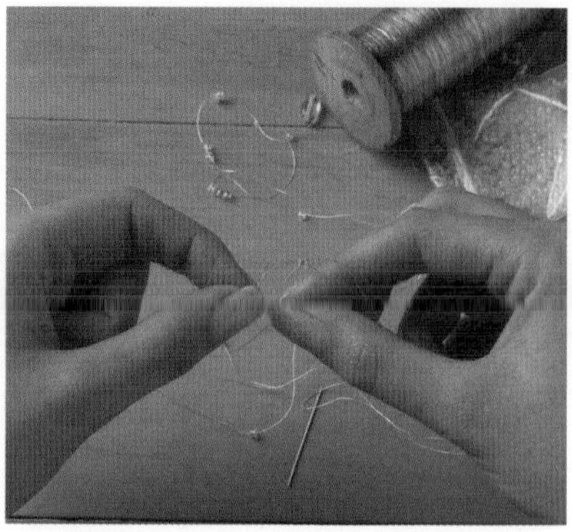

7 Thread the transparent beads in random sequence directly on to a reel of silver thread. Leave 10–30cm/4–12in gaps between groups of beads, knotting the thread after each group.

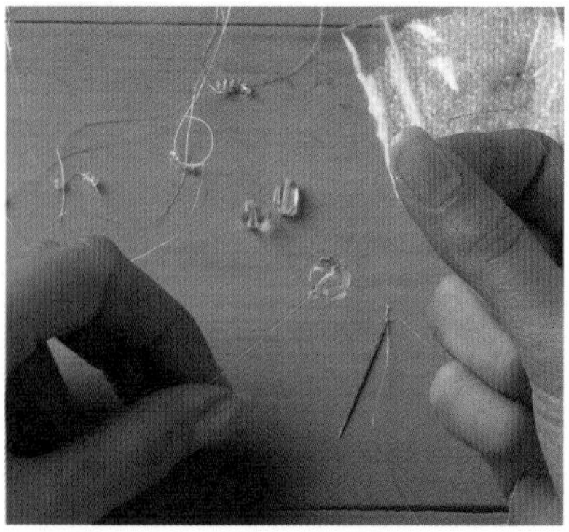

8 Thread on a plastic bead then pass the thread through the bead again. Thread on small silver glass beads in groups of three or more. Fasten off the end of the thread and cut.

9 Unravel a little thread from the other reel. Tie one end to the lower piece of tubing on the first panel. Pass the reel over the tubing at the top, then under the lower tubing. Continue back and forth across the width of the panel.

10 Wrap the beaded thread around the tubing in the same way. Repeat with the other two panels.

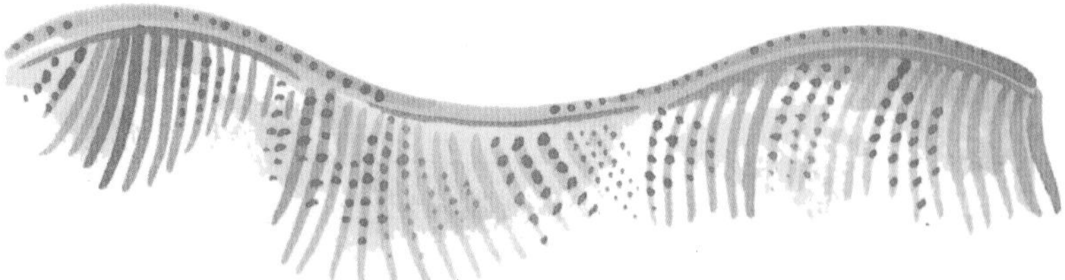

Ribbonwork History and Techniques

For centuries, ribbons were one of the few affordable adornments for all, and from the Middle Ages to the 1800s they were used as fastenings and decorations for garments and hairstyles, crafted into tokens of love and worn as badges of allegiance or awards. From the 1900s ribbon were used less as items of clothing and more as an attractive and widely available craft material. Ribbons in a dazzling variety of colours can now be seen embellishing the smartest gifts, millinery, soft furnishings and fashionable outfits.

From the very earliest times, ribbon has served both practical and decorative purpose. Its history is closely aligned to the history of fashion, but its use and popularity has changed dramatically.

The History of Ribbons

The earliest examples of ribbons – in the broad sense of narrow strips of fabric – are from ancient Egypt and can be dated to about 3000BC. It is impossible to say for certain how or where weaving was first developed, but, having produced lengths of fabric, people began to use them as clothing, and embellished them in various ways.

During the Middle Ages, a variety of elaborate borders began to be used to decorate clothing. In England, gowns had become relatively complex garments. The bodice was slit down either side from arm to hip and fitted with ribbons, which were used to tie the material tightly across the upper part of the body. By the middle of the 12th century, skirts had become fuller with dozens of knife-pleats, and the tightness of the bodice was accentuated with a belt resembling a deep cummerbund, which was tied at the back with ribbons.

Below: A pedlar selling ribbons. A travelling salesman would bring his wares to isolated farms and villages.

By the 16th century, trade with the New World had developed and a middle class emerged, eager to spend its wealth on imitating the style of the aristocracy. Henry VIII loved richly decorated garments and headdresses and, to protect himself and the Court from being copied, he introduced legislation preventing anyone but royalty and the aristocracy from wearing decorative embroidery, ribbons woven with gold and silver thread, brocades and jewellery.

The use of ribbons and other adornments was relatively modest during the Puritan period of the 17th century, but the restoration of the English monarchy in 1660 and the coming of age of France's Sun King, Louis XIV, in 1661 brought about a complete change of attitude in both countries. Louis XIV's powerful and dazzling court in France and the self-indulgent rule of Charles II in England were reflected in the costume of men and women. Men's petticoat-breeches, doublets and shoes were decorated all over with bunches of ribbon. Tight stockings were generally pulled over the breeches and fastened with a garter, which was also decorated with a bunch of ribbons. Women's skirts were divided or drawn up with lavishly tied ribbon to reveal extremely ornate petticoats beneath.

Above: This Flemish woman from the 17th century wears a dress embellished with huge silk ribbon bows.

The Court of Versailles dominated all matters of taste and fashion among the European aristocracy in the early 18th century. At the same time, the middle classes experienced increasing

Right: The interior of Hill Bros Millinery Goods in the 19th century, with hundreds of rolls of ribbon for hat trimming.

prosperity and for the first time fashion became the domain of the majority. Ribbons played an essential role, being used to trim gowns and bonnets, tie up hair for a ball, lace dainty shoes and in the form of waist-bands, sashes, frills, favours and rosettes. Children were smothered in ribbon, and curtains and cushions were embellished with broad bands of silk. Ribbons were produced in a dazzling variety of weaves and colours; plain, striped, checked, watered, shot, shaded and figured ribbons were all widely available. During the Napoleonic wars, weavers were recruited for the army, leaving the trade short of labour. The smuggling of vast quantities of French ribbon almost became an industry in itself in coastal villages, and yet the demand was still not met.

In 1813, a scalloped-edged ribbon became the rage and weavers had never known a time of such fierce demand for their product. In London, for a period of two years while the craze lasted, manufacturers could ask whatever prices they wished.

By the first half of the 19th century, the Industrial Revolution was in full swing and fashion was no longer dictated by nobility. Department stores sprang up in all major cities and off-the-peg clothes appeared for the first time. Parasols, large-brimmed hats and the new fashion accessory, the handbag, were all extravagantly decorated with rosettes and bows.

In 1823, jacquard looms were introduced in Coventry, thus extending the variety of fancy ribbons available. Ribbon factories and mills were built, all making use of steam-powered looms, although workers using hand looms still continued their trade, particularly in the countryside. The increased prosperity of the time meant that working girls had a little money to indulge in a piece of ribbon to trim a hat, and Coventry found a new middle- and lower-class market.

The period between 1850 and 1870 was one of unprecedented prosperity for an enormous number of people. Women's clothes became increasingly complex, made from two or three different materials and trimmed with a medley of folds, frills and pleats. Ribbons and braids were an integral part of the garments, and by the 1880s, bustles became known as the "upholstered style" because they were made from draperies more suited to furnishing a room than trimming a dress. The turn of the 20th century saw a general softening of the silhouette and tucks, frills, ruchings and other ribbon trims were gradually modified. As the size and complexity of dresses diminished, hats grew larger and were trimmed with a profusion of ribbons and feathers. These extravagant hats gradually gave way to more modest creations: the cloche hat of the 1920s was quite plain but often trimmed with a fancy rosette on one side.

From the 1930s until quite recently, the significance of the ribbon as a fashion item diminished, with just the occasional reappearance as trends dictated – during the 1960s for example. There is today a revival of interest in ribbons and ribboncrafts, although the emphasis is now as much on home decoration as on fashion. Ribbon embroidery is the new stitchcraft and ribbon weaving, pleating, plaiting and ruching are all being rediscovered.

Ribbons are an extremely versatile medium and presented here is a selection of work by contemporary designers that illustrates just some of the wide range of effects that can be achieved.

Gallery of Ribbonwork

Textile artists working in techniques from weaving and stitching to leatherwork and millinery are today using lengths of ribbons on their own to create texture and pattern, or in small amounts to add colourful detail to their designs. The simplicity of the ribbon hat on the left makes the most of the natural flow of the coiled ribbon, and the woven cushion overleaf exploits the subtle shades of soft velvet, whilst the gloves and hydrangea picture show a more traditional use of ribbon as embellishment.

Below: WAVES WALL HANGING
Ribbon makes an ideal material for weaving, and offers dramatic effects. The inspiration for this design came from the shapes that are created by the weaving techniques employed. Small-scale undulations, or waves, are produced through the interaction of the bands of a thick wool warp and thin ribbon weft.
PATRICIA TINDALE

Below: CHRISTENING GOWN
Double-face satin ribbon to match the cream lace has been appliquéd on to the gown using various simple techniques.
JENNY BANHAM

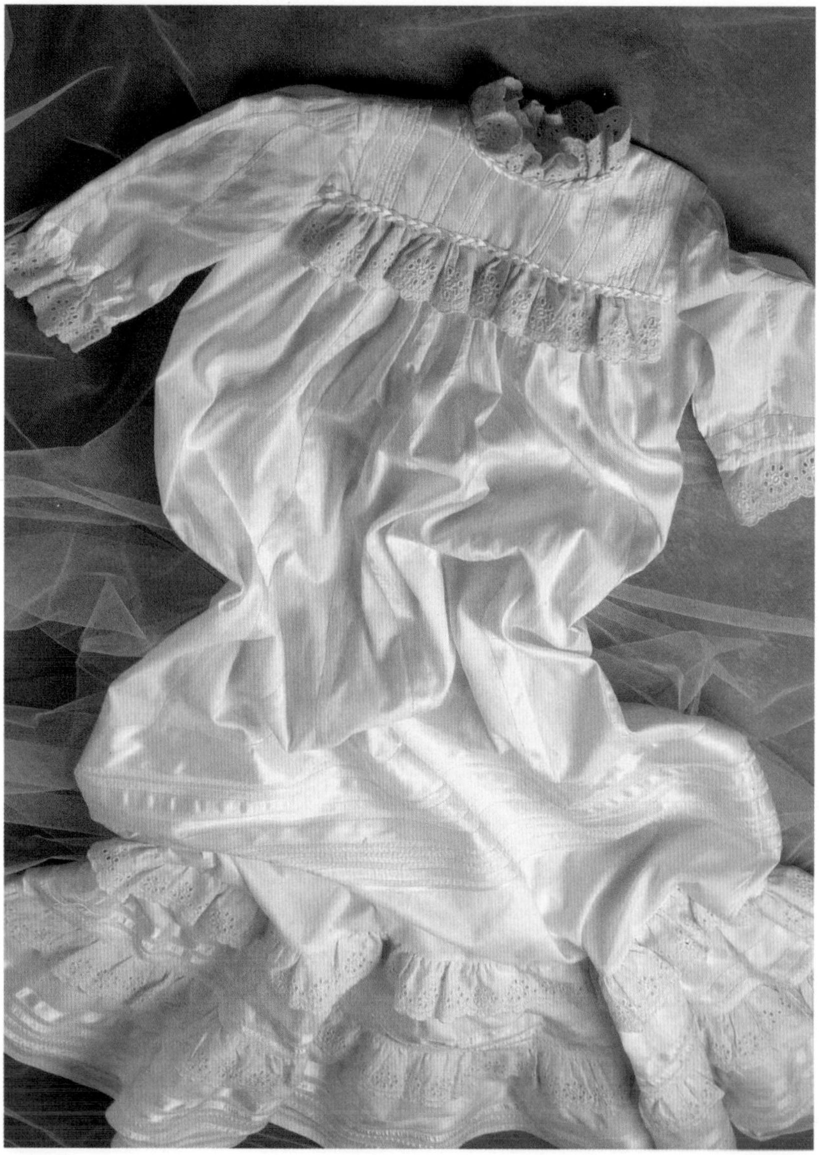

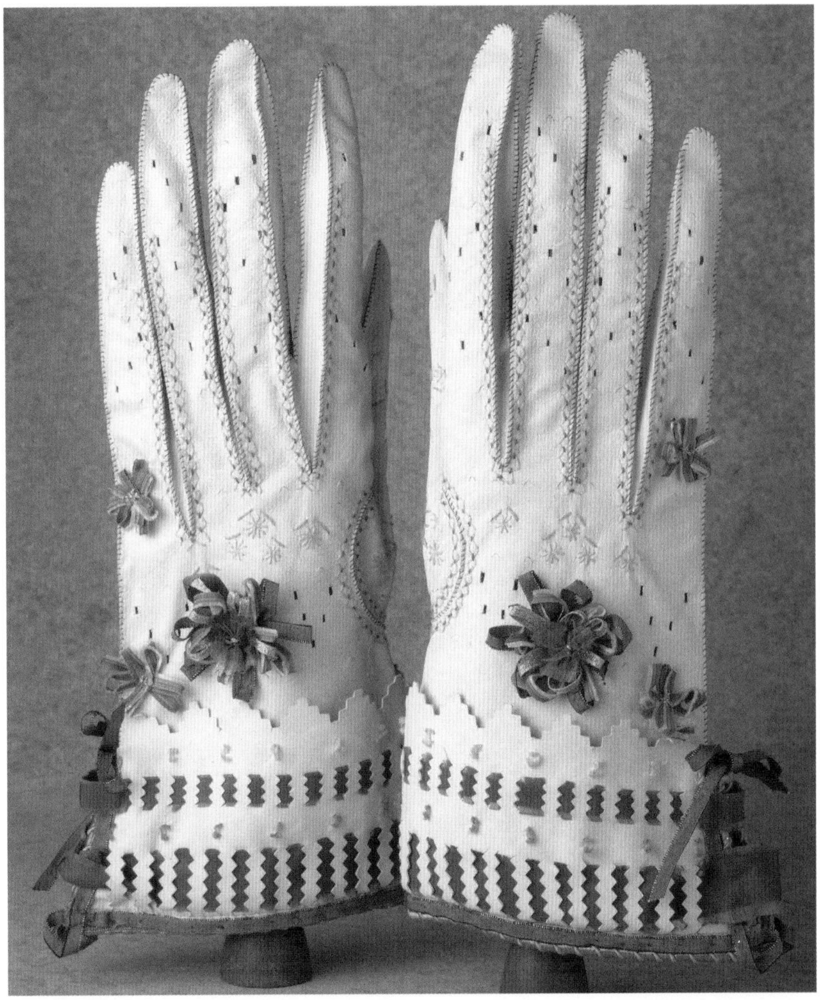

Above: RIBBON SPIRAL HAT
This elegant ribbon hat was inspired by the natural way in which the ribbon spirals when pulled from the roll.
JO BUCKLER

Right: EMBROIDERED GLOVES
These hand-stitched gloves, which are embroidered with ribbons, are based on an original 17th-century pair. The decoration is typical of the period when ribbons were used in profusion.
PAMELA WOODS

Right: RIBBON EMBROIDERY
This beautiful embroidery was inspired by the pretty, delicately coloured hydrangea. It is composed mainly of machine embroidery with ribbon embellishment. First the bracts were drawn, outlined and shaded in. Then the tiny flowers were worked by hand using ribbon, beads and French knots. The foliage was machined without any further drawing on to the fabric.
DAPHNE J. ASHBY

Left: INVITATION
This card was made by drawing a decorative border of delicate roses on to parchment paper. It was then colour-washed in watercolour before being decorated with ribbon rosebuds and bows.
LINDSAY CHALFORD BROWN

Above WOVEN CUSHION
The charm and beauty of this woven cushion lies in the fantastic colour scheme and texture of the velvet ribbons.
HIKARU NOGUCHI

Below: AFRICAN HANGING
This wall hanging was made by stitching together two layers of simple patchwork in a grid pattern. Selected areas of the patchwork were then cut away to reveal the layer underneath. The surface was covered with couched "ribbons" of hand-dyed silk to create geometric patterns.
JENNY CHIPPINDALE

Above: TREASURE CHEST
The lid of the chest is made up of a square of ribbon weaving worked in fine ribbons in shades of blue. It is enhanced with extra ribbons, held in place with single strands of metallic embroidery thread, worked in cross stitch and French knots. To give a three-dimensional effect, the weaving was mounted on to card. This shape suggested the lid of a treasure chest, inspiring the designer to make the rest of the chest.
M. MAUREEN VOISEY

A simple sewing kit of needles, thread and scissors is all that you need for basic ribbonwork, but a few of the projects that follow require more specialized items, which are readily available from craft suppliers.

Equipment

Above: Equipment such as a glue gun, florist's tape and stub wire is required for a few of the projects in the book. However, for many of them a good range of sewing equipment is all that is needed.

Dressmaker's chalk

This makes an easily removed line to mark templates or specific intervals on to fabric or ribbon.

Dressmaker's pins

Long, straight pins have many uses in ribbonwork. Glass- or pearl-headed versions are easier to handle and are used for weaving.

Florist's tape (stem wrap)

Flexible and stretchy, this green self-sticking tape is used to conceal wire stems and bind the stems of fresh flowers together.

Glue

Although not essential, a glue gun will quickly become indispensable once purchased. They apply glue with speed and accuracy, even in tricky areas, and are available in various sizes. A small gun is ideal for beginners. As with any adhesive product, it is important to keep glue guns out of the reach of children. PVA or white craft glue is ideal for larger-scale sticking and dries clear. Double-sided tape is good for paper projects and gives a neat finish.

Sewing thread

Polyester thread comes in a wide range of colours, so you should always be able to find a reel to match the ribbon you are using.

Scissors

Use small, sharp-bladed scissors for trimming thread and cutting ribbons, and larger dressmaking shears for fabric. Keep a third pair especially for cutting paper only.

Stub (floral) wire

Florists use this thick, straight wire for supporting the flower stems. It is used to make the stalks of ribbon roses.

Tape measure

This is useful for checking the length of ribbons before cutting and also for measuring the progress of bead weaving, bracelets or necklaces.

Weaving board

A heat-resistant, fabric-covered soft board that will take pins easily is needed for weaving, although an ironing board is a good substitute.

Wire cutters

An essential tool for cutting florist's and stub wire. Some pliers, such as those illustrated here, can be used to cut wire, as well as to shape it.

Ribbons come in myriad textures, colours and widths, and there is a ribbon for every occasion and season, from baby pastels and frothy sheers to designer prints and brocades.

Types of Ribbon

Cut-edge craft

This ribbon is made from a wide fabric and then cut into strips. It is available wired or unwired and is suitable only for craft applications. The special finish stops the ribbon from fraying but means it is not washable.

Grosgrain

These ribbons have a distinctive crosswise rib and are a stronger, denser weave than most other ribbon types. Grosgrains are made in solid colours, stripes, dots and prints; satin and grosgrain combinations are also available.

Jacquards

An intricate pattern is incorporated in the weave of the ribbon. This can be multicoloured or single-colour combinations, florals or geometric patterns, which give a beautiful tapestry-like effect.

Lace-edged satins and jacquards

These are sometimes embellished with a lace edge that is stitched or bonded on to the selvedge. It is particularly popular for bridal applications.

Merrow-edge

This describes the fine satin-stitched edge, usually incorporating a wire, that is added to elaborate cut-edge ribbons for stability and decoration. It is often in lurex thread but can also be in a contrasting colour.

Metallics

These ribbons are made from or incorporate metallic or pearlized fibres. Many different weaves and finishes result in a number of combinations.

Moiré

This effect is the result of a water-mark finish applied during manufacture. It gives a lustrous finish.

Ombré taffeta

A finely woven taffeta with colour shading across the width. Variations include plaids and interesting colour blends giving a lustrous finish and subtle tonal effects.

Plaids and checks

Popular classics, plaids and checks are usually taffeta weaves but are also available in cut-edge ribbon.

Satins

Satins are either double-face or single-face. They are available in plain colours or printed. Some incorporate edgings such as picot- or feather-edge.

Sheers

These fine, almost transparent ribbons are available as plain ribbons or with satin, lurex or jacquard stripes. A thicker yarn is used along the selvedge to give stability. This is known as a monofilament edge.

Shot-effect taffeta

The use of different, often contrasting colours for the warp and weft results in a shot effect giving a really lustrous, colour-shaded finish, similar to shot silk. This product is available both wired and unwired.

Ribbon Conversions

1.5mm (1/16in)	36mm (1 3/8in)
3mm (1/8in)	39mm (1 1/2in)
5mm (3/16in)	50mm (2in)
7mm (1/4in)	56mm (2 1/4in)
9mm (3/8in)	67mm (2 5/8in)
12mm (1/2in)	70mm (2 3/4in)
15mm (5/8in)	77mm (3in)
23mm (7/8in)	80mm (3 1/4in)
25mm (1in)	

Velvets

The deep, plush pile of velvet is unmistakable and the depth of colour is exceptional. Imitation velvets are also available.

Wire-edged taffeta

A fine weave with a matt rather than shiny finish. This product looks the same on both sides and is available plain or with lurex incorporated. Weaves include plaids, checks and ombrés. Taffeta can also be printed or given a shimmering watermark finish. The wire-edge is usually encased so it is not visible.

Woven-edge ribbon

These ribbons are woven in narrow strips, with a non-fraying selvedge running along both edges. They are ideal for projects that need to be laundered or that will have heavy wear. The ribbon reels should carry laundry instructions and details of crease resistance and colour fastness.

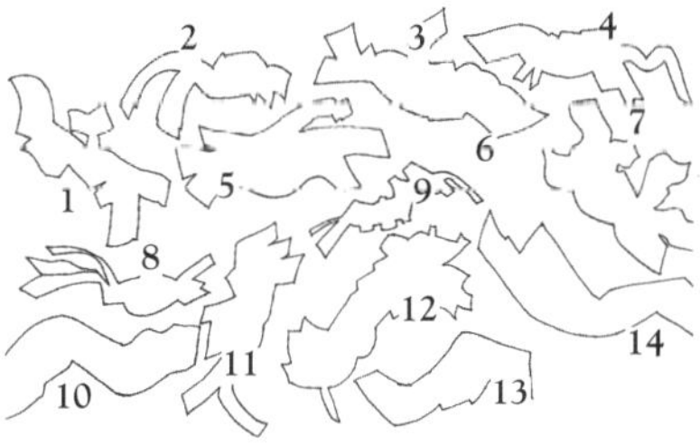

1 Ombré taffeta; 2 Grosgrain; 3 Sheer; 4 Jaquard; 5 Wire-edged taffeta; 6 Lace-edged; 7 Shot-effect taffeta; 8 Plaid and check; 9 Velvet; 10 Merrow-edge; 11 Moiré; 12 Metallic; 13 Cut-edge craft; 14 Satin

Ribbons are a wonderfully versatile craft material with which to work. They can be woven, braided, appliquéd, used in embroidery, or simply made into beautiful rosettes, flowers and bows.

Basic Techniques

Ribbon Bows

Bows are probably the first thing that comes to mind when thinking about ribbon. There are several ways of making a bow; be it large and floaty or small and dainty, all are easy to accomplish. Satin ribbon is the most popular choice, but sheers, prints and lurex all have their own special qualities. As a general rule, if the ribbon can be tied in a tight knot, it is suitable for hand-tying. A stiffer ribbon will need to be pleated and stitched or bound at the neck. The hanging tails of the finished bow need to be in proportion to the loops. Leave them slightly longer than is required, then trim diagonally or into a chevron. This not only looks attractive, but also prevents a woven ribbon from fraying.

You will need

Ribbon
Florist's wire
Craft scissors
Glue gun
Needle and matching thread

Hand-wired Bow

1 Fold each half of the ribbon across the centre to make two loops and two tails. Hold the ribbon at the neck and bind it with wire. Conceal the wire with a narrow ribbon, secured with glue or a couple of stitches.

Double-loop Bow

1 Fold a length of ribbon into the desired number of loops. Form the neck by stitching through the ribbon or binding it tightly with wire, exactly half-way along the loops.

2 Hide the wire or stitches by wrapping a small piece of ribbon around the neck. Secure with glue or a couple of stitches at the back.

Pompom Bow

1 Fold the end of a length of cut-edge ribbon into a loop the diameter of the finished bow. Wrap the ribbon ten times around this loop and flatten into a rectangle. Cut off the corners.

2 Refold so that the cut corners meet in the middle to form the neck. Bind the neck securely with wire. Pull out each of the ribbon loops individually and twist them in different directions. Trim the ends diagonally or in a chevron, as shown here.

Ribbon Roses

Despite their sophisticated look, ribbon roses are deceptively easy to make. There are several techniques, employing various ribbon types, and each method will produce a slightly different flower; for example, satin ribbon roses will be more delicate and less full than those made from wire-edged taffeta. Experiment also by using different widths of ribbon – the wider the ribbon, the larger the finished rose will be. The fuller you wish to make the rose, the more ribbon you will need to use.

Stemmed Wire-edged Rose

This quick and easy flower is perfect for trimming special gifts or evening wear garments. They can also be used as accessories for bridal wear. The addition of a stem makes the rose suitable for use as a buttonhole or as an attachment to a hair-slide. A group of roses can be arranged in a vase.

You will need

Wire-edged ribbon
Needle and matching thread
Stub (floral) wire
Wire cutters
Florist's tape (stem wrap)
Artificial leaves

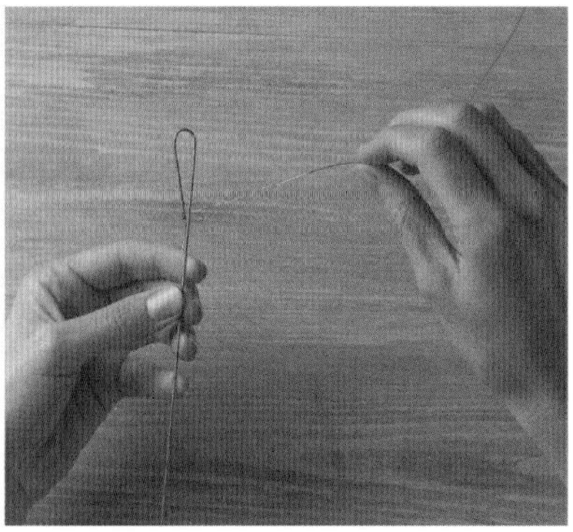

1 Tie a knot at one end of the ribbon and gather it by carefully pulling up one of the wires from the other end. Hold the knot and wrap the gathered edge around it to form the rose.

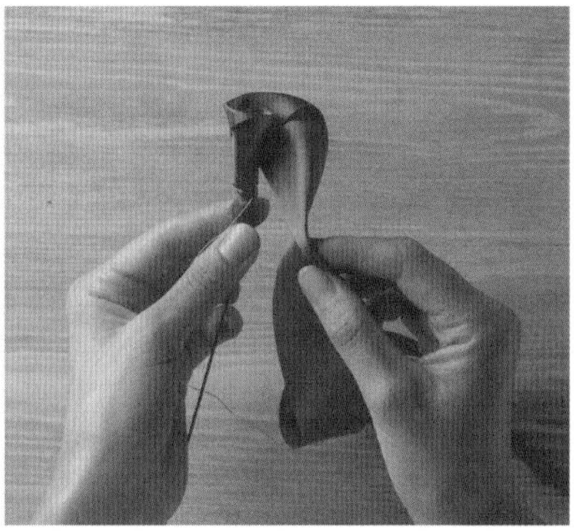

2 Twist the end of a stub wire gently around the stem and wrap the wire strand around the end of the stem. Fold back and wrap the raw end of the ribbon, securing it with a few stitches as necessary.

3 Bind the stem with florist's tape, adding on the leaves as you work. Ease the ungathered edge of the ribbon into the shape of the petals.

Stitched Ribbon Rose

Use this highly decorative rose for adorning fashion accessories or soft furnishings, either singly or in groups for extra romantic appeal. A stem and leaves can be added as before.

You will need

Ribbon
Needle and matching thread
Dressmaker's pins

1 Fold one end of the ribbon at a right angle so it extends 2.5cm/1in below the edge of the remaining ribbon. Stitch through both layers. Working from left to right, turn the ribbon six times to make a tube. Stitch at the base to secure the centre.

2 For each petal, fold the ribbon to the outside at a right angle, 2.5cm/1in from the centre, so the loose end hangs down vertically. Pin the fold and turn the bud into the fold until the ribbon is horizontal. Secure with a stitch and remove the pin.

3 Continue folding and stitching until 8cm/3in of ribbon remains. Fold again and stitch the raw edge to the base, pleating as necessary.

Ribbon Weaving

Weaving ribbons is an immensely satisfying craft, which can produces some dazzling effects, as can be seen in the Basket-weave Cushion and Woven Ribbon Waistcoat projects. It can be used for many different soft furnishings or on a smaller scale in panels on accessories or evening wear. The methods described here are all fused on to iron-on interfacing. Any type of ribbon can be used for weaving, but if the item is to be laundered you should work with washable, woven-edge ribbons. When working with velvet, place the ribbon face down to protect the woven pile and iron the interfacing on to the back of the finished woven piece.

Basic Steps for Weaving

You will need

Felt-tipped pen
Ruler
Tape measure
Iron-on interfacing
Weaving board
Ribbon
Glass-headed pins
Scissors
Steam iron or dry iron with damp cloth

1 Pin the piece of interfacing to the board, glue upwards. Pin the top ends of the warp, or vertical, ribbons along the top edge.

2 Weave in the weft, or horizontal, ribbons and pin down both ends, angling the pins outwards. Cut the interfacing to the size of the weaving area, marking in a 2.5cm/1in seam allowance all around.

3 Pin down the bottom of the warp ribbons, then fuse the completed weave to the interfacing using a moderate dry iron. Press the outer edges with the tip of the iron.

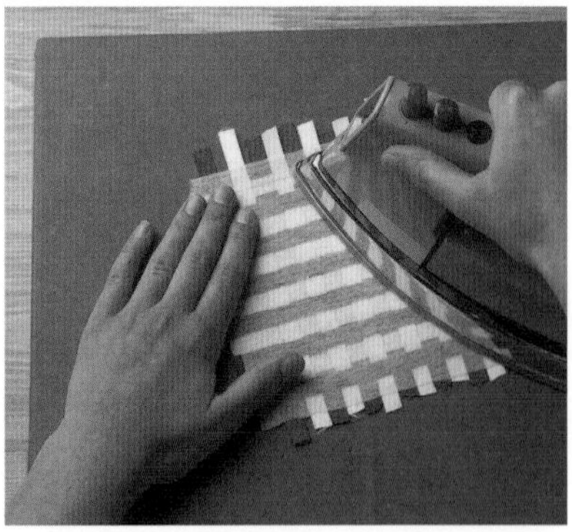

4 When the ribbons are secure, remove all the pins. Turn over and press again with a steam iron or with a damp cloth, then leave to cool.

RIBBON QUANTITIES FOR WOVEN SQUARES

The quantities given are for the whole square. If using two or more colours, divide the quantity by that number. All measurements include a 2.5cm (1in) seam allowance.

RIBBON WIDTH	RIBBON LENGTH		
	10x10CM (4x4IN)	20x20CM (8x8IN)	30x30 CM (12x12IN)
5mm (3/16in)	6m (6½yd)	20m (22yd)	42m (46yd)
7mm (¼in)	4.2m (4½yd)	14.6m (16yd)	30.2m (33 yd)
9mm (⅜in)	3.4m (3¾yd)	11m (12yd)	23.2m (25yd)
15mm (⅝in)	2.2m (2½yd)	6.6m (7¼yd)	14m (15¼yd)
23mm (⅞in)	1.4m (1½yd)	4.6m (5yd)	9.2m (10yd)

Plain Weave

You will need

For a 30cm/12in square:
Lightweight iron-on interfacing, 35cm/14in square
Red ribbon, 15.1m x 6mm/16½yd x ¼in
Blue ribbon, 15.1m x 6mm/16½yd x ¼in

1 Prepare the interfacing as in Basic Steps for Weaving. Cut both ribbons into 15cm/4in lengths. Pin the top ends of the red warp ribbons, edge to edge, along the top of the interfacing.

2 Weave the first blue weft ribbon over the first warp, under the second, then under and over to the end. Push it up to the top line and pin tautly at each end. Weave the next weft under the first warp and over the second, and so on to the end.

3 Alternate the weft ribbons in this way until the whole of the weaving area is covered. Check the ribbons are all neatly lined up before pressing as shown in the Basic Steps.

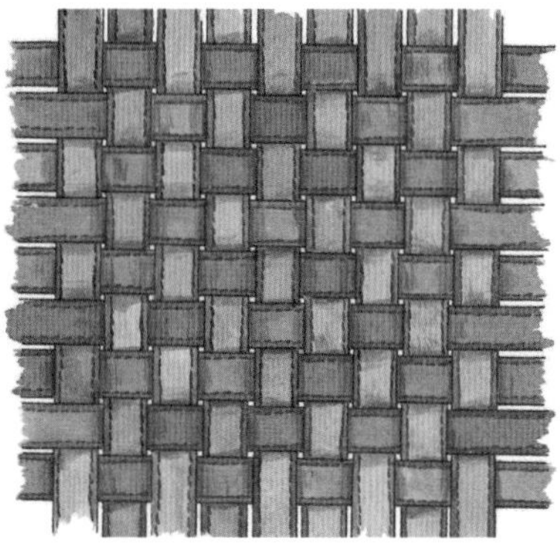

Patchwork Weave

You will need

For a 30cm/12in square:
Lightweight iron-on interfacing, 35cm/14in square
Blue ribbon (A), 8.5m x 10mm/13¼yd x ⅜in
Yellow ribbon (B), 12m x 10mm/13¼yd x ⅜in
Red ribbon (C), 5.5m x 10mm/6yd x ⅜in

1 Prepare the interfacing as in Basic Steps and cut all the ribbons into 35cm/14in lengths. Pin the warp ribbons along the top edge in the following sequence: blue, yellow, red, yellow (ABCB).

2 Starting at the top-left corner, pin the ends of the weft ribbons down the side in the same order.
Weave them in the following sequence of four rows:
row 1: over AB, under C, then over BAB, under C to the end.
row 2: under A, over BCB to the end.
row 3: over A, under B, over C, under B to the end.
row 4: as row 2.

3 When complete, bond the ribbons to the interfacing as in Basic Steps.

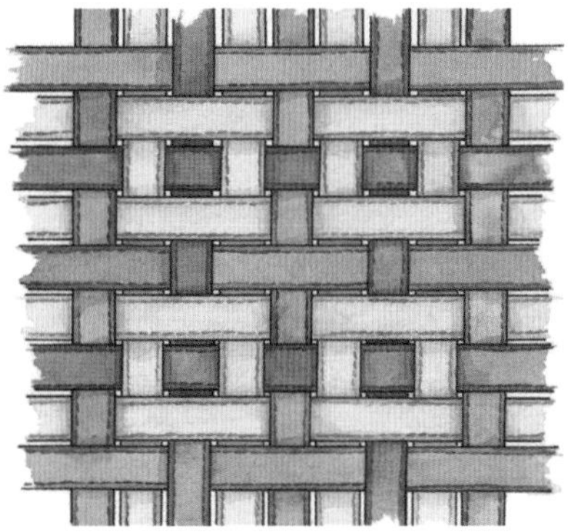

Zigzag Weave

You will need

For a 30cm/12in square:
Lightweight iron-on interfacing, 35cm/14in square
Yellow ribbon, 15.4 x 6mm/16¾yd x ¼in
Blue ribbon 14.6m x 6mm/16yd x ¼in

1 Prepare the interfacing as before and cut the ribbons into 35cm/14in lengths. Pin alternate yellow and blue ribbons along the top and left edges.

2 Weave the weft in the following four-row sequence:
row 1: under two, over two to the end.
row 2: under one, over two, under two, over two to the end.
row 3: over two, under two to the end.
row 4: over one, under two, over two under two to the end.

3 Bond the ribbons to the interfacing as detailed in Basic Steps.

Basic Stitching Techniques

Ribbon embroidery is exactly the same as any other embroidery, the only difference being that the stitches are worked with ribbon. The texture and width of the ribbon produces raised embroidery, and the amazing range of shades available means that very life-like floral results can be achieved. The real secret of successful ribbon embroidery is to remember that you are trying to recreate the look and feel of the original subject, be it daisies, roses or tulips.

Running Stitch

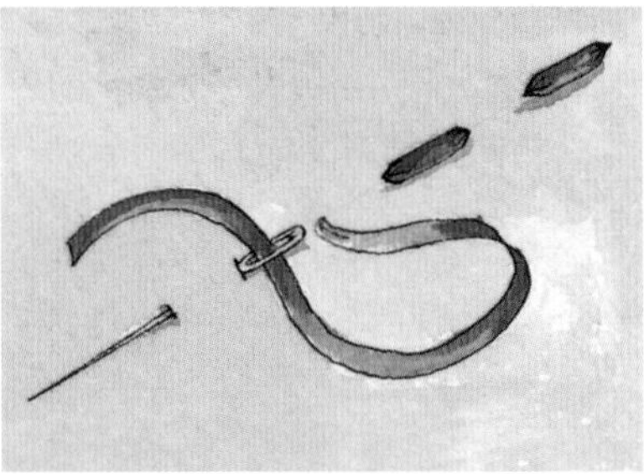

Pass the needle regularly in and out of the fabric, keeping the stitches small and evenly spaced on the back and front.

French Knots

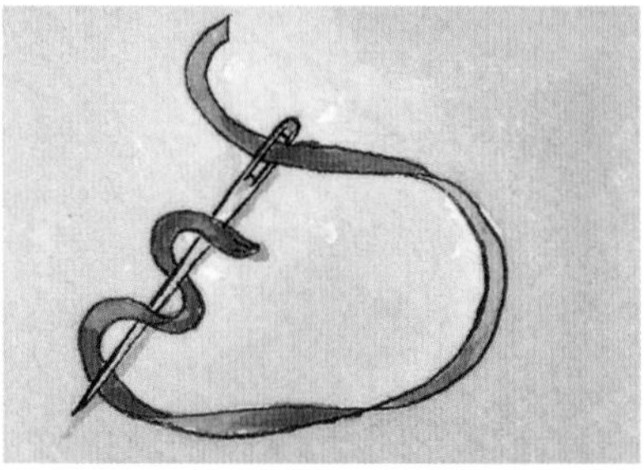

1 Bring the needle up through the fabric to the right side. Hold the ribbon taut with one hand and twist the needle around the ribbon twice.

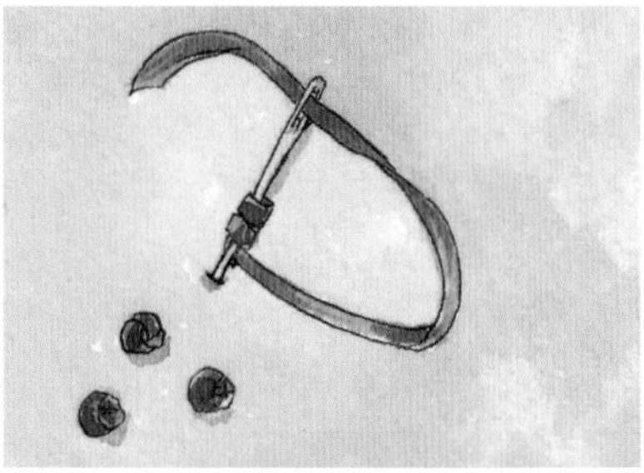

2 Still holding the ribbon, turn the needle to go back down through the fabric close to the point where it emerged. The needle and ribbon should go through the twists.

Spider's Web Rose

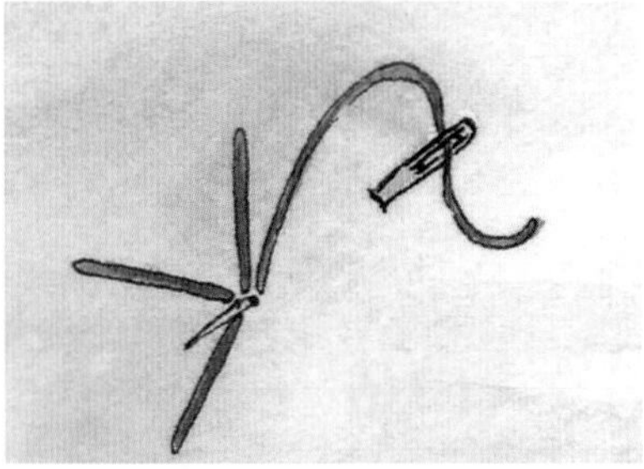

1 Stitch a circle of five spokes in a strong thread. Secure the thread at the back of the fabric and fasten off.

2 Bring the ribbon up through the centre of this circle of spokes and start weaving in and out of the spokes in a spiral. Let the ribbon twist naturally as you form the rose.

3 Pass the needle under the rose and back down through the fabric.

Lazy Daisy Stitch or Detached Chain Stitch

1 Bring the ribbon up through the fabric. Push the needle back down again at almost the same spot, leaving a loop of ribbon. Come back up through the fabric inside the loop and pull the ribbon up gently.

2 Take the needle back down again, over the loop to secure it in place. Bring the needle up at the tip of the next petal. Repeat to the end.

Chain Stitch

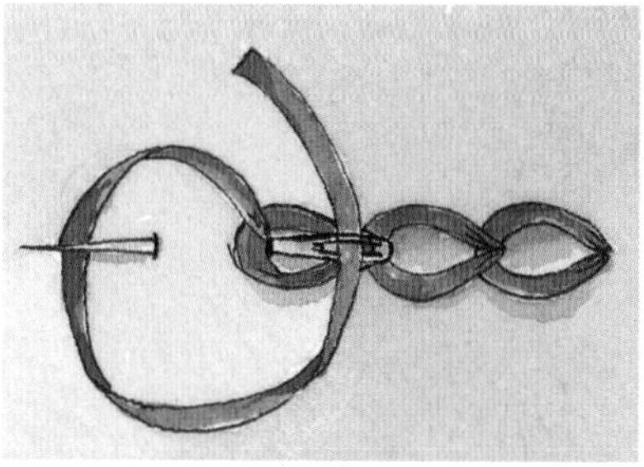

Loop the ribbon under the needle's tip. Hold the ribbon down as you draw the needle through the fabric. Push the needle back through the hole it left to form the next stitch.

Blanket Stitch

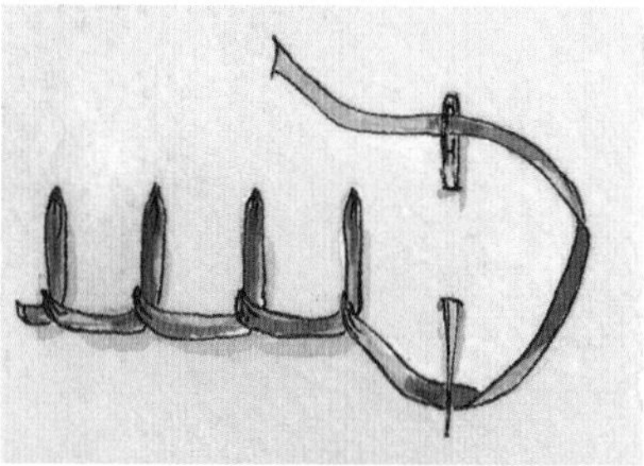

Work a line of vertical stitches and, as you draw the needle through the fabric, catch the ribbon under the needle's tip. Pull the ribbon through then insert the needle into the fabric parallel to the previous stitch.

Cross Stitch

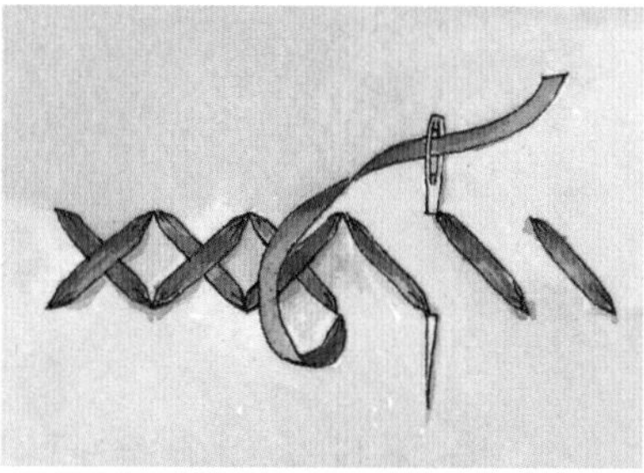

Cross stitch is worked in two parts and the top stitches should always lie in the same direction, usually from bottom left to top right. Work a row of diagonal stitches from right to left, then complete the crosses with a second row of diagonal stitches worked in the opposite direction.

Back Stitch

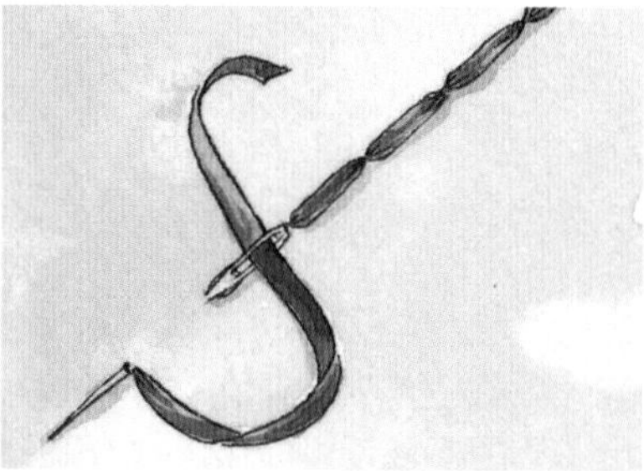

Back stitch produces an unbroken line of stitching suitable for outlining designs. First make a small stitch and pull the needle through the fabric. Insert the needle into the hole at the end of the previous stitch, then bring it up through the fabric a stitch length further on and repeat.

Slip Stitch

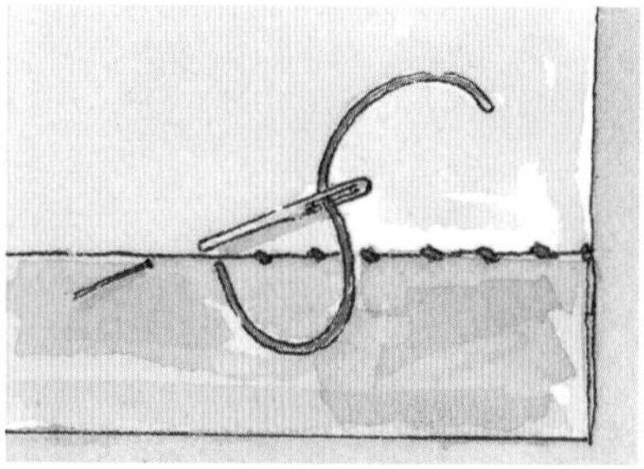

This dressmaking stitch is worked in sewing thread, and should be nearly invisible. Pick up two threads of the single fabric and slip the needle through the fold for about 6mm/¼in. Draw the needle through to make a tiny stitch and repeat to the end.

Tips for Ribbon Embroidery

To thread the needle, pass the end of the ribbon through the eye of the needle. Then push the point of the needle through the same end of the ribbon and pull. As with other types of embroidery, it is best to work with an embroidery hoop. Use your finger or a large needle to prevent the ribbon from twisting. Don't tie knots too tightly in case you need to undo them. Try to weave in the ribbon ends at the back of the embroidery.

Ribbonwork Projects

Ribbon is a surprisingly versatile textile medium, and the creations on the following pages reveal just a few aspects of what can be achieved with them. Small-scale gift boxes, jewellery, Christmas decorations and present-wrapping ideas are shown alongside more ambitious and complex projects, which involve other skills such as basic woodworking, floristry or dressmaking. Today's stunning variety of colours, widths, patterns and styles of ribbon make ribbon projects even more adaptable, innovative and decorative.

Any aspiring young prima ballerina, flowergirl or junior bridesmaid would be delighted with the way that satin ties and a cluster of ribbon roses transform these plain ballet pumps into pretty shoes fit for a princess.

Ballet Shoes

you will need
3 toning shades of double face satin ribbon, 20 x 1cm/ 8 x ½in of each
Scissors
Needle and matching threads
Pair of ballet shoes
Single-face satin ribbon to match ballet shoes, approximately 2m x 15mm/2¼yd x ⅝in

1 For each satin rose you will need a 10cm/4in length of 1cm/½in wide ribbon. Start by rolling one raw end of the first length inwards to the left two or three times. Secure by stitching neatly through the roll at the lower edge.

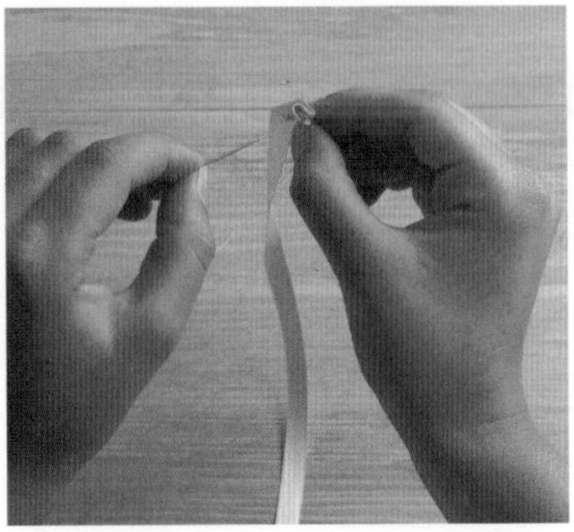

2 To make the first petal, hold the roll in one hand and fold the ribbon away from you with the other. Turn the rolled end from right to left, turning tightly at the bottom and loosely at the top. Stitch the base of the petal in place.

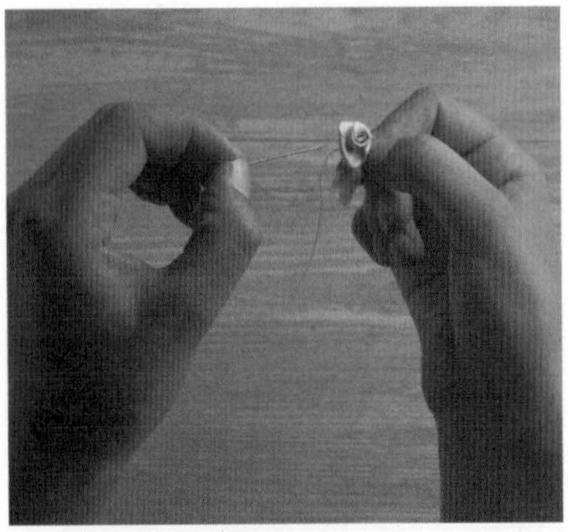

3 Continue folding the ribbon, rolling the rose and stitching each petal until the rose is the desired size. Cut the ribbon square approximately 5mm/¼in from the rose. Fold the end neatly on to the rose and stitch to secure.

4 Make five more roses from the remaining ribbon in the same way. Stitch three roses, one of each shade, to the front of each shoe, just below the bow. Use a double length of thread for extra security.

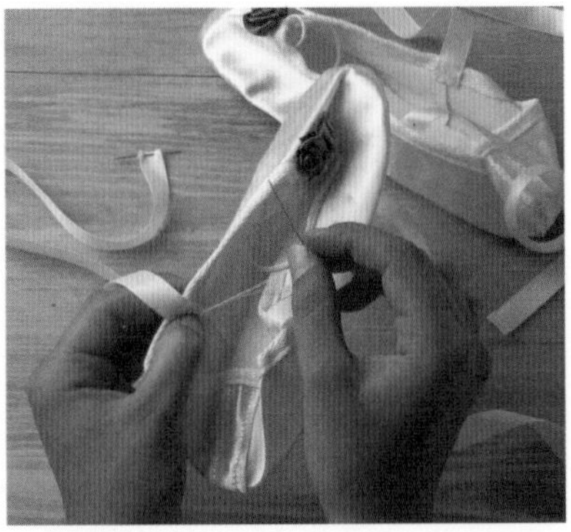

5 Cut the 15mm/⅝in ribbon into four equal lengths. Stitch one length inside each side of the ballet shoes to form ties. Neatly hem the end of each tie to prevent fraying.

Extravagant bows and rosettes add true distinction to special gifts. Choose wrapping paper in interesting textures to complement them, and combine ribbons in several different shades for enchanting effects.

Luxurious Giftwrapping

you will need

- Gold wire-edged ribbon in two shades
- Scissors
- Organza ribbon in three colours
- Bead-edged ribbon, 5cm/2in wide
- Tape measure
- Double-sided adhesive tape
- Gold corded ribbon
- Thin card (stock)
- Stapler

1 Wrap a length of wire-edged ribbon around the gold parcel and tie in a single knot on top. Tie a length of another shade in the other direction and knot as before. Tie all four ends together in a bow. Open out and adjust the loops, then cut the free ends into fishtails.

2 For the multicoloured bow, place organza ribbons in three colours one on top of the other and tie around the parcel together. Open out the loops and cut the free ends into fishtails.

3 To make the pompom, cut a length of bead-edged ribbon 126cm/49in long and fold into seven concertina (accordion) pleats, each 18cm/7in long. Trim the ribbon ends diagonally. Holding the pleats together, carefully make a 2cm/¾in cut in the centre of each long edge.

4 Cut a second length of ribbon long enough to wrap around the parcel plus 15cm/6in. Tie this length around the centre of the pleats, then wrap it around the parcel and secure the ends underneath with double-sided adhesive tape. Open out the folds of the pompom to form puffed loops.

5 Make the rosette from a 3cm/1¼in circle of cardboard and 110cm/43in of ribbon. Fold under one end of the ribbon, make a pleat and staple to the centre of the circle. Continue pleating and stapling in a spiral. Staple the raw end underneath. Wrap the parcel in ribbon and tape the rosette to the top.

It's easy to make ribbon roses and they always look gorgeous. You simply wrap, roll and tweak. Here, they are randomly applied to a plain lampshade to add splashes of colour.

Rosy Lampshade

you will need

Wire-edged ribbon in pink and red
Tape measure
Scissors
Needle and matching thread
Plain lampshade
Ribbon trim
Strong glue or glue gun

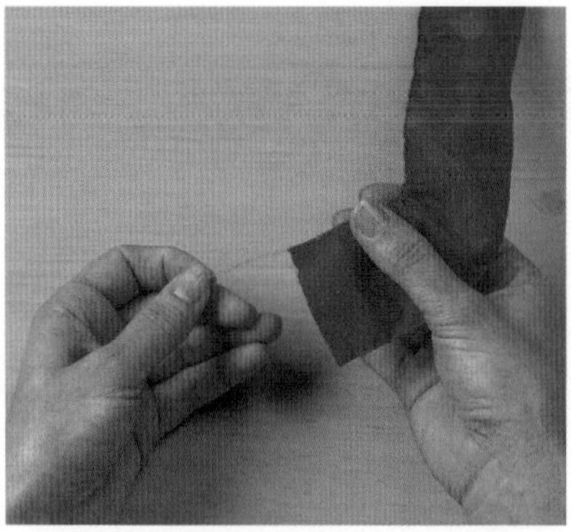

1 Cut a 40cm/16in length of wire-edged ribbon. Ruche the ribbon by pulling up the wire along one edge from both ends.

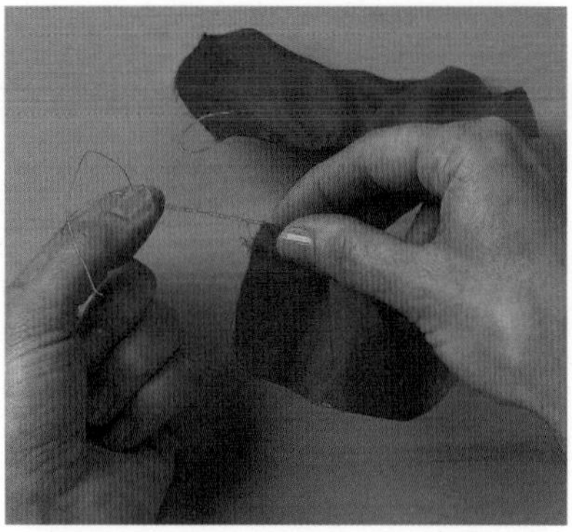

2 Keep pulling until the ribbon is evenly ruched and the wire ends even.

3 Fold the ribbon in half and roll it up loosely, starting at the raw ends. Fan out the ribbon edge to create the rose, and secure the base with a few small slip stitches.

4 Make enough roses to cover the surface of the lampshade. To give it an informal look, fix them in place at random, but regularly spaced, intervals.

5 Cut a length of ribbon to fit the lower edge of the lampshade, allowing a 2cm/¾in overlap. Glue in place with strong glue or a glue gun.

Glamorize plain bedlinen by edging a pile of pillows with ribbon bands and bows. Bright ginghams work well in a child's bedroom, but you could adapt the idea using cooler colours for a more sophisticated look.

Pillowcase Edgings

you will need

- Plain white cotton pillowcases
- Plain and gingham ribbons of various widths
- Tape measure
- Scissors
- Fusible bonding web
- Iron
- Needle and matching thread
- Dressmaker's pins

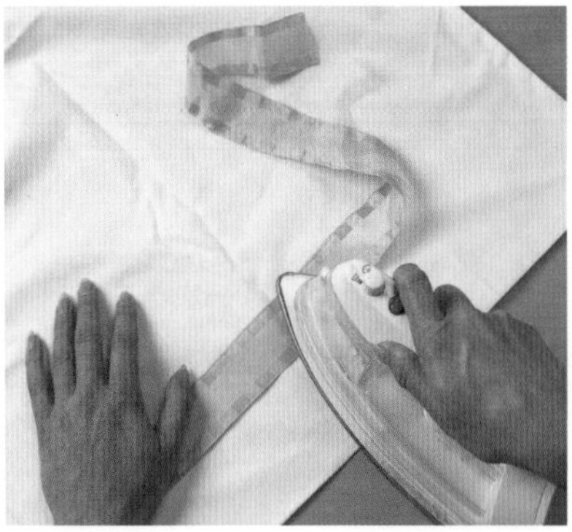

1 For the banded pillowcase, cut lengths of three different ribbons about 5cm/2in longer than the width of the pillowcase. Cut three lengths of fusible bonding web to size and use to attach each of the ribbons.

2 Turn in the raw edges and stitch the ribbons to the pillowcase at each end. Hand sew with tiny stitches along each long edge of the pillowcase.

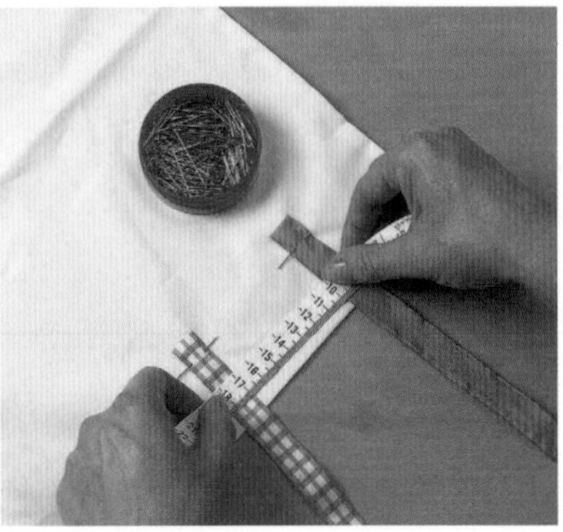

3 For the pillowcase with ties, cut two 30cm/12in lengths from each of five different narrow ribbons and pin one of each pair at regular intervals along the folded edge of the pillowcase opening. Stitch in place at the ends.

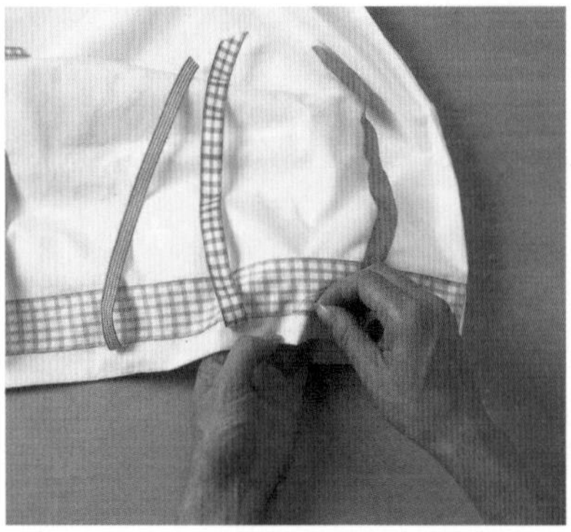

4 Use fusible bonding web to attach a length of wide ribbon to conceal the stitched ends of the ties. Hand or machine stitch around all four edges.

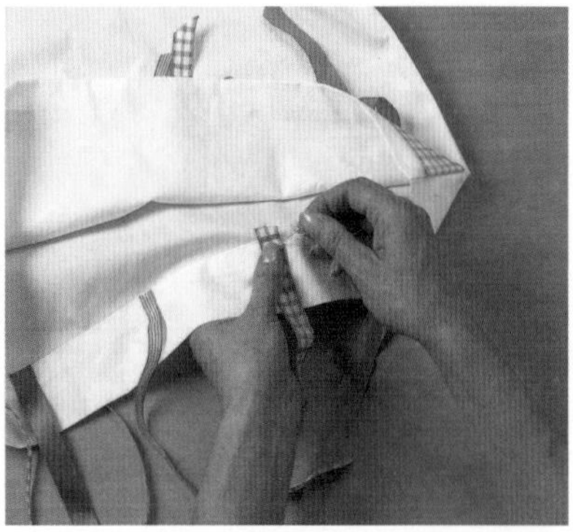

5 Attach the matching ribbon lengths to the other side of the pillowcase opening, folding in the raw edges and stitching neatly to secure.

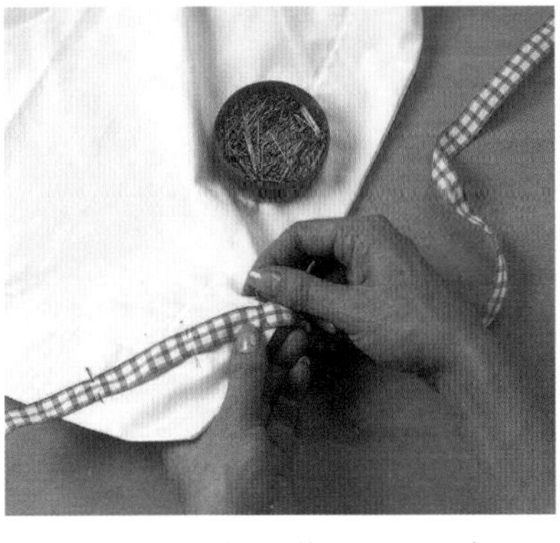

6 To decorate the pillowcase with ties, cut lengths of ribbon of differing widths and pin them across the corners. Slip stitch to secure.

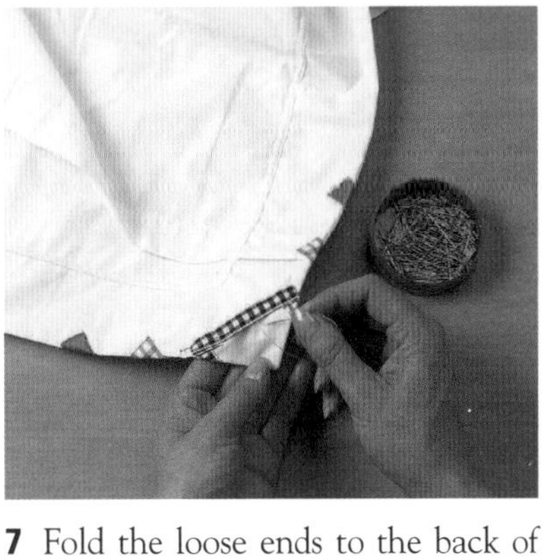

7 Fold the loose ends to the back of the pillowcase. Cut a second length of each ribbon, tuck under the ends to conceal the raw edges and slip stitch in place.

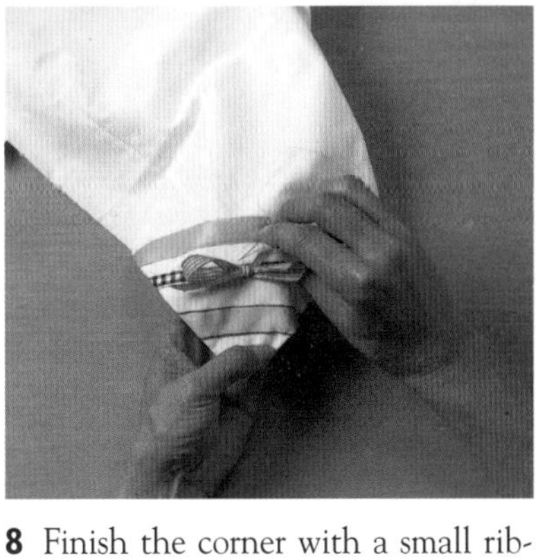

8 Finish the corner with a small ribbon bow, stitched through the knot to prevent it from coming undone.

The pleasure given by your gifts will be doubled when they are presented in these gorgeous wrappings. Plain boxes – new or recycled – can be painted brightly and adorned with ribbons to suit any occasion.

Gift Boxes

you will need

- Wire-edged shot-taffeta ribbons in various widths
- Gift boxes
- Scissors
- Tape measure
- PVA (white) glue
- Needle and matching threads

Red gift box

1 Cut a 105cm/41in length of 4cm/1½in ribbon and fold into seven 15cm/6in concertina pleats. Trim the ribbons into chevrons. Carefully cut a small nick in the centre of each long side and tie a small piece of ribbon around the middle to secure the loops.

2 Open out each fold to make a rounded loop. Hold the bow in place on the gift box lid. Tuck the ends of the ribbon under the box lid and glue in place. Cut off the excess ribbon.

Large purple gift box

Cut four lengths of green ribbon. Wrap each length around one side of the box and tie in a single loop bow at one corner. Slip each new ribbon under the previous bow. Cut the end of each ribbon into a chevron.

Green gift box

1 Wrap a length of purple wire-edged shot-taffeta ribbon around the gift box and cut off, leaving a little extra for tying a knot. Fold the ribbon into small pleats widthways at regular intervals. Secure the pleats with neat stitches in matching thread.

2 Wrap the ribbon around the box, gluing in place at the points where the ribbon is tied. Tie the ribbon in a knot close to one corner of the box and cut the ribbon ends in chevrons.

Small purple gift box

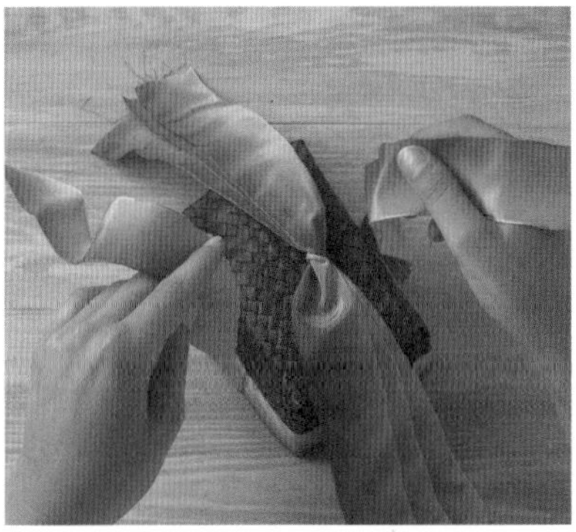

1 Glue a length of pink ribbon around the edge of the lid. Cut two equal lengths of ribbon and glue one end of each to the inside of the lid on opposite sides. Cut three 38cm/15in lengths of ribbon and twist together in the middle. Place the twist in the centre of the lid and tie the two glued ribbons together over the twisted ribbons.

2 Making sure that the ends are all level, tie all eight ribbons together with an overhand knot. Cut the ends at a diagonal angle and ease the ribbons apart to give depth to the trim.

Dark purple gift box

Cut two lengths of pink ribbon. Tie one length around the box in one direction and the other ribbon in the opposite direction. Holding the ribbons together in pairs, fasten in a single-loop bow. Pull the loops and tails apart. Cut the extending ribbon ends into chevrons.

Pamper yourself with these co-ordinating accessories – easily and quickly made by adding pretty ribbons to bathroom basics – but don't forget to check that both the ribbon and accessory are washable.

Bathroom Set

you will need

White hand towel:
Dressmaker's pins
Tape measure
Crewel needle
Red double-face satin ribbon, 3.5m x 3mm/4yd x 1/8in
Scissors

Black mesh container:
Dressmaker's pins
Tape measure
Red spotted double-face satin ribbon, 11.75m x 3mm/13yd x 1/8in
Red double-face satin ribbon, 1.5m x 3mm/1 2/3yd x 1/8in
Small red starfish
PVA (white) glue
Scissors
Crewel needle
Needle and matching threads

Wash mitt:
Black spotted double-face satin ribbon, 25cm x 1cm/10 x 1/2in
Scissors
Needle and matching thread
Black spotted ribbon, 1.5m x 2.5cm/1 1/2yd x 1in

White hand towel

Place pins 2.5cm/1in apart along all four edges of the towel. Thread a crewel needle with the red ribbon. Insert the needle at one pin and bring it out at the next. Knot the ends of the ribbon together neatly so that the ribbon lies flat against the towel. Cut off the excess ribbon, leaving short tails.

Black mesh container

1 Decorate the rim of the lid and base of the container with the spotted ribbon, as for the towel. Glue the starfish around the sides.

2 To make a tassel, bunch together 26 x 38cm/15in lengths of red spotted ribbon. Cut two 30cm/12in lengths of the red ribbon. Fold one length in half and wrap it around the middle of the bunch. Thread the ends through the loop and pull tightly.

3 Thread a crewel needle with the remaining ribbon. Bind it tightly around the tassel, then slip the needle behind the binding ribbon and pull tightly. Trim the tassel ends level, then sew it to the centre of the lid.

Wash mitt

Cut a length of 1cm/1/3in black spotted ribbon to fit the strap, adding an extra 1cm/1/2in. Turn under 6mm/1/4in at each end and stitch the ribbon to the strap. Cut three long lengths of 2.5cm/1in black spotted ribbon. Place them on top of each other and tie in a bow around the strap.

This project uses simple ribbon-embroidered flowers to great effect. To vary the bag, embroider multi-coloured flowers directly on to striped cotton and tie with matching ribbon.

Ribbon-embroidered Bag

you will need

White loose-weave waffle fabric, 30 x 25cm/12 x 10in
Embroidery hoop
Deep blue, pink, purple and yellow satin ribbons, 1m x 3mm/1yd x ⅛in of each
Chenille needle
Iron
Scissors
Emerald green satin ribbon, 70cm x 3mm/27½ x ⅛in
Bright blue satin ribbon, 1.75m x 3mm/2yd x ⅛in
Green and white striped fabric, 25 x 13cm/10 x 5in
Dressmaker's pins
Matching thread
Pot pourri

1 Place the fabric in an embroidery hoop. Starting 10cm/4in in from one long edge, work a row of eight lazy daisy stitch flowers in deep blue, pink, purple and yellow ribbon (see Basic Techniques) over 20cm/8in. Space them evenly and make each flower 2cm/¾in in diameter. Work a French knot in the centre of each flower.

2 Press the fabric lightly and trim to 25 x 20cm/10 x 8in so the flowers lie 7.5cm/3in from the bottom. Thread the needle with emerald green ribbon and weave two horizontal lines through the top threads of the fabric to form a border on either side of the flowers. With bright blue ribbon, weave seven vertical lines.

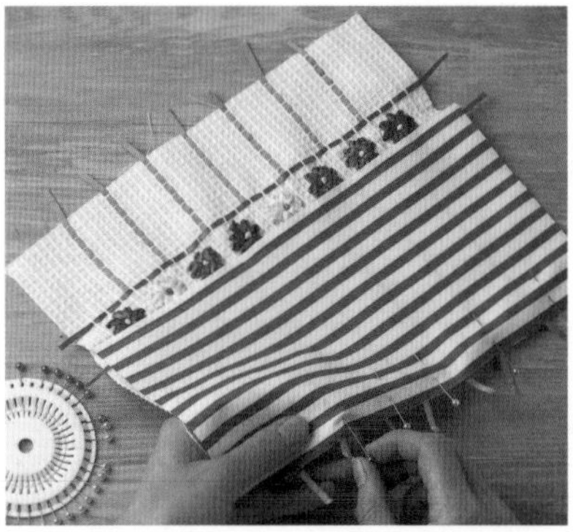

3 Pin and stitch the green and white fabric along the top edge of the waffle fabric, right sides facing, with a 1cm/½in seam allowance. Open out and press the seam. Fold in half vertically, right sides of the lining facing. Pin and stitch a side seam along the edge.

4 Pin and stitch along the bottom edge. Clip the corners and turn right-side out. Push the green lining to the inside and press the top edge. Fill with pot pourri. Complete by tying the remaining ribbons into a bow around the neck of the bag.

Inspired by fond memories of 1950s raffia baskets, this design uses ribbon embroidery to emblazon a plain shopping basket with a scattering of simple coloured daisies.

Embroidered Basket

you will need

Thin card (stock)
Pencil
Craft (utility) knife
Fabric marker
Straw basket
Large-eyed tapestry needle
Narrow embroidery ribbons
Needle and matching threads
Matchstick (wooden match)

1 Cut out the template at the back of the book from card. Following the main picture as a guide, mark two rows of flowers around the basket, changing the angle of each one as you work, to give variety to the pattern.

2 Thread the tapestry needle with green ribbon, then make a long stitch from one end of the stem to the other. Finish off with a knot on the wrong side. Using a sewing needle and matching thread, couch down the ribbon along the marked line with small straight stitches.

3 To make the centre of the flower, thread the tapestry needle with a length of ribbon and make a small stitch over a matchstick. Do not pull the ribbon tight. Make a second small stitch over the matchstick and then remove it. Work five more "knots" around the centre.

4 For the petals, thread the tapestry needle with ribbon and knot the end. Insert the needle on the wrong side and bring it out next to the centre knots. Insert the needle at the same point and return to the wrong side leaving a loop about 2.5cm/1in long.

5 Thread a sewing needle with matching thread and, bringing it out to the right side at the tip of the petal, sew down the loop. Repeat all around the flower. Continue stitching the flowers until the bag is complete.

Trimming is the main function of ribbon, and here a plain place mat is transformed to brighten up a simple table setting. As with any other item that will be laundered, check the ribbon is washable.

Ribbon Table Mats

you will need

Woven table mats
Ruler
Contrasting grosgrain ribbon, 1cm/½in wide
Contrasting checked ribbon, 2.5cm/1in wide
Toning grosgrain ribbon, 15mm/⅝in wide
Scissors
Dressmaker's pins
Needle and contrasting and matching threads
Iron and damp cloth

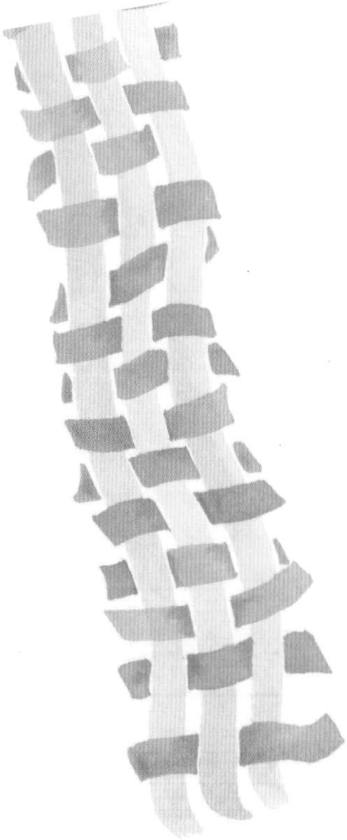

1 Calculate the ribbon requirements by measuring all around the edges of the table mats, adding 20cm/8in for turnings. Cut each colour of ribbon into four lengths, one for each edge of the mat plus a 2.5cm/1in turning allowance at each end.

2 Starting from the outside edge, lay the ribbons in place around the mat. Use the ruler to ensure the ribbons are parallel to the edge. Pin each one in place, leaving the ends free.

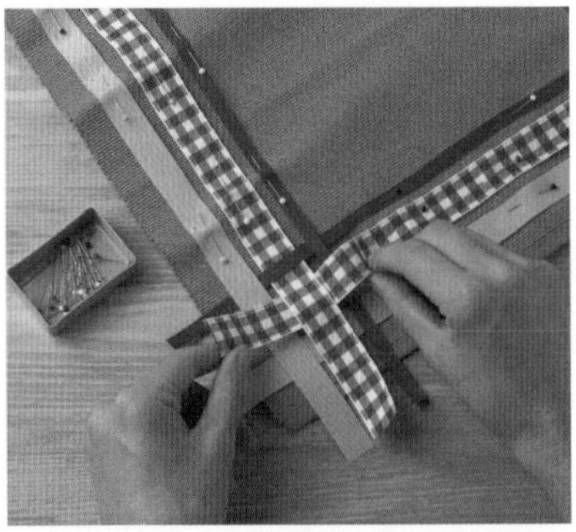

3 Interlace the ribbons to produce a woven effect where they meet and overlap at the corners and pin in place. Tack (baste) them down with contrasting thread and remove the pins.

4 Sew the ribbons down with matching thread using an invisible slip stitch along each edge, working the stitches closely together. Turn under the raw ends and sew to the back of the table mat. Press the piece under a damp cloth with the right side down.

Let fresh air in and keep flies out with a brilliant Mexican-style curtain. Each length ends with a large glass bead to add weight and substance: the number required depends on the width of the door frame.

Ribbon Door Curtain

you will need

Tape measure
Length of 2.5 x 2.5cm/1 x 1in wooden batten (furring strip)
Hacksaw
Drill and drill bit
Ruler
Pencil
Double-face satin ribbon in six bright colours, 15mm/⅝in wide
Scissors
Coloured glass disc-shaped beads
Staple gun
2 wood screws
Screwdriver

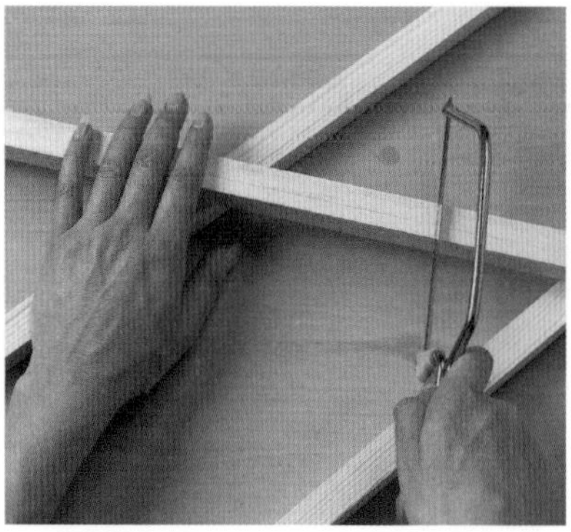

1 Measure the width of your door frame. Mark the distance on the wooden batten, then use the hacksaw to cut it to the correct length. It should fit snugly inside the top of the door frame.

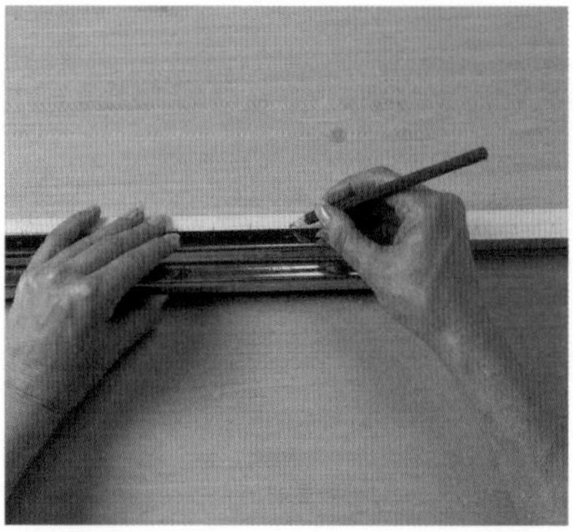

2 Draw a pencil line along the centre of the batten. Make a mark every 2.5cm/1in along the batten to indicate the positions where the ribbons will be attached. Drill a hole through the mark closest to each end to hold the screws.

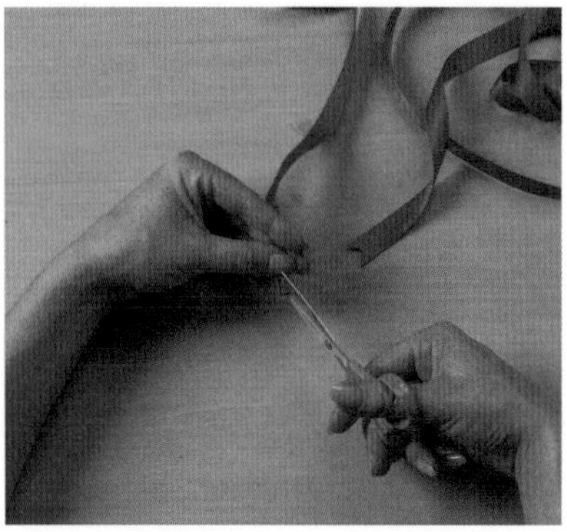

3 Cut a length of satin ribbon for each point marked on the batten, about 15cm/6in longer than the door measurement to allow for attachment and tying on the glass beads. Trim one end of each length into neat points.

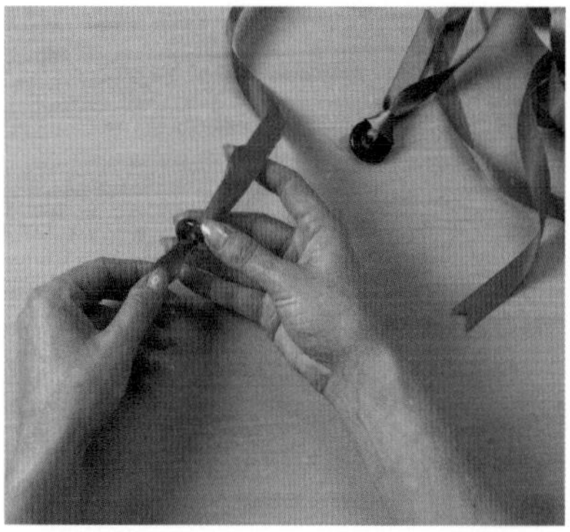

4 Fold the trimmed end over for about 10cm/4in, then push the folded end through the hole in the centre of a glass bead. Pull the whole length of the ribbon through the loop and pull taut to hold the bead securely. Repeat with all the ribbon lengths.

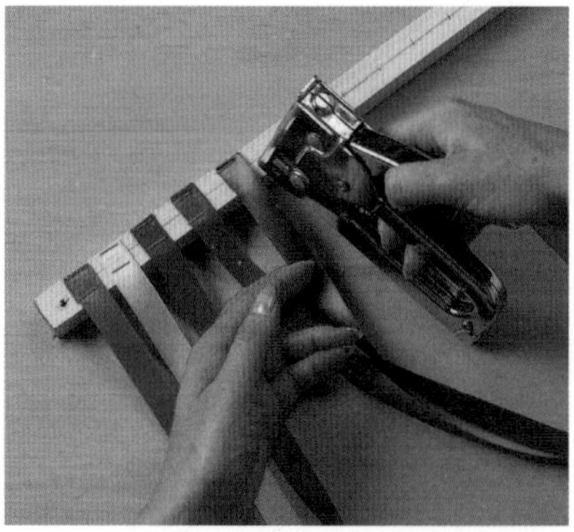

5 Fold under 15mm/⅝in at the other end of each ribbon and staple to the batten at a pencil mark, checking they are all the same length as you go. Follow the same colour sequence all across the curtain. Finally, attach the batten to the door frame with two long woodscrews.

Bring instant colour and a touch of Asian opulence to your home with this dazzling cushion. The richly textured woven metallic braids have a luxurious feel and many interesting combinations can be achieved.

Golden Braid Cushion

you will need

Approximately 18 different patterned gold braids, 1m/40in of each
Red and green satin ribbons, 1.75m x 15mm/2yd x 5/8in
Tape measure
Scissors
Striped ticking, 75 x 40cm/30 x 16in
Dressmaker's pins
Needle and matching threads
Iron
Co-ordinating backing fabric, 60 x 30cm/24 x 12in
Cushion pad, 60 x 30cm/24 x 12in
Heavy gold furnishing cord, 1.75m/2yd

1 Cut the braids and ribbons into 40cm/16in lengths. Starting at the centre and using the woven lines of the ticking as a guide, pin the braid and ribbon in place. Arrange the colours for dramatic effect, interspersing the gold braid with red and green satin ribbons. Sew down using a narrow zigzag stitch, working slowly and carefully to avoid puckering.

2 When the ticking is completely covered, press from the back with a cool iron. Trim the edges so that the piece measures 60 x 30cm/24 x 12in. Turn under a 1cm/⅓in allowance on one short edge and hem. Make a 1cm/½in hem along one short edge of the backing fabric. With right sides facing, pin then sew the front and backing together around the three raw edges.

3 Clip the corners, turn through and press lightly. Insert the pad and slip stitch the opening (see Basic Stitching Techniques).

4 Slip stitch the furnishing cord around the edge of the cushion, making a small decorative loop at each corner.

A relatively small amount of expensive ribbon makes a big difference to this natural linen throw. Antique-style crushed velvet ribbon applied diagonally across the throw brings an element of real luxury.

Ribboned Throw

you will need

Natural linen, 1.5m/5ft square
Fabric marker
Ruler
Iron
Crushed velvet ribbons, 3cm/1¼in and 15mm/⅝in wide
Scissors
Dressmaker's pins
Tape measure
Sewing-machine
Matching thread
Silk lining, 167cm/5ft 7in square (widths joined if necessary)
Needle

1 Lay the linen flat, then use a ruler and fabric marker to mark a border all around the square, 7cm/2¾in from the edge. Fold two opposite corners together and press along the crease to make a diagonal fold across the centre.

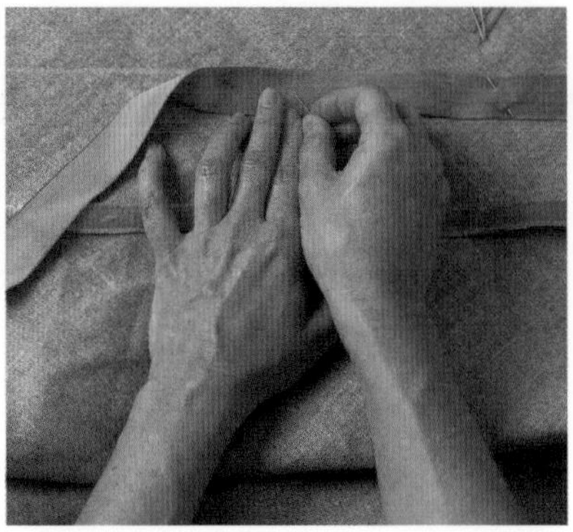

2 Using the picture as a guide, pin the velvet ribbon diagonally across the linen following the direction of the fold and alternating the widths. Cut the ribbon to overlap the border by 2.5cm/1in at each end.

3 Machine stitch the ribbons in place, stitching close to the edges. To ensure that the ribbon lies flat, stitch both edges in the same direction.

4 With right sides together, match two opposite edges of the lining fabric to the border line marked on the linen. Pin and machine stitch the seams, starting and finishing 2cm/¾in from each end of the marked lines.

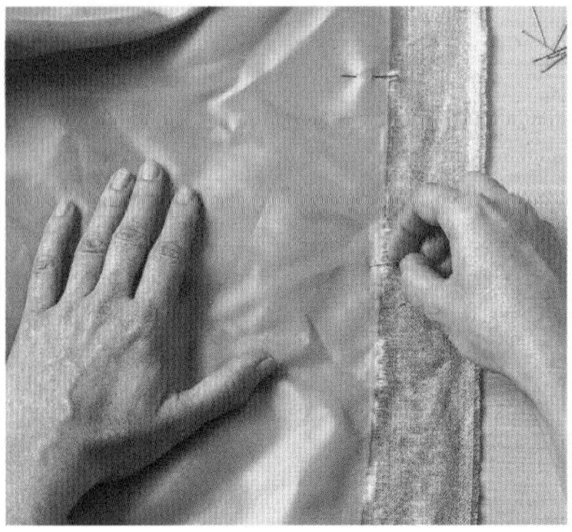

5 Match the two remaining edges in the same way. Machine stitch the edges together, leaving a 30cm/12in gap on one side.

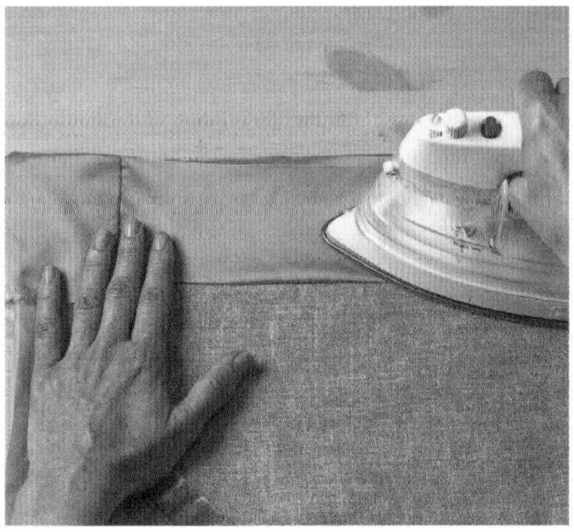

6 Turn the fabric through to the right side. Centre the linen to give an even border 7cm/2¾in wide and press with a warm iron.

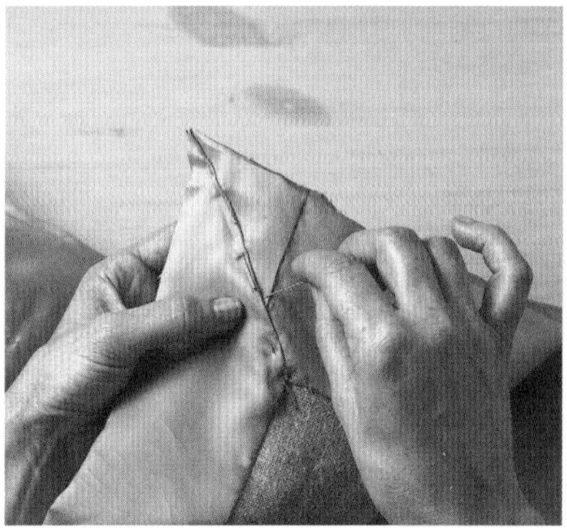

7 Turn in the lining along the opening edge and press. Slip stitch the gap closed. At the corners, trim and tuck in the excess fabric to form a mitred seam. Press and ladder stitch or slip stitch the folded edges together.

Bands of satin, velvet and taffeta ribbon across this silk cushion make up a symphony of rich textures. Though all the tones are similar, light plays on the ribbons in different ways, creating dramatic contrasts.

Striped Ribbon Cushion

you will need

Silk fabric, 80 x 45cm/32 x 18in
Tape measure
Dressmaking scissors
Iron
Selection of satin, velvet and taffeta ribbons
Dressmaker's pins
Needle and tacking (basting) thread
Stranded embroidery thread (floss) in complementary colours
Velvet, 20 x 40cm/8 x 16in
Sewing-machine, with zip foot
Matching thread
Piping cord; 2m/2yd
Zip, 40cm/16in
Cushion pad, 40cm/16in square

1 For the cushion front, cut a 45cm/18in square from the silk fabric. Fold diagonally through the centre and press. Arrange lengths of ribbon side by side across the fabric, using the fold as a guide, and pin in place. When you are satisfied with the ribbon positions, tack (baste) the ribbons to the front of the cushion.

2 Using stranded embroidery thread in a range of colours to complement the ribbons, work rows of feather stitch to join the edges, varying the direction of the stitches. Fold the velvet diagonally and cut 4cm/1½in wide strips parallel with the diagonal.

3 Stitch the short edges together with a 6mm/¼in seam allowance and press open to make a length of bias binding. Pin the binding around the piping cord and machine stitch in place.

4 Pin the covered cord all around the cushion front with the raw edges matching. Clip the seam allowance at the corners so that it lies flat. Tack, then machine stitch close to the cord.

5 Unpick 2cm/¾in of the machine stitching from the beginning of the piping. Trim the cord so the ends butt together and lap one end of the casing over the other, turning under the raw edges. Pin to the cover and machine stitch. Slip stitch the casing edge.

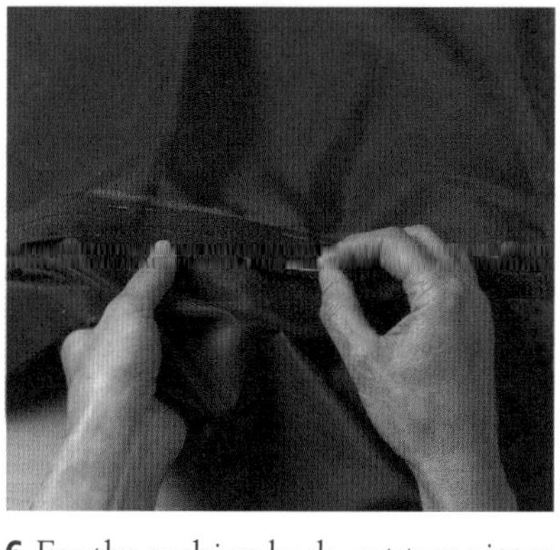

6 For the cushion back, cut two pieces of silk 23 x 45cm/9 x 18in. With right sides together, match the two long edges and machine stitch using a long stitch setting. Press the seam open. Centre the zip over the back of the seam and tack in place.

7 Using a zip foot on the sewing-machine, top stitch around the zip. Unpick the temporary seam. Undo the zip. With right sides together, pin and machine stitch the cushion back and front together, following the line of piping. Clip the corners, turn through and insert the cushion pad.

Customize a child's denim jacket with this colourful sunflower. Ribbon appliqué is deceptively simple to work, as the woven edges mean no fussy hemming, and tricky curves and angles are easy.

Sunflower-motif Jacket

you will need
Denim jacket
Brown double-face satin ribbon, 1.5m x 1cm/1⅔yd x ½in
Needle and matching threads
Yellow double-face satin ribbon, 1m x 4cm/40 x 1½in
Scissors
Leaf-green double-face satin ribbon, 50 x 4cm/40 x 1½in
Embroidery threads (floss)

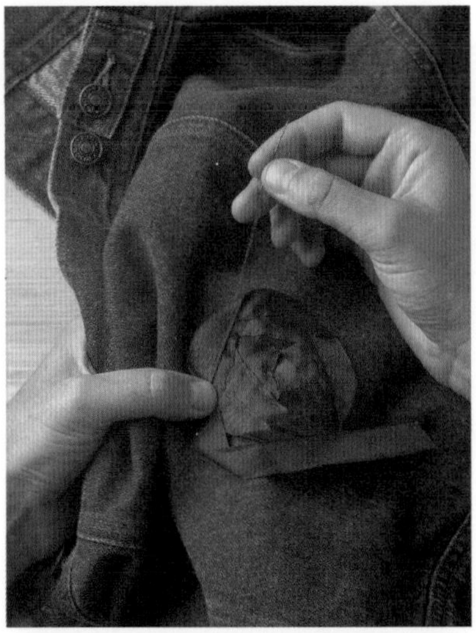

1 Mark the design area on the jacket as a rough guide for the appliqué work. Start by stitching the end of the brown ribbon to the centre of the design area. Sew the ribbon in a spiral, overlapping the coils and turning the ribbon over itself to form a circle. Sew along the inside edge of the ribbon as you make the spiral, using back stitch or running stitch to secure the outer edge of the previous coil (see Basic Techniques). Leave the outer edge of the completed spiral unsewn.

2 Make 11 flower petal shapes from yellow ribbon, snipping a curve along each side of the tip without cutting the straight edges.

3 Stitch the petals around the flower centre, turning under the raw edges and tucking the base of each petal under the unsewn edge of the centre of the flower.

4 Continue adding petals around the centre, overlapping some of the edges. Leave a gap at the bottom for the last two flower petals to be added after the flower stem.

5 Cut the flower stem from the leaf-green ribbon. Tuck one end under the outer edge of the flower centre and sew the stem in place, using green embroidery thread. Turn under the bottom raw edge before stitching. Sew the last two petals over the stem.

6 Sew down the outer edge of the flower centre, securing the petals and the top of the stem. Decorate the centre with French knots of various sizes worked in brown embroidery thread.

7 To finish off, cut two leaves from the green ribbon and stitch to either side of the stem. Stitch veins on the leaves using a small running stitch and green embroidery thread.

A great advantage of ribbon is its versatility. Here pieces of richly patterned ribbon have been fashioned into a stunning necklace – an idea that could be extended to make a bracelet or earrings to match.

Ribbon Jewellery

you will need

Thin white card (stock)
Pencil
Ruler
Scissors
Wire-edged patterned ribbon, 40 x 5cm/16 x 2in
Super epoxy clear glue
Glue spreader or paintbrush
Needle and matching thread
Round and tubular beads, 15mm/⅝in wide
Plastic-coated garden wire
Toning ribbon, approximately 75cm x 3mm/30 x ⅛in
Small gold beads
Necklace clasp

1 Cut six 7 x 4cm/2¾ x 1½in rectangles from the card and roll each one carefully into a tube.

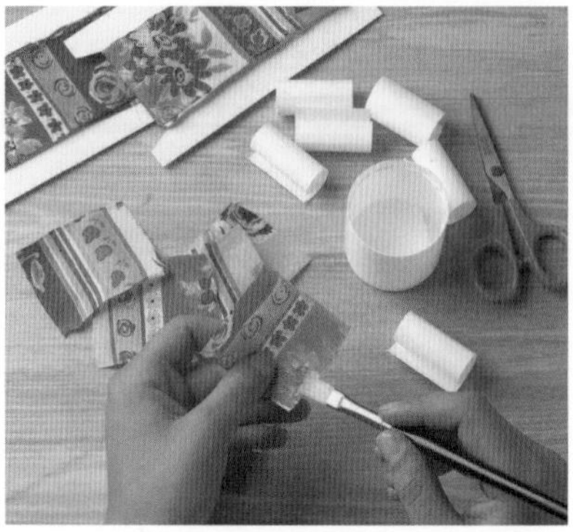

2 Cut six 7cm/2¾in strips of patterned ribbon, selecting the pattern area you want to use along the ribbon. Glue one end of each piece of ribbon on to the outside end of each tube of paper. Allow to dry.

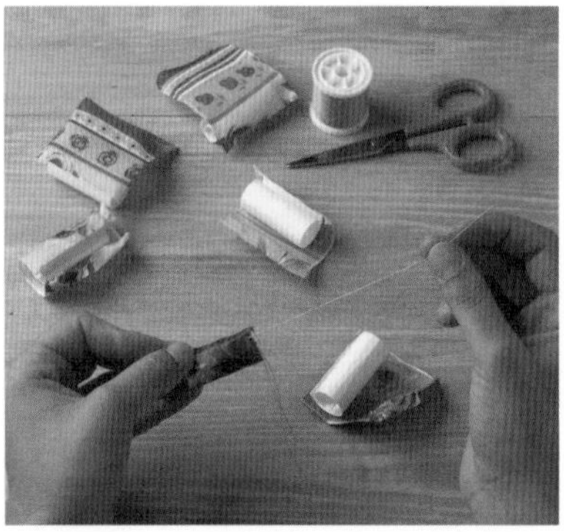

3 Fold over the other end of the ribbon by 6mm/¼in. Roll the ribbon around the tube so that the edges of the ribbon meet. Stitch down the join. Push the wired edges of the ribbon into the tube. Apply glue to both ends of the tubes and press on a bead.

4 Hold the beads in place while the glue dries by threading a piece of wire through each tube and bending the end around. Thread the ribbon-covered tubes on to the 3mm/⅛in ribbon with gold and coloured beads arranged in a repeating pattern in between.

5 Thread a clasp on to the ends of the ribbon. Fold each ribbon end back on itself and stitch down, wrapping the thread over the stitching. Knot the end of the ribbon and wrap again with thread to cover the knot. Secure the thread firmly before cutting it off.

Fun to make and bound to be a conversation piece, these plaid roses can be adapted to suit many festive occasions: as part of a garland, as a table centrepiece or stitched to a bag, gown or satin slippers.

Tartan Ribbon Roses

you will need

For one rose:

Tartan ribbon, 60 x 4cm/24 x 1½in

Stub (floral) wire, 20cm/8in

Needle and matching thread

Craft scissors

Tartan wire-edged ribbon, 30 x 4cm/12 x 1½in

Fine florist's wire

Florist's tape (stem wrap)

1 Bend the end of a piece of stub wire to form a hook equal in depth to the ribbon width. Holding the tartan ribbon with the cut end to the right, hook the wire through the upper right-hand corner of the ribbon, approximately 6mm/¼in from the edge. Close the hook to hold the ribbon in place.

2 Roll the ribbon around the hook two or three times from right to left to enclose the wire. Stitch at the base to secure. Then, holding the wire stem in your right hand and the loose ribbon in your left, fold the ribbon so that it runs downwards, parallel to the wire.

3 Roll the covered hook end from right to left into the fold, turning tightly at the bottom and loosely at the top until the ribbon is once again horizontal to the wire.

4 With the wire stem facing towards you, stitch the base of the rose to secure the petal in place.

5 Continue folding the ribbon and rolling the rose in this way, stitching the base after each fold until you have the desired shape and size of rose. To complete the rose, cut the ribbon squarely, fold it back on to the rose and stitch in place.

6 To make a leaf, cut the wire-edged ribbon into 10cm/4in lengths. Cut three 20cm/8in lengths of florist's wire and make a small loop 2.5cm/1in from the end of each one. Fold two corners of a piece of ribbon down and forward into a triangle. Place a wire in the centre with the short end upwards and stitch it in place.

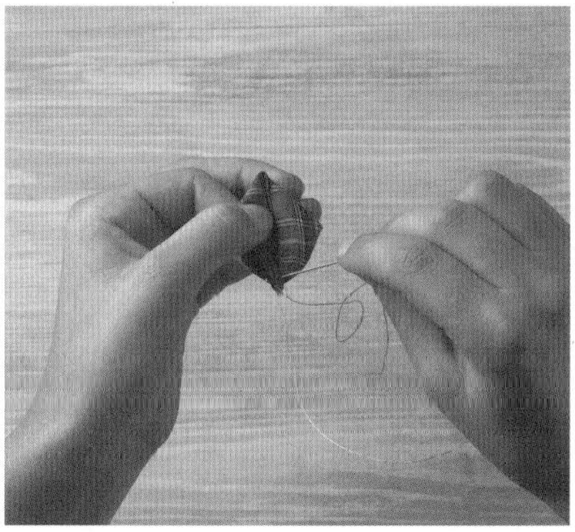

7 Fold the lower corners of the ribbon triangle under and backwards to create a leaf shape. Gather the lower part of the leaf neatly around the long wire stem and stitch to secure in place. Make two more leaves in this way.

8 Bind the wire stems of two leaves with florist's tape for 1cm/½in. Bind the wire stem of the third leaf for 2.5cm/1in. Join the three leaves together at this point and continue binding all three wires to create a single stem. Bind the rose stem, adding in the triple leaf about 10cm/4in down from the flower.

Lantern frames are available in many different shapes and sizes, so this idea is very versatile. Measure the four sides of the frame and select a width of ribbon that can be multiplied to fit into this length exactly.

Ribbon Lantern

you will need

Basic lantern frame
Tape measure
Ribbon, length and width depending on size of frame
Scissors
Iron
Needle and matching threads
Beads (one small, one large and one rocaille per ribbon)
PVA (white) glue

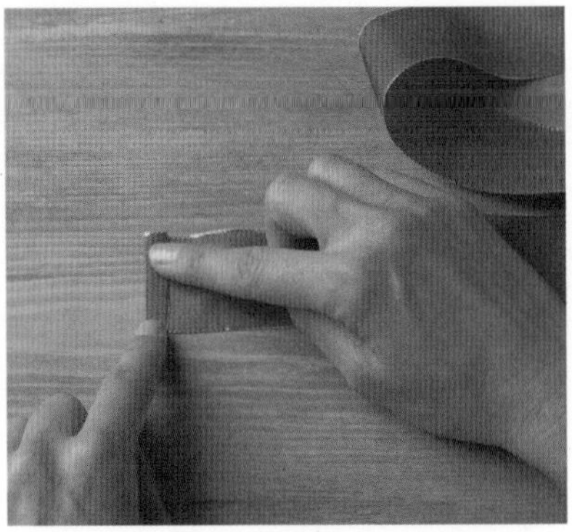

1 Cut pieces of ribbon to twice the finished frame length. To mitre one end of each ribbon, turn in 1cm/½in along the raw edge and press lightly with a dry iron to hold in place.

2 Fold in one corner to the centre of the ribbon, then fold in the other corner to make a triangular, mitred point. Iron to hold in position.

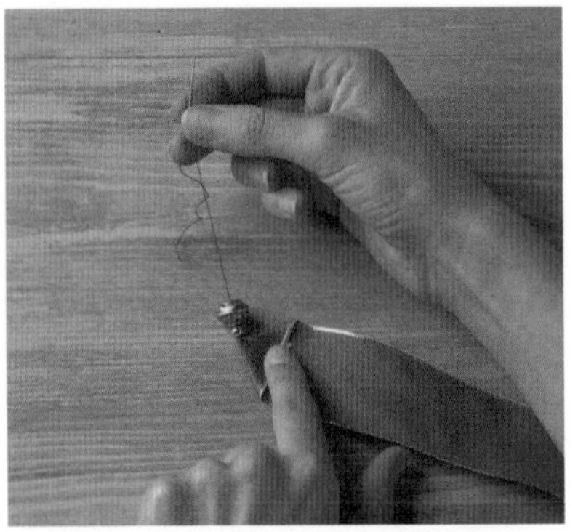

3 Thread a needle and tie a knot in one end. Pass the needle through the point of the mitre, then thread a small bead followed by a large bead and a rocaille. Pass the needle back through the large and small bead so the rocaille forms a stopper. Secure with a small stitch on the inside of the point.

4 Starting close to the final stitch, slip stitch along the central join of the mitre, keeping a neat point at the end of the triangle (see Basic Techniques).

5 Turn the other end of the ribbon over, and loop the ribbon over one side of the frame. Fold under and slip stitch the other end of the ribbon to the top of the mitre, making sure that the wrong sides of the ribbon will be inside the frame. Make all the other ribbons in this way.

Give your prettiest clothes the care they deserve with these luxurious padded hangers, decorated with roses and bows made from exquisite silk and brocade ribbons in beautiful muted shades.

Ribbon-Rose Coat Hangers

you will need
Polyester wadding (batting)
Scissors
Wooden coat hangers
Needle and matching thread
Satin ribbon, 8cm/3in wide
Selection of organza, silk, petersham or grosgrain and brocade ribbons

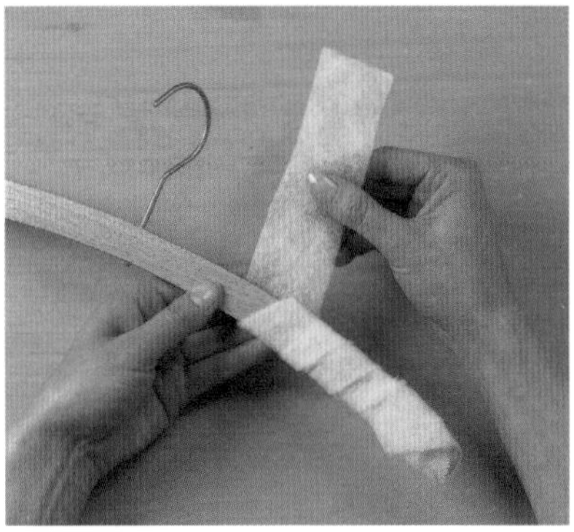

1 Cut a 5cm/2in wide strip of polyester wadding and wind it around the wooden part of a hanger. Secure it with a few stitches at each end.

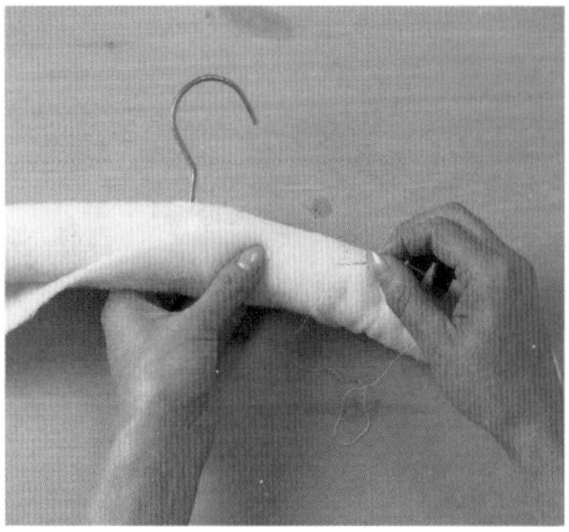

2 Cut a long, narrow rectangle of wadding to cover the hanger. Fold it over the bound wadding and sew in place along the top edge, folding over and neatening the ends as you go.

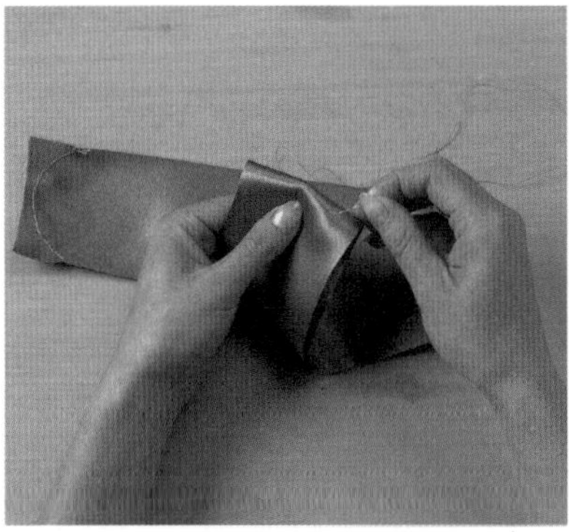

3 Cut two lengths of wide satin ribbon to make the cover for the hanger and, with right sides together, stitch each end in a gentle curve.

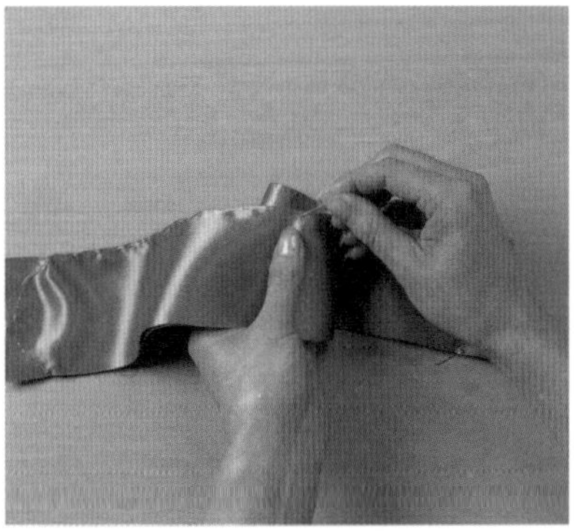

4 Stitch the two ribbons together along one long edge of the satin cover and turn to the right side.

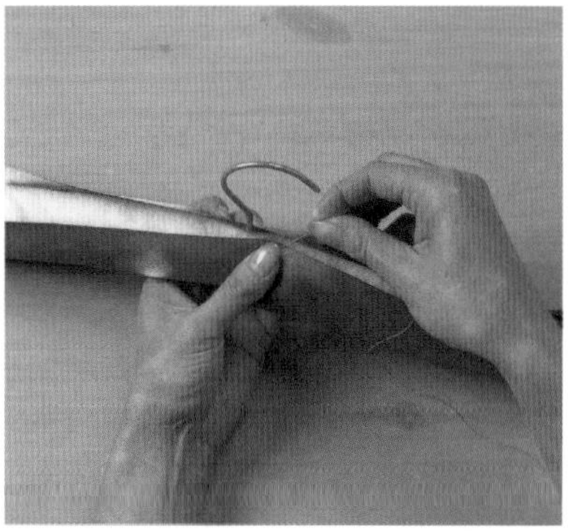

5 Fit the cover over the hanger and slip stitch the top edges neatly, gathering the ends gently and easing in the fullness as you sew.

▶

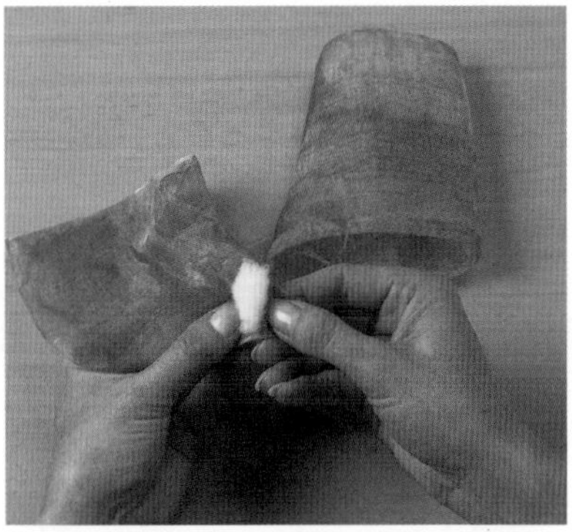

6 To make a rose to decorate the hanger, fold a tiny piece of wadding into the end of a length of organza ribbon and secure with a stitch.

7 Fold and wind the rest of the ribbon around this central bud, stitching through the layers to secure. Tuck in the raw edge and stitch down. Make two roses for each hanger.

8 To make a rosette, cut a length of silk ribbon about five times its width and join the raw edges.

9 Gather the ribbon with a running stitch slightly above the centre. Pull up and secure. Flatten the ribbon out with your fingers to complete the rosette. Make two for each hanger.

10 To make a leaf, take a small piece of green petersham or grosgrain ribbon and fold both ends down to the side. Work a running stitch along this side and pull up the gathers tightly, securing with a stitch. Make four for each hanger.

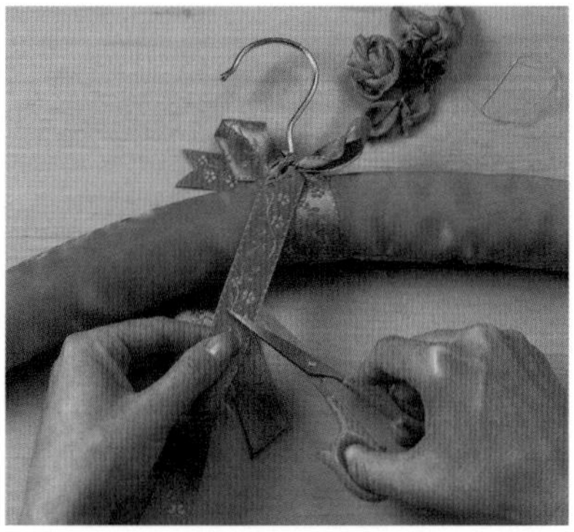

11 Tie a length of brocade ribbon around the centre of each hanger to finish in a bow around the hook. Use this as a foundation to attach the roses, leaves and rosettes. Decorate with loops of ribbon to make a pleasing arrangement.

Hat boxes make ideal storage containers for all sorts of items beside hats. The basic boxes can be bought from stationery or gift shops and, with a little imagination, the decorative possibilities are endless.

Ribbon Hat Box

●●●

you will need

35cm/14in diameter hat box
Patterned fabric, 1.5m x 115cm/1⅔yd x 45in
Dressmaking scissors
Iron
Glue gun or contact adhesive
Heavy gold cord, 1.75m/2yd
Thin card (stock)
Lining fabric, 40 x 90cm/16 x 36in
Polyester wadding (batting), 38 x 75cm/15 x 30in
Matching sewing thread
Plain ribbon, 1m x 10cm/1yd x 4in
Wire-edged gilded ribbon, 1.8m x 10cm/2yd x 4in
3 bunches artificial grapes
2 gold tassels

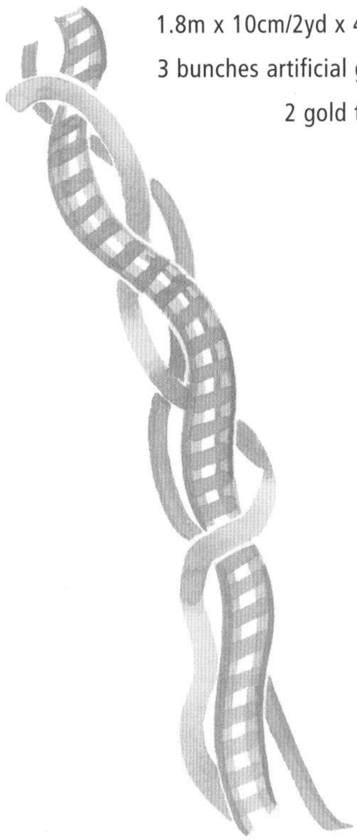

1 Cut a length of patterned fabric slightly longer than the circumference of the box and 2½ times its height. Press under 1cm/½in along one short side, then glue the fabric to the box using a glue gun or impact adhesive. Overlap the folded edge to make a neat join.

2 With the point of a pair of scissors, make a small hole ⅔ of the way up each side. Cut a 75cm/30in length of gold cord, and insert through the holes to form a carrying handle. Knot securely on the inside and glue in position if necessary.

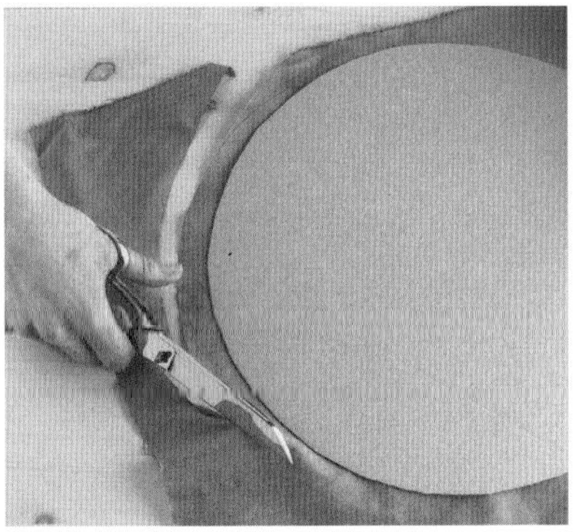

3 Cut a circle from card measuring 1cm/½in less in diameter than the base of the box. Cut out a slightly larger circle of lining fabric and use it to cover one side of the card. Smooth the fabric to prevent any wrinkles forming, then turn over and glue down the edges.

4 Fold the excess patterned fabric into the box to line the inside, smoothing the fabric so it lies neatly. Stick the covered circle to the base of the box, with the fabric-covered side uppermost. Any surplus lining fabric will be hidden underneath the card circle.

▶

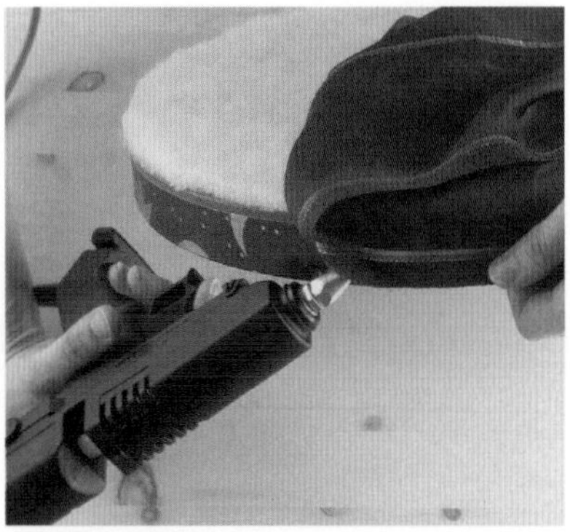

5 Cut a circle of wadding to fit the top of the box lid and glue in place. Cut a circle of the remaining fabric, slightly larger than the radius and circumference of the box lid. Glue this around the outside of the lid, matching the edge of the material with the edge of the lid to leave excess for gathering.

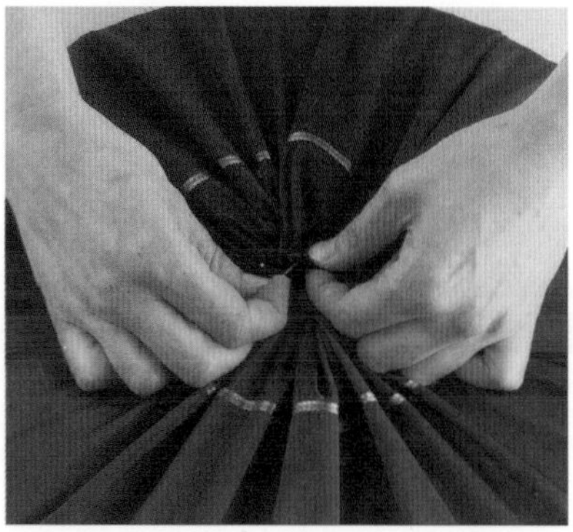

6 Run a gathering thread through the fabric 18cm/7in from the rim, draw up and secure.

7 Cut the plain ribbon in half and stretch one piece across the lid, gluing the ends inside the rim. Knot the other piece to the centre and glue the ends inside the rim, at right angles to the first.

8 Glue gold cord around the outside of the rim. Butt the two ends together and cover with a narrow strip of fabric to neaten the join.

9 Make a bow from the wire-edged ribbon. Cut the ends in fishtails and shape the loops. Glue to the centre of the lid, then stick on the grapes.

10 Finish off by sewing a tassel to each end of the handle.

The cover for this striped lampshade consists entirely of ribbons, allowing you to introduce a rich variety of colour and texture. They are simply stuck side by side on to a piece of lampshade backing material.

Satin and Velvet Ribbon Shade

●●●

you will need

Graph paper
Pencil
Drum-shaped lampshade frame with reversible gimbal, top diameter 18cm/7in, bottom diameter 20cm/8in, height 20cm/8in
Scissors
Self-adhesive lampshade backing material
Satin bias binding
Selection of coloured velvet and satin ribbons
White (PVA) glue
Clothes pegs (pins)
Needle
Matching thread
Ceramic lamp base
Spray enamel paint and face mask

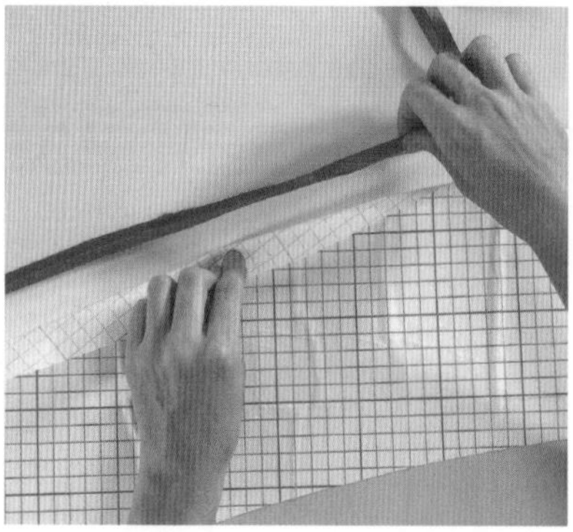

1 Make a paper pattern to fit the frame. Cut a piece of self-adhesive backing material to the size of the pattern. Remove the backing paper from the lower edge of the backing material to expose the adhesive. Cut a piece of satin bias binding to the length of the lower edge plus 2cm/¾in. Press one edge of the bias binding to the lower edge of the backing material.

2 Cut lengths of satin and velvet ribbon to fit the circumference of the shade, leaving a 1cm/½in overlap at one end. Lay a length of ribbon alongside the bias binding, following the curve of the pattern. Lay more lengths of ribbon across the backing until the last one is 6mm/¼in from the top edge. Alternate velvet with different coloured satin, and remove the paper.

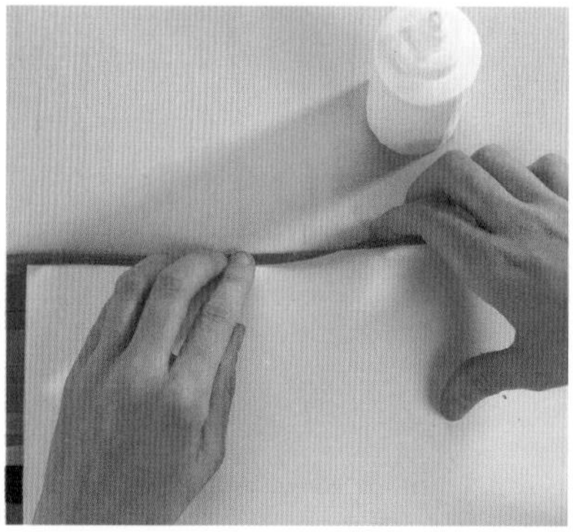

3 Cut a piece of binding to fit the top edge, with a 2cm/¾in allowance. Lay one edge of the bias binding along the top edge. Apply glue to the wrong side of the backing at top and bottom. Fold over to the wrong side.

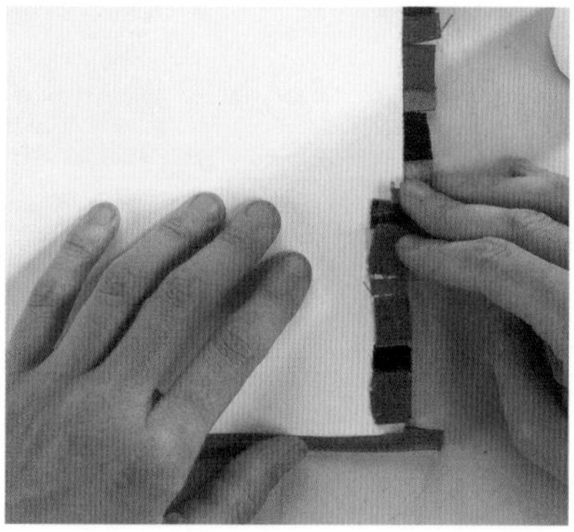

4 Apply glue to the side edge and fold the raw ribbon ends to the wrong side. Leave to dry. If the ribbons begin to curl away from the backing, place under a heavy object. Neaten untidy edges or hanging threads with scissors.

5 Apply a thin line of glue to the underside of the same edge. Take care to wipe away any glue that squeezes on to the ribbons. Roll into a drum shape and lap the glued edge over the opposite edge, matching up the stripes of colours perfectly. Use two clothes pegs to hold the edges together firmly at the top and bottom until the glue is completely dry.

6 Where the raw edges of the bias binding meet, turn under 1cm/½in of one raw edge and stick it down so that it overlaps the other raw edge. Use the clothes pegs to hold the bindings together until the glue is dry. Slip stitch the folded edge in place. Apply a line of glue to the outside edge of the frame and insert it into the cover.

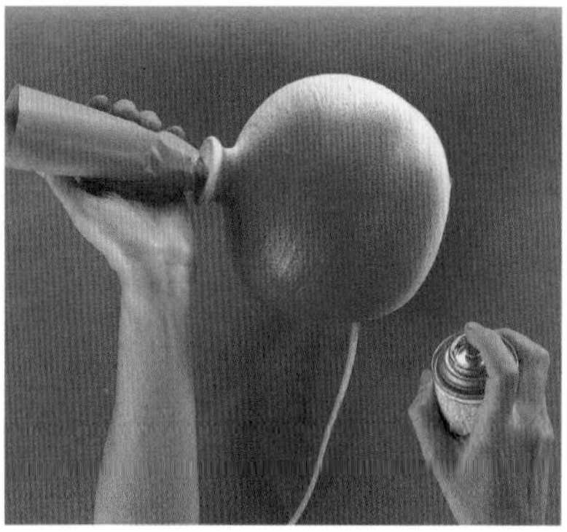

7 Working in a well-ventilated space, and wearing a face mask, spray the lamp base with a thin coat of pink enamel paint. Leave to dry before applying a second coat. Spray the shade with flame retarder if necessary, before attaching to the base. Use a medium-wattage bulb.

These subtle ribbon decorations – a combination of earthy colours and natural textures – make a welcome change from glitzy baubles. Hang them from a tree or wreath, or string them along the mantelpiece.

Ribbon Christmas Decorations

you will need

Baubles:

Polystyrene (styrofoam) balls, 7.5 or 5cm/3 or 2in diameter
Pencil
Tape measure
Gold, brown and cream ribbons, 1m x 3–9mm/40in x 1/8–3/8in
Dressmaker's pins
Scissors
Toning patterned ribbon, 2m x 3–10mm/2 1/4yd x 1/8–1/2in
Tiny gold beads
Gold-coin pendants
Brass lace pins
Large, ornate gold beads

Pine cone parcels:

Gold, lemon or brown ribbon, 4cm/1 1/2in wide
Gold or brown ribbon, 3mm/1/8in wide
Pine cones
White (PVA) glue

Golden tassel:

Cotton-pulp ball, 2.5cm/1in in diameter
Scissors
Gold grosgrain ribbon, 10m x 3mm/11yd x 1/8in
Crewel needle
White (PVA) glue

Baubles

1 Draw lines on a polystyrene ball to divide it vertically into four segments, then mark horizontally round the sphere to divide it into eighths. Place a length of ribbon along one quarter, pin the ends on the lines and trim. Fill in the section with a patchwork of assorted ribbons, taking care to overlap the edges.

2 Fill in each section. Lay the patterned ribbon over the pins and ribbon ends, following the guidelines, and pin at each point where the lines cross. Fold under the ends to neaten. Make a hanging loop by slipping a 25cm/10in length of ribbon under one intersection and knotting the ends.

3 Slip a tiny gold bead and a coin pendant on to each of 15 brass lace pins. Pin them in a row around the centre. Thread a small and a large bead on to the last pin and stick into the base of the ball to complete. Make other baubles in the same way, using different ribbons.

▶

Pine cone parcels

Tie the wide ribbon into a bow (see Basic Techniques). Wrap the narrow ribbon around a pine cone, as if wrapping a parcel, tying off at the tip. Dab with glue to secure. Make a hanging loop by tying the ends together 10cm/4in from the knot. Glue the bow to the top of the cone.

Golden tassel

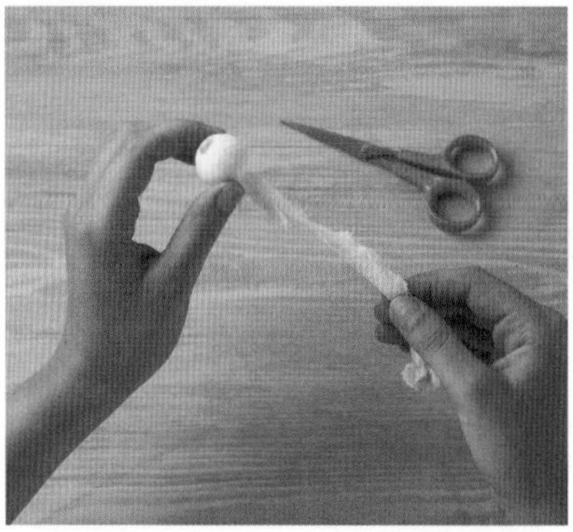

1 Use scissors to make a hole through the centre of the cotton-pulp ball. Pull out some of the fibre to enlarge the hole to 1cm/½in in diameter. Cut 25cm/10in grosgrain ribbon, then cut the rest into 30cm/12in lengths.

2 Put the 25cm/10in and a 30cm/12in length aside and use the crewel needle to thread the others through the hole. Allow 12.5cm/5in of each ribbon to hang below the ball. Spread glue thinly over the ball. Fold down the ribbons protruding from the top to cover the ball completely.

3 Thread the needle with the 25cm/10in length of ribbon. Glue one end around the ribbons close to the base of the ball. Wrap the ribbon tightly around the tassel.

4 Insert the needle behind the binding ribbon and pull tightly. Unthread the needle, allowing the ribbon end to hang down with the other ribbons. Do not trim at this stage.

5 To suspend the tassel, double the 30cm/12in length of ribbon and thread it through the needle. Insert the needle down through the hole in the ball. Remove the needle, knot the ends neatly together and trim. Gently pull the loop taut, hiding the knot among the ribbons. Trim the ends.

Ruched organza ribbons, sewn on to translucent voile in a fine tracery of delicate spirals, give an interesting, three-dimensional effect to this light and airy curtain.

Appliquéd Ribbon Café Curtain

●●●

you will need
Tape measure
Voile
Dressmaking scissors
Dressmaker's pins
Sewing-machine
Matching thread
Iron
Thin card (stock)
Pencil
Fabric marker
Needle
Organza ribbons in green and pink

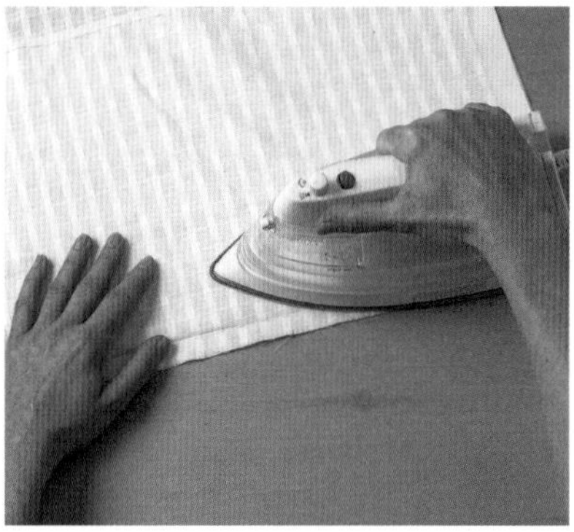

1 Calculate the width and drop of the curtain and cut out the voile, adding 5cm/2in to the width and 15cm/6in to the length. To make the facing, cut a second piece of voile to the same width by 30cm/12in. Turn under and machine stitch a 6mm/¼in hem along the lower edge of the facing. Press. With right sides together, pin the facing to the curtain, matching the top edges.

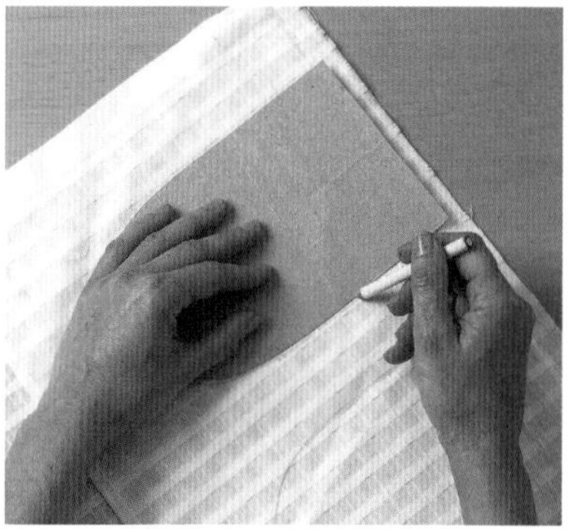

2 Enlarge the scallop template at the back of the book, and cut out of thin card. Add the width of the template to the proposed width of each fabric loop (4–7cm/1½–2¾in) and divide the finished curtain width by this figure to calculate the number of scallops required. Allow for a strip at each end of the curtain. Draw around the template along the top of the curtain, using a fabric marker.

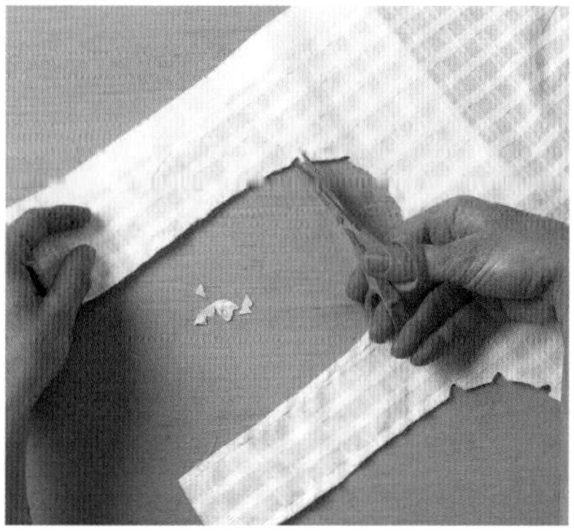

3 Machine stitch the facing to the curtain along the marked lines. Cut out the scallops, leaving a 1cm/½in seam allowance. Clip the corners and snip into the curves.

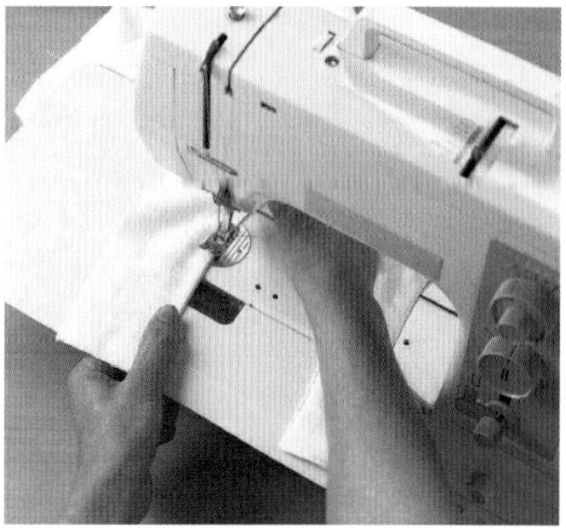

4 Turn the curtain through to the right side and press. Topstitch around the seams, 4mm/⅕in from the edge.

►

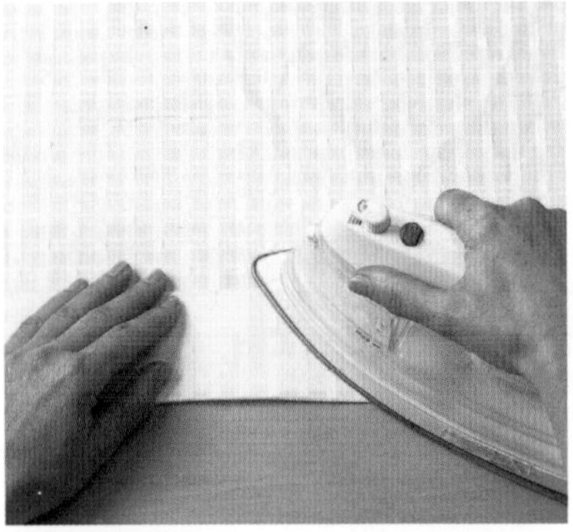

5 Turn under and press a double hem 1cm/½in wide down each side edge of the curtain. Turn under and press a 5cm/2in double hem along the bottom edge.

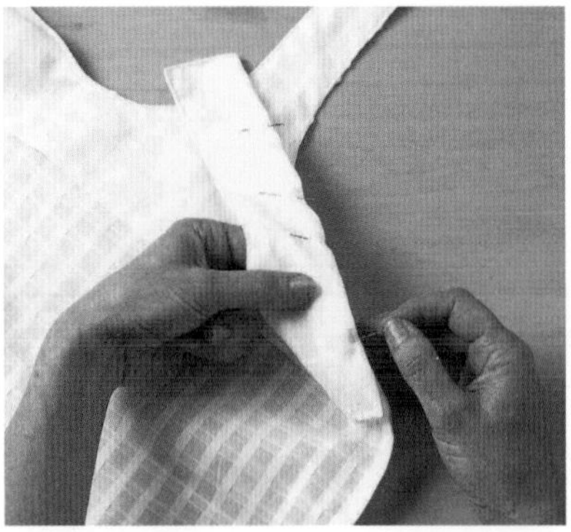

6 Mitre the corners and slip stitch them neatly in place. Turn under and press a 1cm/½in single hem down both side edges of the facing. Slip stitch the facing and all the hems in place.

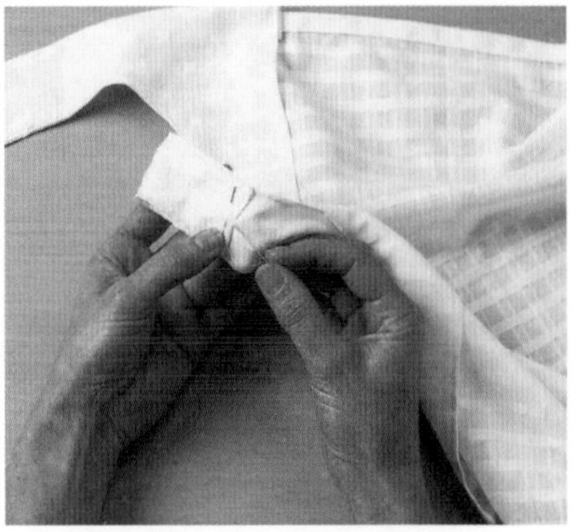

7 To make the fabric hanging loops, turn 5cm/2in of each strip to the wrong side of the curtain. Pin and slip stitch them to the facing, taking care not to let the needle pass through to the right side.

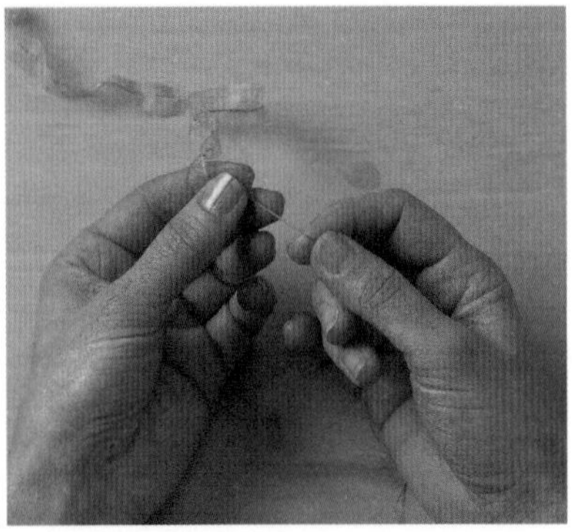

8 Cut the green ribbon into 1m/1yd lengths. Set the machine to a long straight stitch and sew down the centre of each length. Pull up the bobbin thread from each end to gather the ribbon, then adjust the ruffles so that they lie evenly.

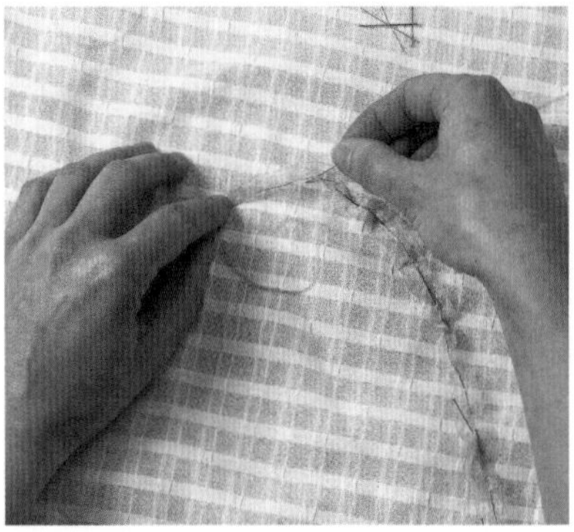

9 Draw a series of freehand spirals randomly across the curtain, using a fabric marker. Pin the ruched ribbons along the lines. Machine stitch along the gathering threads, being careful not to trap the ribbon under the stitches.

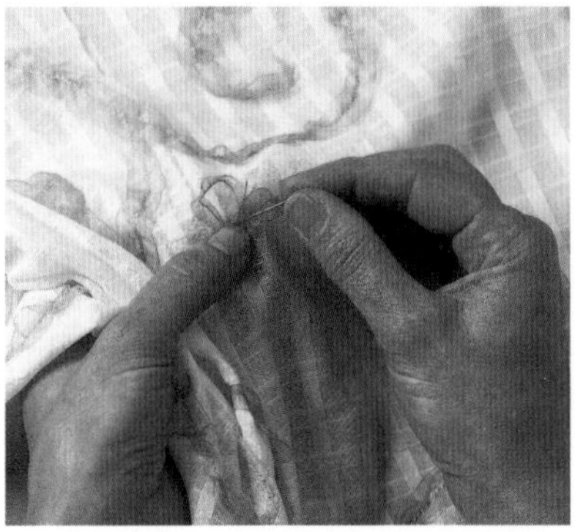

10 Gather the pink ribbon as before and cut a strip 15cm/6in long for each flower. Fold each one into three small loops and pin the flowers to the curtain in the spaces between the spirals. Machine stitch, securing the loops in place. Insert a narrow pole through the hanging loops and fix it in place at the window.

An old deckchair can be transformed with a new cover and an interesting way to make this is with grosgrain ribbon. Here, two contrasting colours have been interwoven to make a chequerboard effect.

Deck-chair Cover

you will need
Deckchair
Claw hammer or pliers
medium-grade abrasive paper
Large sheet of card (stock)
Tape measure
Pencil
Grosgrain ribbon in white and blue, 4cm/1½in wide (10m/11yd is sufficient for a small chair)
Scissors
Drawing pins (thumb tacks)
Dressmaker's pins
Needle and tacking (basting) thread
Sewing-machine and matching thread
Staple gun

1 Remove the existing canvas from the chair frame, setting it aside to use as a template and carefully prising out any old fabric fixings with a claw hammer or pliers. Sand down any rough edges on the frame and repaint if necessary.

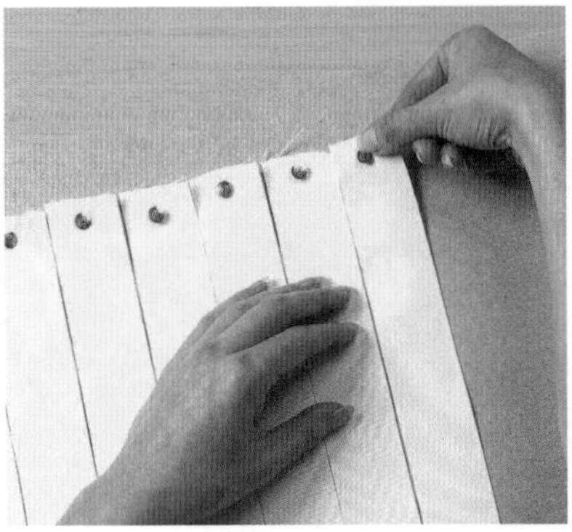

2 Mark the dimensions of the cover on the sheet of cardboard. Cut lengths of white grosgrain ribbon to the length of the measured rectangle, plus about 10cm/4in for fixing. Pin the ribbons to the board side by side along the top of the rectangle to form the "warp".

3 Cut lengths of blue ribbon to fit across the rectangle and form the "weft". To weave the cover, pin a blue ribbon to the warp length at one side, weave it under and over the warp until you reach the other side, then pin securely again.

4 Continue weaving until you have the size required. When complete, tack (baste) across the edges of the woven piece to hold the warp in place. Cut two lengths of blue ribbon to fit down each side of the new cover. Lay one length over the raw edges of the weft at each side and tack in position.

5 Remove the cover from the board and machine-stitch the blue and white ribbons together, stitching very close to both edges. Attach the new cover to the wooden frame by wrapping the ends of the ribbons around the horizontal rungs and stapling them securely in place.

The openweave effect used to make this plush cover allows the dark blue moiré taffeta backing fabric to show through the complementing richness of the brocade, velvet and jacquard ribbons.

Basket-weave Cushion

you will need

Dark blue moiré taffeta, 1m x 38cm/1yd x 15in
Dressmaking scissors
Ruler
Black rosebud brocade ribbon, 1.15m x 2cm/1$\frac{1}{4}$yd x $\frac{3}{4}$in
Claret rosebud brocade ribbon, 1.15m x 2cm/1$\frac{1}{4}$yd x $\frac{3}{4}$in
Dressmaker's pins
Claret velvet ribbon, 1.15m x 23mm/1$\frac{1}{4}$yd x $\frac{7}{8}$in
Purple marble-print ribbon, 1.15m x 23mm/1$\frac{1}{4}$yd x $\frac{7}{8}$in
Dark red ribbon, 1.15m x 25mm/1$\frac{1}{4}$yd x 1in
Claret jacquard ribbon, 1.15m x 7mm/1$\frac{1}{4}$yd x $\frac{3}{8}$in
Green velvet ribbon, 2.5m x 2cm/2$\frac{3}{4}$yd x $\frac{3}{4}$in
Needle and matching threads
Iron and pressing cloth
Cushion pad, 36cm/14in square

1 Fold a 35cm/14in square of taffeta into quarters. Cut all the ribbons into 35cm/14 in lengths. Lay a brocade ribbon along each crease, then put a velvet ribbon 3mm/$\frac{1}{8}$in away from each side of the cross. Interweave the ribbons, pinning them down at the ends and the crossing points.

2 Using a ruler to ensure that all the lines are straight, continue to weave in the other ribbons, following the design of the completed cushion. When the weave is complete, pin all the loose ribbon ends to the backing fabric.

3 Starting at one edge, sew the ribbons to the taffeta by making two small, neat overstitches across each point where the ribbons overlap. Sew the ribbons firmly in place but avoid pulling the thread too tightly across the back, as this will distort the weave.

4 Cut two 35 x 25cm/14 x 10in taffeta rectangles. Hem one long side of each. Right sides facing, pin to the cushion front so the hems overlap in the centre and the cut edges match. Stitch all round 2cm/$\frac{3}{4}$in from the edge. Clip the corners, turn through, press and insert the cushion pad.

Ribbon is ideal for weaving, and wonderful effects can be achieved with subtle combinations of colour and texture. This headboard sets the tone for a minimalist bedroom in neutral shades.

Woven Ribbon Headboard

●●●●

you will need

Length of 25 x 25mm/1 x 1in wooden batten (furring strip)
Hacksaw
medium-grade abrasive paper
Drill and bit
Tape measure
Pencil
Wood glue
Dowels
4 right-angled fixing brackets
Screws
Screwdriver
Grosgrain ribbon in blue, brown and beige, 5m x 12mm/5½yd x ½in
Cream satin or taffeta ribbon, 20m x 2.5cm/22yd x 1in
Satin striped ribbon in blue, brown and beige, 5m x 3cm/5½yd x 1¼in
Grosgrain ribbon in blue, brown and beige, 5m x 15mm 5½yd x ⅝in
Scissors
Staple gun

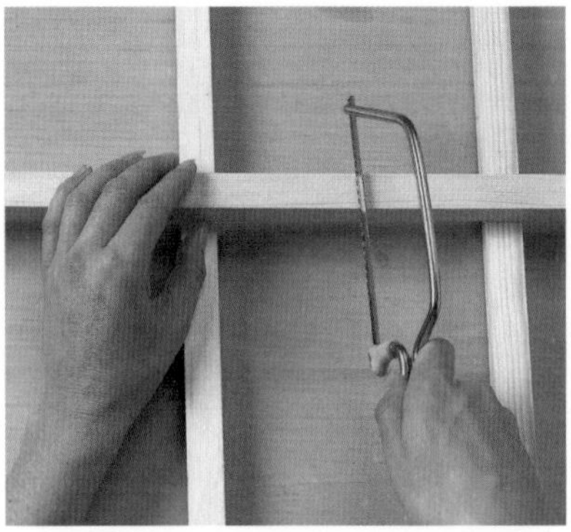

1 Using the hacksaw, cut the softwood batten into four lengths, each measuring 90cm/36in. This will make a headboard to fit a single bed: increase the width of the board for a larger bed and increase the amount of ribbon proportionately. Sand the cut edges.

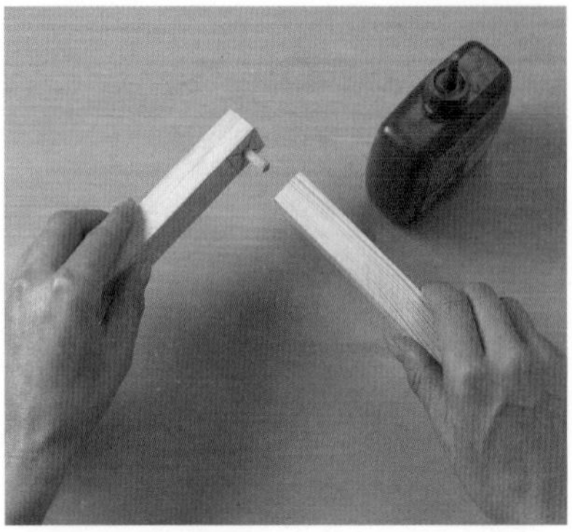

2 Use a drill with a bit to fit the dowels to make a hole at each end of the two battens that will form the horizontal pieces of the frame. Drill a hole 1cm/½in from the top of each side piece and a second hole 60cm/24in down. Glue the dowel joints and assemble the frame.

3 Screw four right-angled fixing brackets to the reverse side of the headboard frame to reinforce the joints and hold the frame rigid while you work. This will help to keep the woven pattern symmetrical.

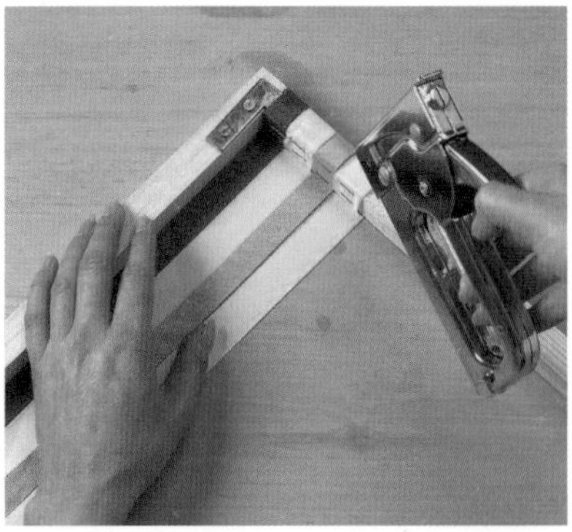

4 Cut the ribbons into 70cm/28in lengths. Lay them vertically on the frame in a symmetrical pattern: start at the centre with a wide grosgrain overlaid with a light satin striped ribbon, then work outwards with alternate narrower satin and grosgrain ribbon.

5 Repeat the sequence to fill the frame. Staple the ribbons to the frame, pulling each piece taut. Cut two short pieces of cream satin or taffeta ribbon and staple to cover the wooden batten at the top two corners.

6 Interweave ribbons horizontally across the headboard in a pattern sequence similar to the warp. Turn the headboard over and staple the raw ends securely to the frame as before, making sure that the ribbons are pulled quite taut.

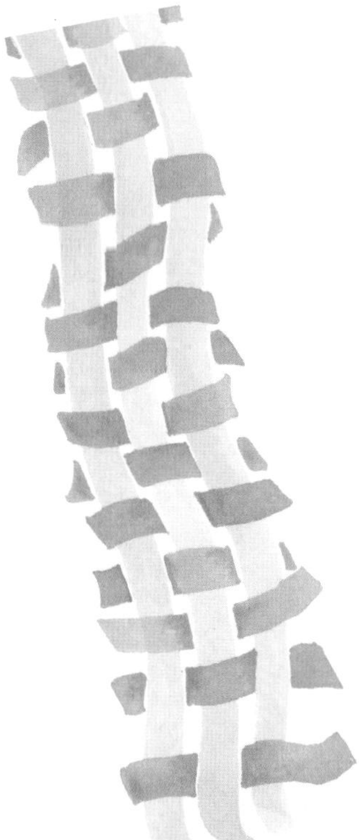

Join lengths of Fortuny-style pleated ribbon to make this sculptural bag, which is lined with iridescent fabric and, as a pretty finishing touch, embellished with sparkling beads.

Ribbon Evening Bag

you will need

- Pleated wire-edged ribbon, 1.6m x 5cm/$1\frac{7}{8}$yd x 2in
- Scissors
- Tape measure
- Needle and matching thread
- Pleated wire-edged ribbon, 40 x 6cm/16 x $2\frac{1}{2}$in
- Matching organza fabric
- Plate, 14cm/$5\frac{1}{2}$in diameter
- Pencil
- Sewing-machine
- Dressmaker's pins
- Fine matching cord, 38cm/15in
- Decorative glass beads

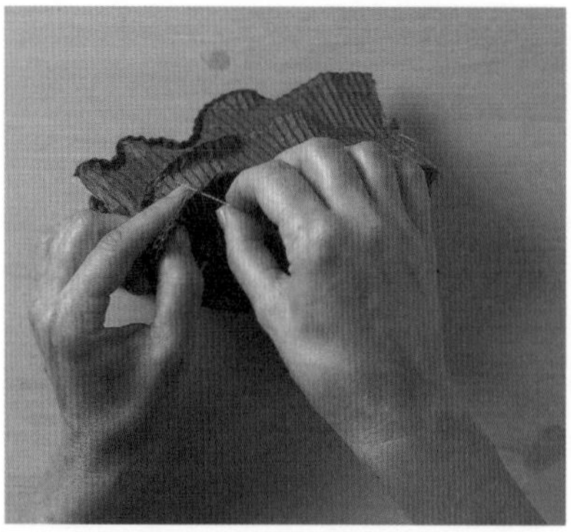

1 For the main bag, cut eight pieces of 5cm/2in wide pleated ribbon. Using a matching thread, oversew the long edges of the pieces of ribbon together to form a rectangle, then join the two outside edges together to make a cylinder.

2 To make the bottom of the bag, stitch the two ends of the 6cm/$2\frac{1}{2}$in wide ribbon together with a 1cm/$\frac{1}{2}$in seam. Run a gathering stitch along one edge and pull up tightly. Secure the ends on the wrong side.

3 Slip stitch the outer edge of the bottom of the bag to the lower edge of the side, turning in the raw edges.

4 For the lining, cut a rectangle 18 x 40cm/7 x 16in and a circle with a 7cm/$2\frac{3}{4}$in radius from the organza, using a plate.

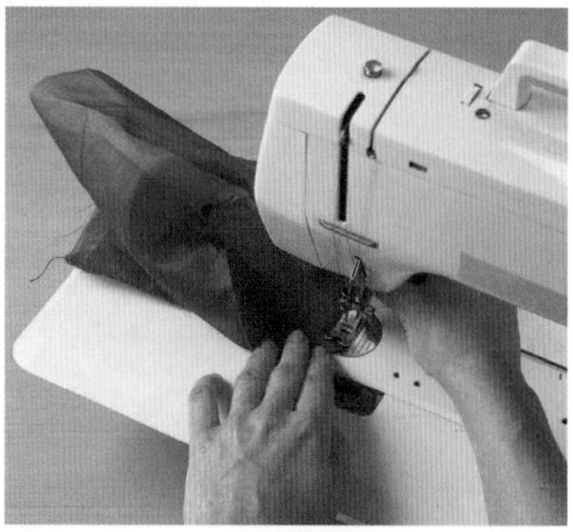

5 Machine stitch the side seam, and pin and tack (baste) the side to the bottom of the bag. Machine stitch together.

6 With the wrong sides facing, fit the lining into the bag. Fold in the top edges of both the lining and the ribbon and slip stitch the two together.

7 To make the carriers for the tie, cut two 6cm/2½in lengths of cord and poke the raw ends through a side seam on either side of the bag, 4cm/1½in from the top. Stitch in place. Cut a piece of cord 25cm/10in long, fold it in half and knot the ends.

8 Thread the loop through the carriers and pass the knotted ends through the loop. Hand stitch decorative glass beads around the top edge of the bag at regular intervals.

Whether containing a collection of drawings, school project, or college thesis, this beautiful folder is bound to enhance its contents. The book cloth and lining paper are available from good craft suppliers.

Woven Ribbon Folder

you will need

2 pieces of stiff board, 36 x 25cm/14 x 10in
Sheet of artist's black lining paper
PVA (white) glue
Glue spreader or paintbrush
Book cloth or stiffened fabric, 1m x 50cm/1yd x 20in
Pencil
Ruler
Scissors
Wood chisel
Hammer
Piece of wood
Black ribbon, 90cm x 6mm/36 x ⅜in
Iron-on interfacing, 35 x 23cm/14 x 9in
Masking tape
Burgundy fleur-de-lis ribbon, 4.6m x 4cm/5yd x 1½in
Iron

1 Line the two boards with black paper, glueing it in place. To make the gusset, cut an 86 x 10cm/34 x 4in strip of book cloth or stiffened fabric and line it with artist's black paper. Fold the strip in half lengthways, then fold the two halves in half again to create a concertina.

2 Mark a point 27cm/10½in from each end of the strip. Fold the strip lengthways at the first point so that you have a double layer. Carefully cut a triangle out of each corner. Open out, then fold and cut the strip at the other 27cm/10½in point in the same way.

3 Fold the strip at the two 27cm/10½in points so that the two end sections of the gusset strip are at right angles to the middle section.

4 Glue the two boards inside the gusset so the edges lie within the two outermost folds. Press all the creases firmly. Cut two pieces of cloth 5cm/2in longer than the boards and slightly narrower. Stick these to the outside of the boards, leaving the excess at the open edge to be turned over later.

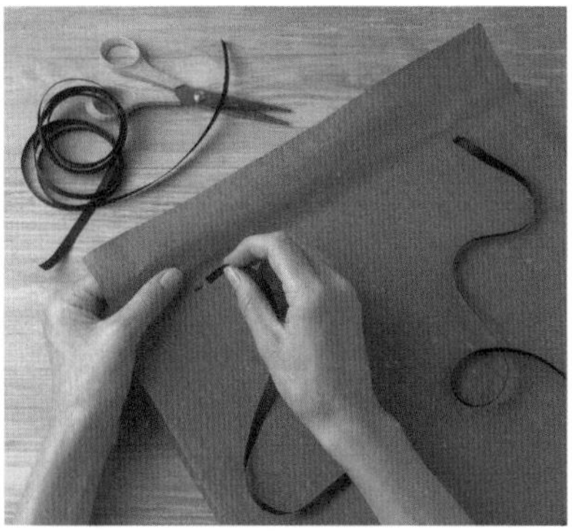

5 Chisel two holes into each side of the top edge of the folder. Protect the boards while you do this by placing a piece of wood between them. Cut the 6mm/¼in ribbon into four equal lengths and thread one through each hole. Turn over the excess lining and glue down to secure the ribbons inside the folder.

6 Tape the interfacing to a weaving board, glue side up. Cut the fleur-de-lis ribbon into eight 27cm/10½in strips and six 40cm/16in strips. Place the eight shorter ribbons side by side over the interfacing and hold them in place with masking tape.

7 Weave the six longer ribbons, plain side up, through the fleur-de-lis ribbons, following the plain-weave technique (see Basic Techniques). Make sure the weaving is even and tight. Press with a dry moderate iron when complete to fuse the ribbon to the interfacing.

8 Trim the edges of the weaving to 2cm/¾in. Fold this allowance over the interfacing and iron carefully. Glue down the edges as necessary, then glue the woven panel to the front of the folder to complete.

Create an heirloom gift for a new baby by combining the freshness of pure white cotton and broderie anglaise with the silky soft appeal of floral ribbon embroidery in delicate pastels.

Ribbon-embroidered Baby Pillow

you will need

White cotton piqué, 90 x 30cm/36 x 12in
Dressmaking scissors
Tape measure
Lightweight iron-on interfacing, 23cm/9in square
Iron
Fabric marker
Embroidery hoop
Chenille needle
Satin ribbon in pale pink, dusky pink, pale mint green, pale lime green and pale aqua, 1.75m x 3mm/2yd x 1/8in of each
Narrow broderie anglaise insertion, 1.4m/1 1/2yd
Broderie anglaise edging, 1.4m x 7.5cm/1 1/2yd x 3in
Dressmaker's pins
Needle and matching and contrasting threads
Ribbon, 1.4m x 6mm/1 1/2yd x 1/4in
Tapestry needle
Cushion pad, 30cm/12in square

1 Cut a 23cm/9in square of cotton piqué and iron the interfacing to one side. Trace the template at the back of the book and mount in a hoop. For the rose centre, sew a star of four pale pink straight stitches. In dusky pink work a ring of stitches around the star.

2 Work the leaves in straight stitch with the green ribbons and the rose-buds in lazy daisy. Complete the rest of the design using a range of random stitches, and add a bow to the space at the bottom edge. Trim the fabric down a 15cm/6in square.

3 Cut four 9cm/3½in squares and four 15 x 9cm/6 x 3½in pieces of piqué. From the broderie anglaise insertion, cut four 9cm/3½in, two 15cm/6in and two 33cm/13in lengths. Position the pieces and the lace around the embroidered square, following the diagram opposite.

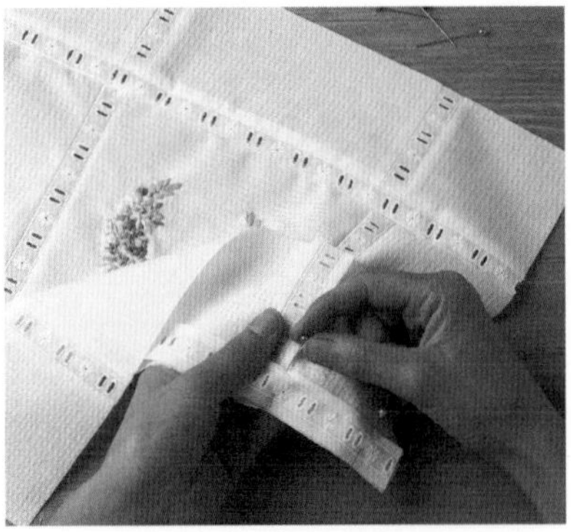

4 Make the front panel by joining the pieces together in three rows with the short lengths of lace insertion, leaving a 1cm/½in seam allowance. Use the two long strips to join the three rows together. Press the seams away from the insertion. Join the two ends of the broderie anglaise edging and run a gathering thread along the raw edge.

5 Fold the edging into four equal sections, marking each quarter division with a small scissor cut. Pin each of these cuts to one corner of the front panel on the right side. Draw up the gathering thread to fit the front panel. Distribute the gathers evenly, allowing a little more fullness at the corners. Pin the broderie anglaise around the outside edge so that it lies on top of the cushion.

6 Tack (baste) and sew in place. Thread the 6mm/¼in ribbon through the insertion using the tapestry needle. Secure each end with a few tacking stitches.

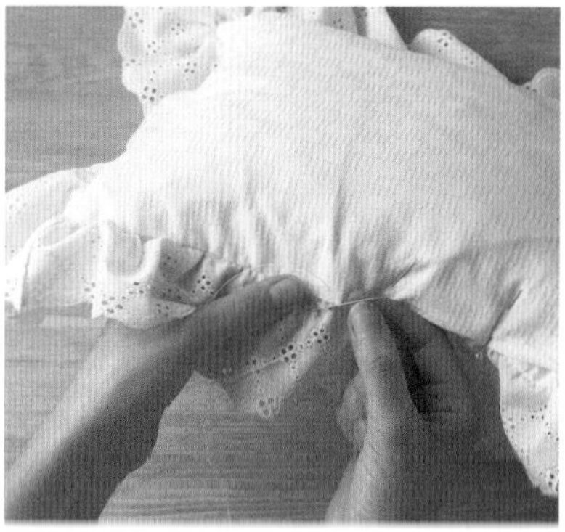

7 Cut a 30cm/12in square of cotton piqué for the panel back. Pin to the right side of the front panel, ensuring that the lace is free of the seam line. Sew around three sides then turn to the right side. Insert the cushion pad and slip stitch the fourth side closed.

This handy case brings together types of needlework: patchwork, embroidery and sewing. The crazy design will be unique for every case made and requires only a little planning to create a stunning look.

Roll-up Needlework Case

●●●●

you will need
Lightweight canvas, 60 x 30cm/24 x 12in
Pencil
Ruler
Dressmaking scissors
5 different toning ribbons, 1m/1yd of each
Needle and matching threads
Toning embroidery threads (floss)
Dressmaker's pins
Ribbon for binding, 1.5m x 2.5cm/1⅔yd x 1in
Ribbon for ties, 50cm x 6mm/20 x ¼in

1 Cut the canvas into four rectangles, two measuring 30 x 20cm/12 x 8in and two 30 x 10cm/12 x 4in. Cut the toning ribbons into various lengths between 2.5 and 7.5cm/1 and 3in.

2 Use running stitch or back stitch to sew the ribbon pieces on to one of the 30 x 20cm/12 x 8in canvas rectangles, turning under the raw edges (see Basic Stitching Techniques). Continue until the entire panel is covered. Don't worry about any small gaps: these add to the crazy patchwork look and can be filled with embroidery stitches.

3 Oversew the edges of the patchwork pieces using three or four different embroidery threads and a range of stitches. Cross stitch, running stitch and chain stitch all work well.

4 Work blanket stitch around three edges of one of the 30 x 10cm/12 x 4in rectangles, leaving one of the long edges unsewn.

5 Draw lines across the second small rectangle to mark the pockets. Blanket stitch along the top edge and position the panel along one edge of the second large rectangle. Join the two together by stitching along the pocket lines.

6 To assemble the case, place the patchwork panel face downwards. Place the pocket piece on top, right side up. Tack together and bind the side and bottom edges with the 2.5cm/1in ribbon. Use a small running stitch to secure the ribbon, stitching through all the layers.

7 Place the remaining rectangle above the pocket piece to form a flap, with the unsewn edge at the top. Pin in place and bind the top edge with ribbon as described in step 6.

8 Fold the length of 6mm/¼in ribbon in half and at the centre point stitch it inside one side edge of the case. Use this ribbon to secure the needlework case, when rolled up.

Shocking pink ribbon in a variety of styles – embroidery, satin, velvet and wire-edged – makes up this pretty tie-back. A satin band holds the curtain in place, while the tassel hangs decoratively to one side.

Tasselled Tie-back

●●●●

you will need

Large-eyed tapestry needle
Narrow embroidery ribbon
Wooden beads in two sizes
Scissors
Selection of satin, velvet and wire-edged ribbons
Needle and strong thread
2 brass rings

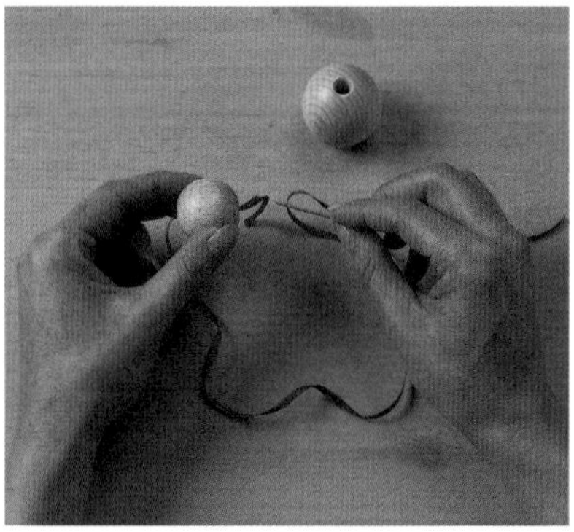

1 Using a large-eyed tapestry needle, thread narrow embroidery ribbon around two large wooden beads to make the tassel head.

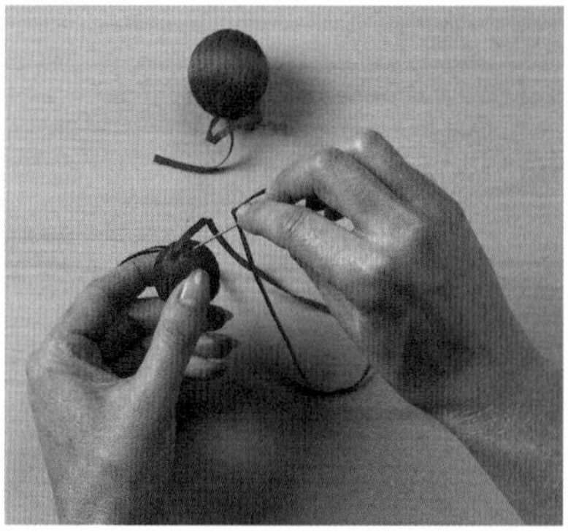

2 When the beads are completely covered, tie off the ends securely. Create a hanging loop at the top of the smaller bead.

3 To make a rosette, cut a length of satin ribbon and join the ends neatly together, turning in the raw edges. Work a running stitch along both edges of the ribbon.

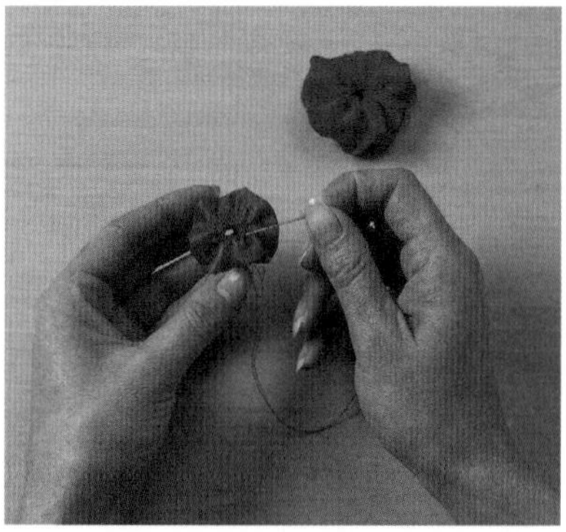

4 Gather up the edges tightly to make a puff shape and secure the threads. Make a second rosette, using ribbon of a different width and colour.

►

5 To make a loop rosette, cut two pieces of narrow velvet ribbon: 30cm/12in lengths will make a rosette that is 15cm/6in across – cut longer lengths for a larger rosette. Fold the raw ends of the first to the centre and secure with a few stitches.

6 Fold and stitch the second length in the same way. Place this loop at right angles across the centre of the first to form a cross, then stitch through all the layers to form the rosette.

7 Select satin and wire-edged ribbons for the skirt of the tassel, cutting them to twice the finished length: this will depend on the size of the tassel head, so experiment until the tassel looks right. Arrange the ribbons in a star shape and secure by stitching through all the layers in the centre.

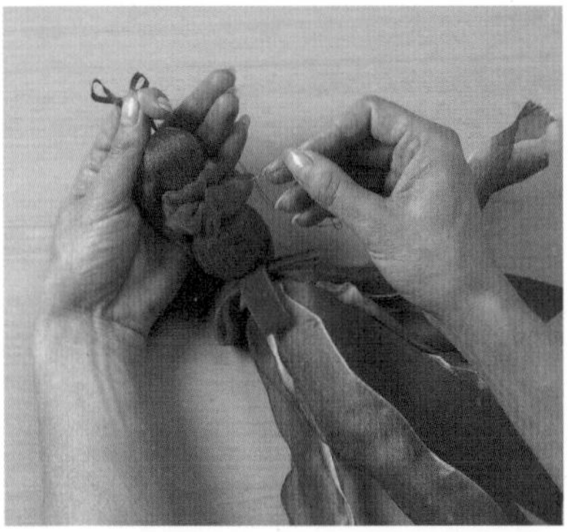

8 To assemble the tassel, thread the large needle with several lengths of strong thread and stitch through the centre of each element, starting with the skirt. Fasten off securely when you reach the top of the smaller bead.

9 To make the tie-back, cut a suitable length of wide satin ribbon. Neaten the raw edges and stitch a brass ring securely to each end. Cut a second piece of the same ribbon twice the length of the tie-back and gather by working a line of running stitches along the centre.

10 Draw up the fullness to fit the foundation ribbon and stitch down the centre. Sew the tassel's hanging loop to one end of the tie-back, so that it will hang at the side of the curtain.

This luxurious little evening bag exudes style and elegance. The velvet is painted with luxurious gold stripes, then woven through with complementary coloured ribbons.

Classic Evening Purse

you will need

Black velvet, 40cm/16in square
Black lining fabric, 20cm/8in square
Scissors
Large sheet of paper
Masking tape, 2.5cm/1in wide
Gold fabric paint
Paintbrush
Thin card (stock)
Fabric marker
Small sharp-pointed scissors
Silver ribbon, 1.6m x 6mm/1¾yd x ¼in
Green ribbon, 1.75m x 6mm/2yd x ¼in
Maroon ribbon, 1.75m x 6mm/2yd x ¼in
Tape measure
Tapestry needle
Dressmaker's pins
Needle and matching threads
Iron

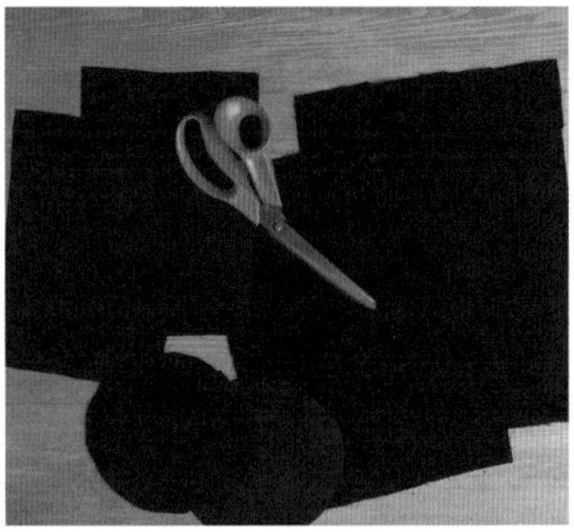

1 Enlarge the three pattern pieces at the back of the book to size. A seam allowance of 1cm/12in is included. Cut two of the larger rectangles from black velvet, two of the smaller rectangles from the black lining fabric and one circle from each fabric.

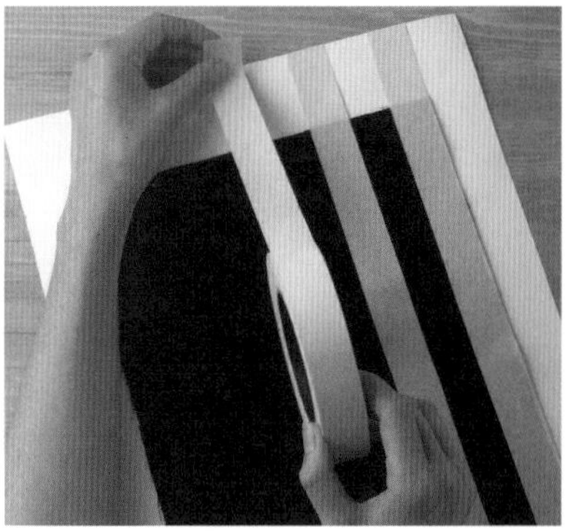

2 Place one rectangle of velvet fabric face up on a sheet of paper (to protect the work surface). Lay vertical strips of masking tape over the velvet, leaving a gap of 2.5cm/1in between them. Lay a double strip of masking tape across the centre of the fabric.

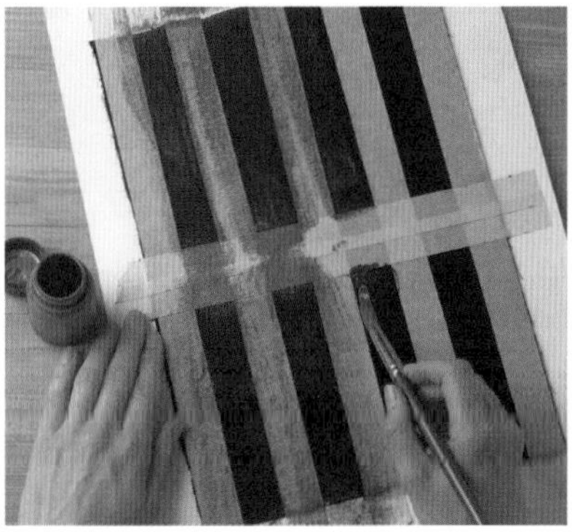

3 Apply gold paint lightly and evenly to the exposed areas of fabric with a dry brush. Leave to dry completely, then peel off the tape carefully. Follow the manufacturer's instructions for fixing the paint.

4 Make a template for the ribbon insertion, cutting points from a strip of card cut to the length of the painted stripes. Mark six evenly spaced points along one edge of the strip. Transfer these points to the velvet with a fabric marker along both sides of each painted strip. Mark only the bottom half of the whole piece of velvet.

▶

5 Use sharp scissors to cut 6mm/¼in slits in the fabric at the marked points. Cut the ribbons into 20cm/8in lengths. Use a tapestry needle to thread one through each row of slits, alternating the colour with each row. Thread the ribbon loosely, allowing it to fall naturally.

6 Secure the ends of each ribbon on the back of the velvet with a few stitches. Repeat steps two to six with the second rectangle of black fabric to make the other half of the bag.

7 With right sides facing, pin, tack (baste) and sew the long sides of the two rectangles together, leaving a space in each seam where indicated on the pattern. Sew both lining rectangles together along the short edges, leaving a gap in one seam for turning.

8 With right sides facing, pin, tack and sew the long sides of the lining to the upper edge of the bag, matching up the seam lines. Press lightly and stitch the seam.

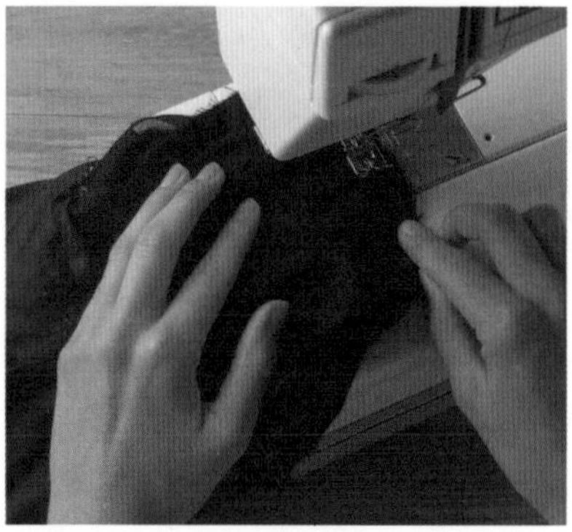

9 Turn the bag inside out and, with right sides facing, pin, tack and sew the circle of velvet to the bottom edge of the bag. Join the circle of lining fabric to the bottom edges of the lining. Turn the bag through the opening to the right side. Fold along the fold line and press gently.

10 Tack along the stitching lines indicated on the pattern to form the drawstring channel, then stitch. Close the side opening with slip stitch (see Basic Stitching Techniques). Thread the remaining ribbon through the channel and tie the ends together to form a drawstring.

The beautiful blooms that make up this romantic coronet will require special care to keep them pristine: give them a long drink before use and mist the finished headdress lightly with a water spray.

Flower and Ribbon Headdress

●●●●

you will need

12 small clusters of *Aronia melanocarpa* berries
Scissors
Stub (floral) wire, 0.38mm/28g
12 small clusters of hydrangea florets
12 *Leycesteria formosa* flower heads
Small garden roses
12 Lizianthus flower heads
12 single Antirrhinum florets
Florist's tape (stem wrap)
Burgundy sheer ribbon, 8m x 23mm/ $8\frac{3}{4}$yd x $\frac{7}{8}$in
Tape measure
Stub wire, 0.71mm/22g

1 Trim the berry stems. Cut short lengths of fine stub wire to double leg mount them. Holding the stem between finger and thumb, place a wire behind and at a right angle to the stem, one third of the way up. Bend it into a "U" so that one leg is twice as long as the other.

2 Holding the short leg against the stem, wrap the long leg twice around both the stem and the other wire. Straighten both legs, which should now be about equal and in line with the stem. Mount the roses, hydrangeas and leycesteria in the same way.

3 Wire each lizianthus flower head by piercing the seedbox with a length of stub wire. Push it about one third of the way through, then bend the wire legs down and wrap the legs around the stem as described for double leg mounting in step 1.

4 Remove the flower heads of the antirrhinum from the main stem and cut two short stub wires for each one. Fold one wire in half and twist into a loop at the bend. Push the legs down through the throat of the flower and out at the base to create a stem.

▶

5 The loop will sit in the narrowest part of the flower, preventing the wire from pulling all the way through. Use the second piece of wire to double leg mount the protruding wires and any natural stem that remains, as shown in steps 1 and 2.

6 Cover all the stems and wires with florist's tape. Hold the end against the top of the stem. With the other hand, hold the rest of the tape at an angle to the stem. Slowly rotate the stem and, keeping the tape taut so that it stretches slightly, wrap it in a downwards spiral, overlapping and pressing it in place.

7 Make 14 three-loop ribbon bows, each with two tails. For each bow, cut a 55cm/22in length of ribbon and divide it into six equal sections. Fold the ribbon accordion-style, pinching the folds together at the base. Double leg mount each bow using stub wire.

8 Cut several equal lengths of heavy stub wire to make the headdress foundation. Group four wires together so each overlaps the next by 3cm/1¼in. Starting at one end, bind them together with florist's tape. As the tape reaches the end of the first wire, add in another length.

9 Continue in this way until the wire measures 3cm/1¼in more than the circumference of the wearer's head. Tape the wired flowers and ribbons to the foundation in your chosen arrangement. Continue to within 3cm/1¼in of the end, curving the wire as you work.

10 Overlap the undecorated end of the stay wire with the decorated beginning. Tape the wires together under the flowers.

A project for a dressmaker, this lined waistcoat will fit a medium adult: adjust the ribbon requirements accordingly for another size. Choose a paper pattern without any darts in the front panels.

Woven Ribbon Waistcoat

you will need

Iron-on interfacing
Commercial waistcoat pattern
Scissors
Pencil or fabric marker
Ruler
Masking tape
Gold ribbon, approximately 20m x 2.5cm/22¼yd x 1in
Steam iron or dry iron and damp cloth
Needle and matching threads
Small gold beads
Blue lining fabric, 1.5m x 115cm/1⅔yd x 45in
Dressmaker's pins
Sewing-machine, with zip foot
Three buttons

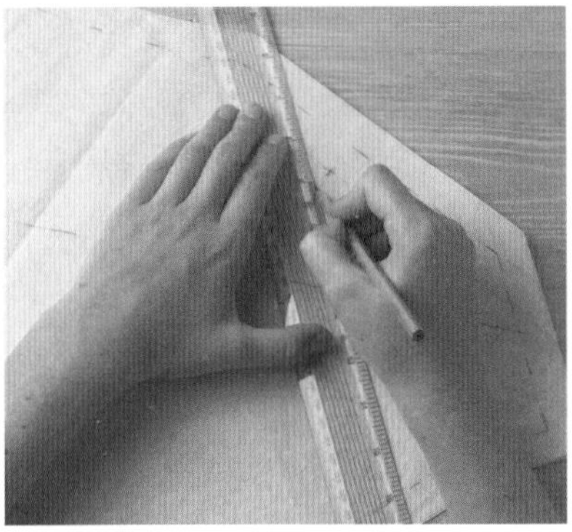

1 Lay the iron-on interfacing, glue side down, on top of the waistcoat front pattern piece. Cut the interfacing around the pattern. Transfer the markings to the interfacing. Turn the pattern piece over and repeat to cut out the second waistcoat front. Draw two crossing diagonal lines as a guide for weaving.

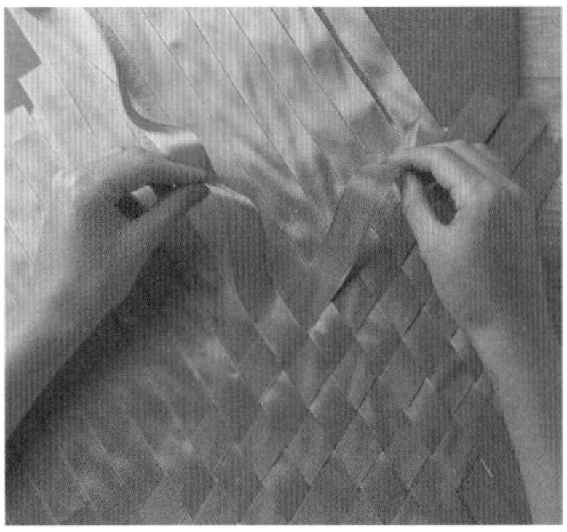

2 Tape the interfacing, glue side up, on a board. Following the pencil lines, lay and cut ribbons side by side in one diagonal direction, overlapping the edges. Tape one long ribbon on the opposite diagonal at both ends and weave in further lengths of ribbon (see Basic Techniques). Adjust the ribbons to keep the weave neat as you work.

3 Continue weaving until the interfacing is covered. Press with a dry iron. Remove the tape, turn over and press again with a steam iron or under a damp cloth.

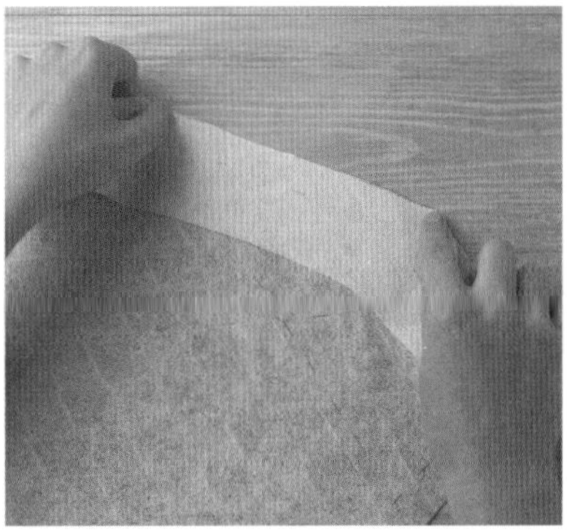

4 Trim the ribbons to the edge of the interfacing. Iron an extra strip of interfacing to the front edge of each piece to provide a firm base for the buttonholes and buttons. Overlap the seamline slightly.

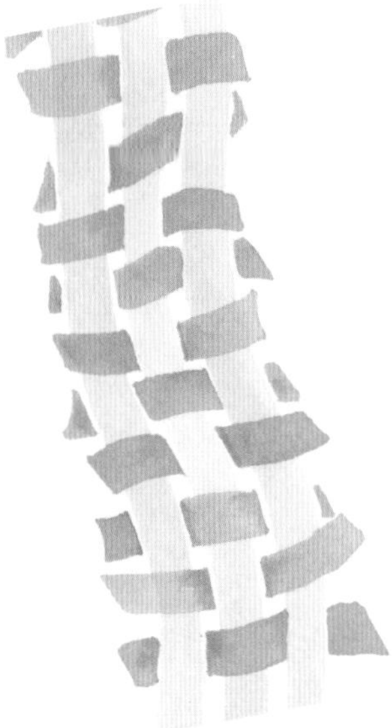

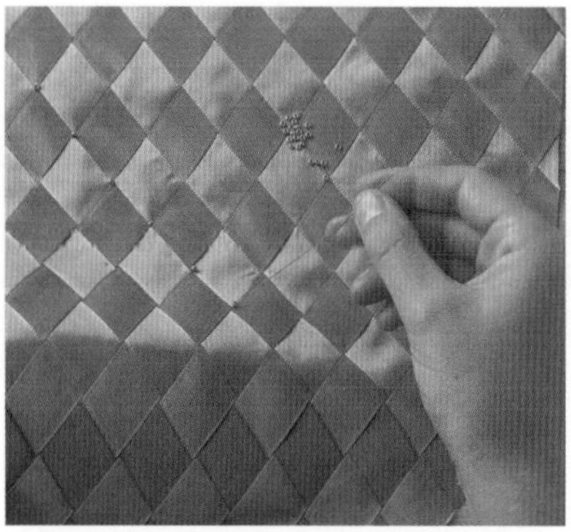

5 Using a double thread with a knot at the end, sew a small gold bead to each point where the ribbons cross. Work along the diagonal and keep the seam allowances free of beads. Secure each bead with a double stitch before going on to the next bead.

6 Cut an outer back, a back lining, and two front pieces from the blue lining fabric. Mark the position of the back ties and buttonholes. Pin and machine stitch the front lining and woven fronts together, right sides facing. Fit a zip foot, and machine stitch around the front edge, along the bottom and around the armholes, leaving the shoulder and side seams open. Trim the seams and corners, clipping the curves. Turn right-side out.

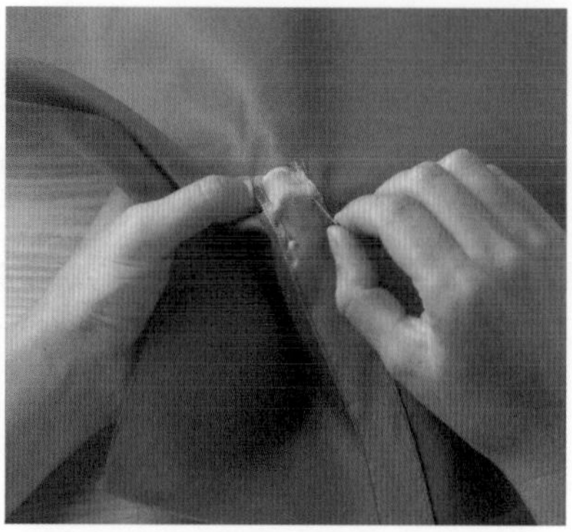

7 Cut two 60cm/24in lengths of ribbon for the back ties. Fold in half and sew down both sides, stitching in the same direction to avoid puckering. Hand sew in place on the waistcoat back, trimming the raw ends to 6mm/¼in and folding them neatly under.

8 Join the waistcoat back to the back lining with right sides facing. Stitch around the neck and armholes. Trim and clip the seam allowances and turn to the right side. With right sides facing, sew the front and back together along the shoulder seams.

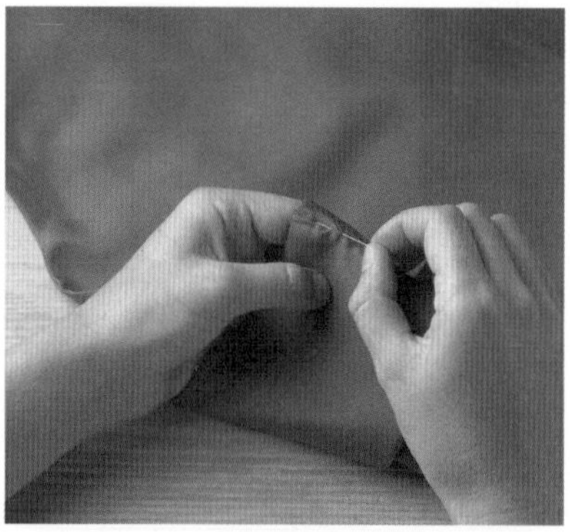

9 Stitch through one layer, leaving the linings free. Trim and press the seam open. Fold the lining seam allowance inside and slip stitch closed. Sew the side seams in the same way. Slip stitch the bottom edge of the waistcoat back closed.

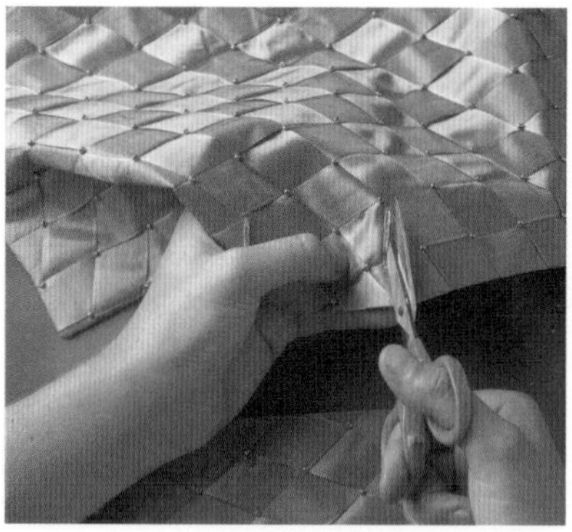

10 Make three buttonholes, using gold thread on top of the machine and blue in the spool case, so that the thread matches the fabric on both sides. Snip the buttonholes and sew the buttons in position.

Templates

Enlarge the templates on a photocopier. Alternatively, trace the design and draw a grid of evenly spaced squares over the tracing. Draw a larger grid on to another piece of paper and copy the outline square by square. Draw over the lines to make sure they are continuous.

Victorian Earrings p64

Victorian Earrings p64

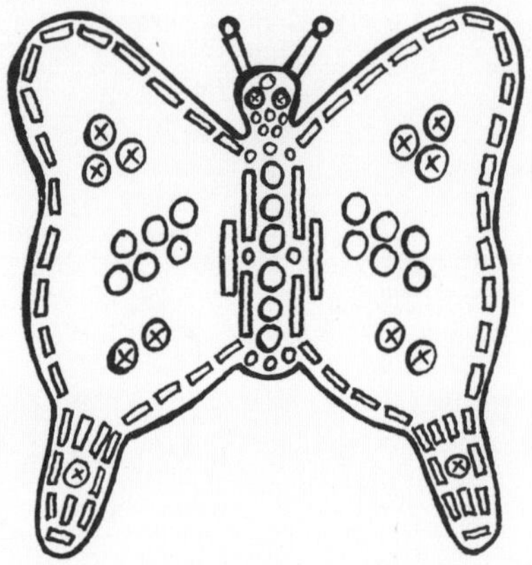

Butterfly Brooch p65

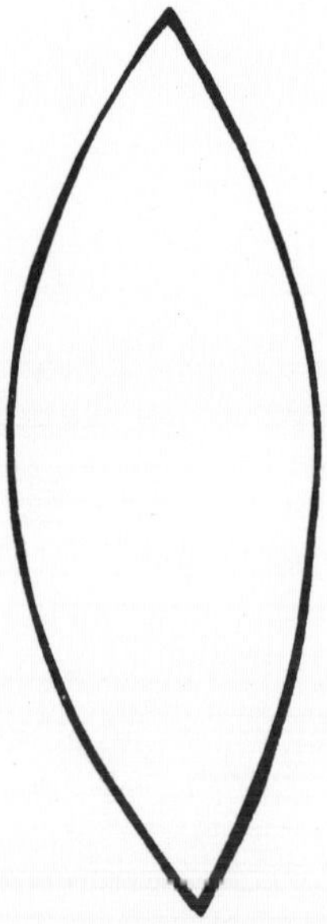

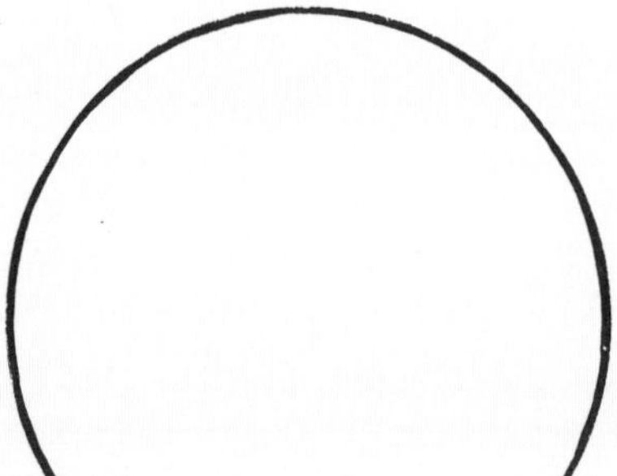

Bead-encrusted Appliqué Flower p106–7

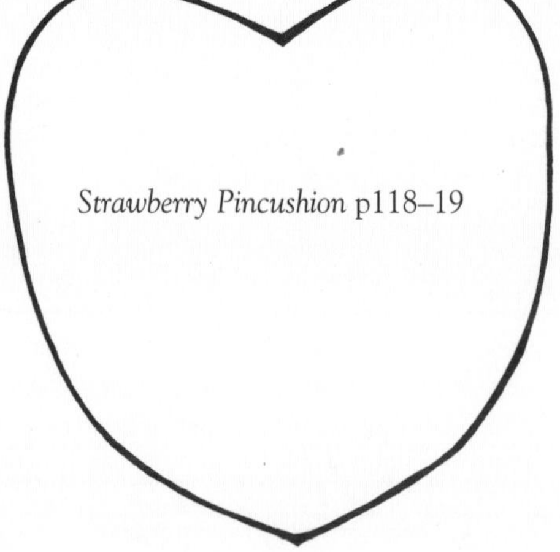

Strawberry Pincushion p118–19

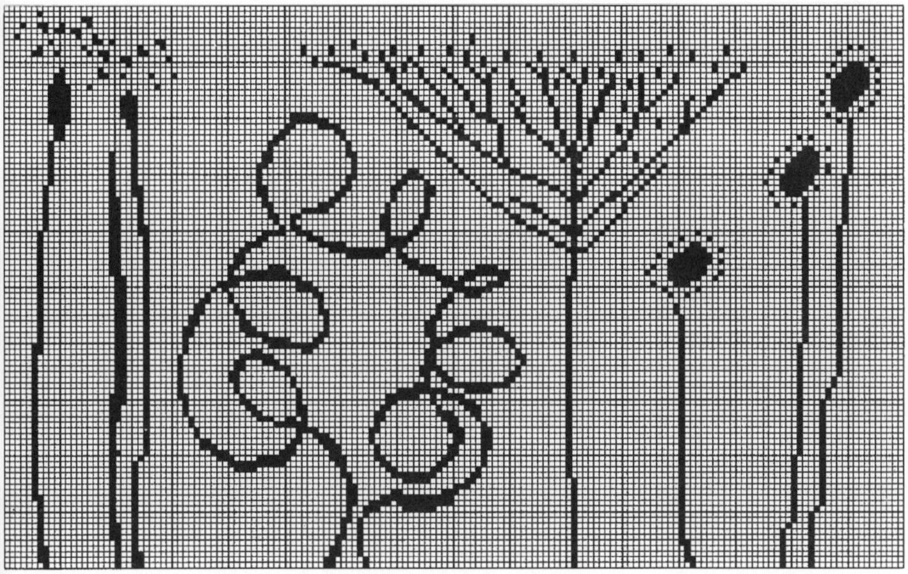

Needlepoint Photograph Album p150–151

Child's Slippers p66–7

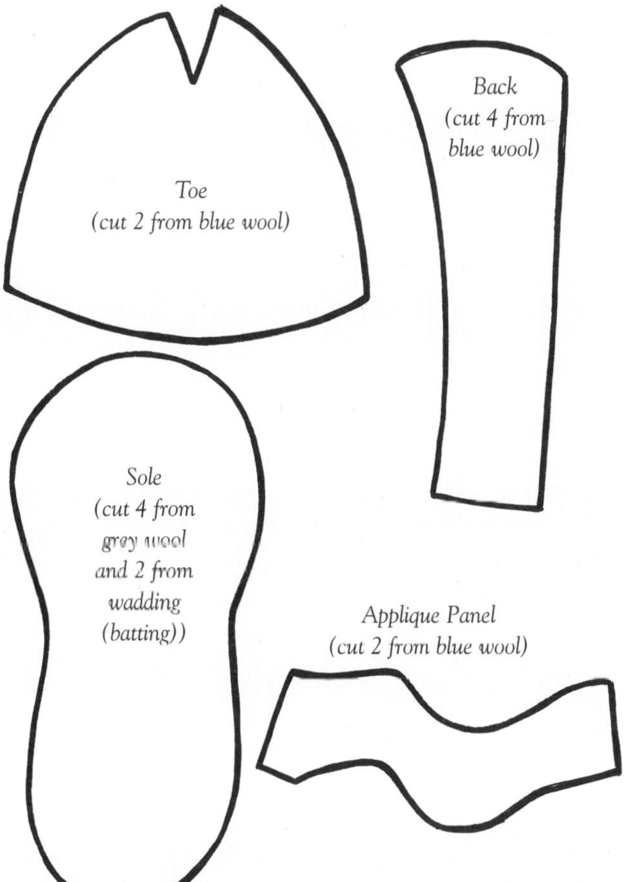

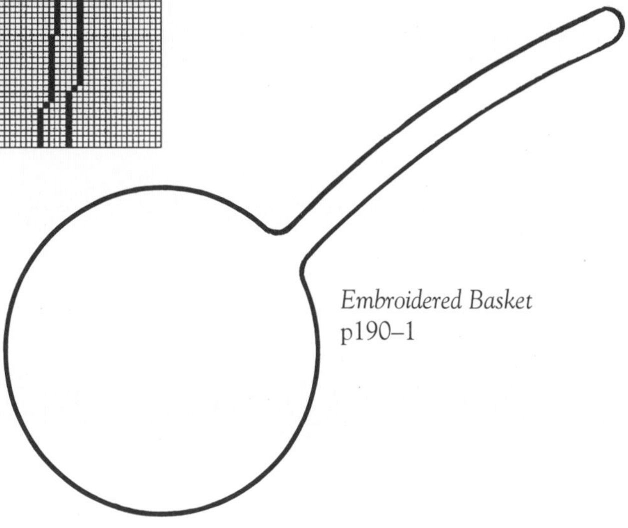

Embroidered Basket p190–1

Baby Pillow p234–5

Woven Bracelet p62–3

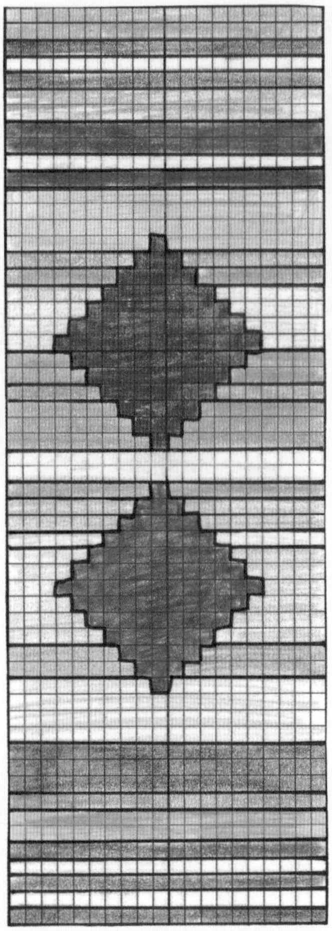

Woven Bead Trim p128–9

Beaded Boat Tapestry p126–7

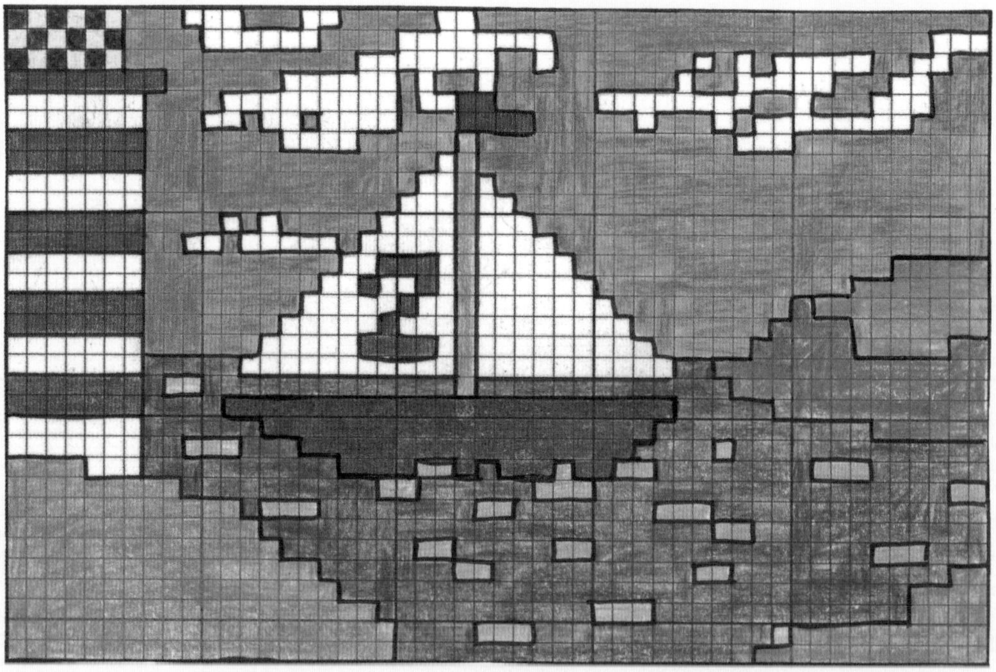

Choker p78–9

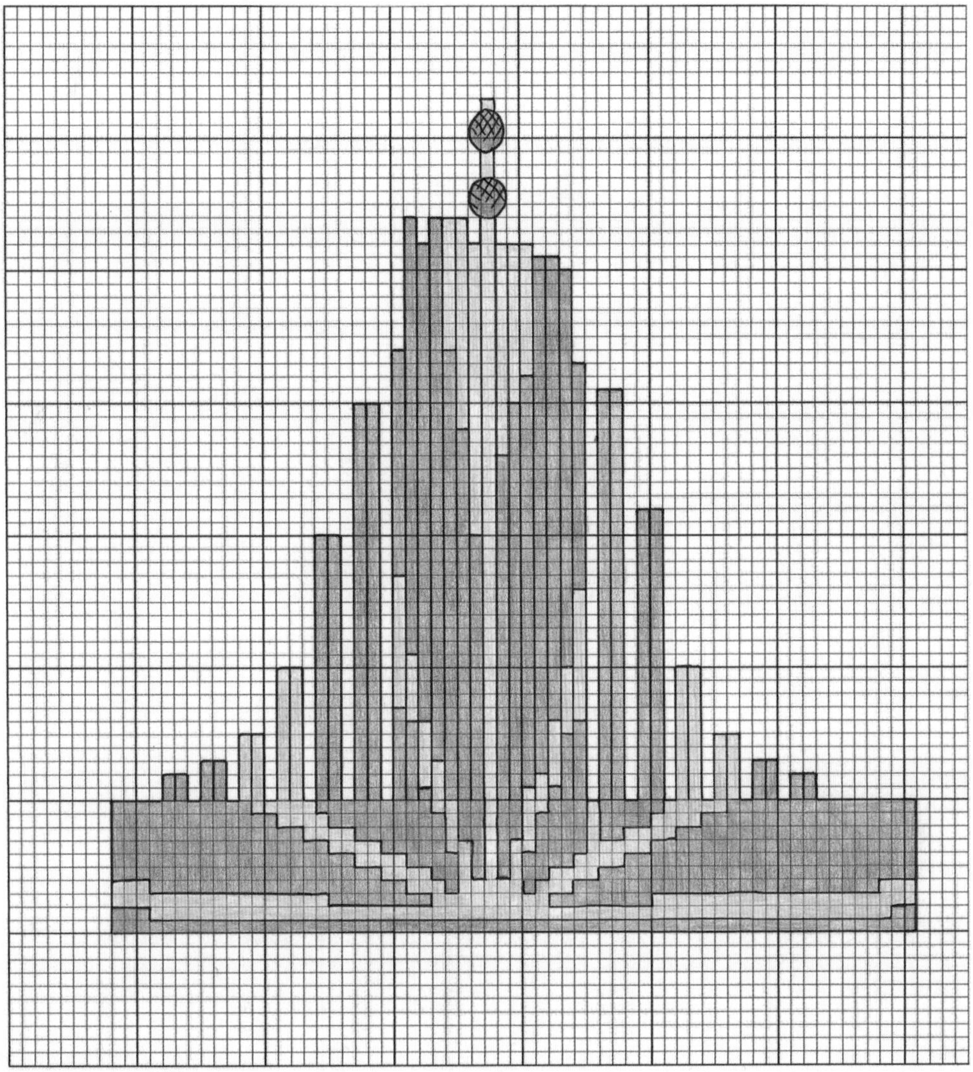

Repeat line 1 35 times
Repeat line 63 35 times

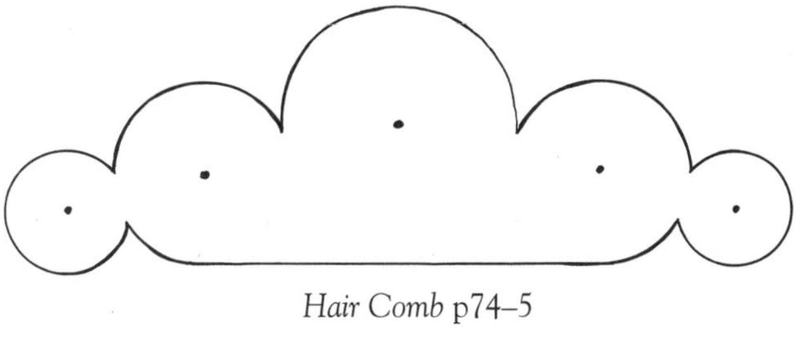

Hair Comb p74–5

Heart-shaped Bag p70–1

Acknowledgements

The publisher would like to thank the following people for the projects and photography in this book:

LISA BROWN, Monogrammed Bag 38, Bead-encrusted Frames 84, Beaded Wire Candlesticks 86, Bead-trimmed Voile Jug Covers 88, Simple Door Curtain 92, Beaded Throw 94, Bead Window Hanging 96, Giant Bead Cord-pulls 101, Table Decoration Set 103, Bead-encrusted Appliqué Flower 106, Chunky Bead Tie-backs 112, Beaded Wall Sconce 114, Glittering Bead Spheres 116, Strawberry Pincushion 118, Silken Key Tassels 120, Beaded Boat Tapestry 126, Woven Bead Trim 128, Fish Mosaic Splashback 132, Lacy Bottle Covers 142, Beaded Cushion Trims 147, Luxurious Giftwrapping 178, Rosy Lampshade 180, Pillowcase Edgings 182, Embroidered Basket 190, Ribbon Door Curtain 194, Ribboned Throw 198, Striped Ribbon Cushion 200, Ribbon-rose Coat Hangers 211, Appliquéd Ribbon Café Curtain 221, Deck-chair Cover 224, Woven Ribbon Headboard 228, Ribbon Evening Bag 230, Tasselled Tie-back 239,

VICTORIA BROWN, Sequin and Bead Frame 140.

LOUISE BROWNLOW, Libran Earrings 52

LUCINDA GANDERTON, Pearl and Crystal Necklace 40, Beaded Charm Bracelet 42, Cascade Earrings 44, Beaded Hatpins 53, Silver Chain Belt 57, Off-loom Mesh Bracelet 68, Heart-shaped Bag 70, Crystal Butterfly 72, French Beading Corsage 80, Edwardian-style Pincushion 122, Ribbon Hat Box 213.

ALISON HARPER, Victorian Earrings and Brooch 64

ALISON JENKINS, Glittering Window Decoration 90

LINDSAY KAUBI, Loom-woven Choker 78,

CHRISTINE KINGDOM, Ballet Shoes 176, Gift Boxes 185, Bathroom Set 186, Ribbon-embroidered Bag 188, Ribbon Table Mats 192, Golden Braid Cushion 196, Sunflower-motif Jacket 202, Ribbon Jewellery 204, Tartan Ribbon Roses 206, Ribbon Lantern 208, Ribbon Christmas Decorations 219, Basket-weave Cushion 226, Woven Ribbon Folder 232, Ribbon-embroidered Baby Pillow 234, Roll-up Needlework Case 236, Classic Evening Purse 241, Flower and Ribbon Headdress 245, Woven Ribbon Waistcoat 247

ISABEL STANLEY, Venetian Necklace 36, Chinese-style Necklace 46, Little Fringed Bag 48, Cord-beaded Bracelet 50, Beaded Buttons 55, Spiral Bracelets 58, Devoré Scarf 60, Woven Bracelet 62, Child's Slippers 66, Pearl Hair Comb 74, Wrapped Earrings 76, Christmas Beadwork Decorations 98, Spiralled Chandelier 108, Bead Candle-holder 110, Velvet Bolster Cushion 124, Fringed Lampshade 130, Beaded Tassels 134, Chunky Beaded Lampshade 136, Bead Pendant Light 138, Bead-fringed Cushions 145, Needlepoint Photograph Album 150, Flowered Frame 153, Waterfall Screen 155, Satin and Velvet Ribbon Shade 216

DOROTHY WOOD, Butterfly Brooch 65

Photography: Lizzie Orme, Michelle Garrett, Lucinda Symons, Peter Williams.

Index

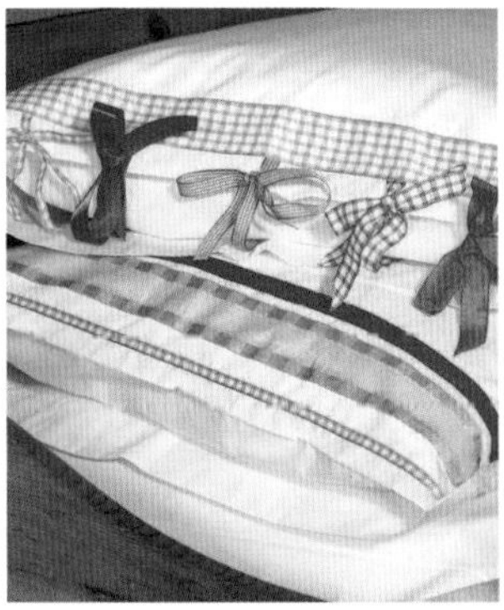